D1389440

Mysteries of the Lost Lands

Great Mysteries

Aldus Books London

Mysteries of the Lost Lands

by Eleanor Van Zandt
and Roy Stemman

Series Coordinator:	John Mason
Design Director:	Günter Radtke
Picture Editor:	Peter Cook
Designer:	Ann Dunn
Editors:	Damian Grint Mary Senechal Nina Shandloff Maureen Cartwright
Research:	Sarah Waters
General Consultant:	Beppie Harrison

New enlarged edition
SBN: 490 004229

Printed and bound in Yugoslavia by
Mladinska Knjiga, Ljubljana

Introduction

Mysterious cities and civilizations of the past, whether buried, submerged, or simply vanished, have a fascination not only for scholars and archaeologists, but for all of us. From the strange Hittite Empire, which lay forgotten from biblical times until the last century, to the enigmatic stone-built complex of Zimbabwe; from the elegant Etruscans, silent predecessors of the Romans, to the colossal temples of the vanished Khmers—here is a feast of archaeological mysteries, some solved, some mysteries still. The book then tackles the riddle of Atlantis, one of the world's great unsolved mysteries. Starting from Plato's fragmentary description of a lost land that was apparently "the nearest thing to paradise on Earth," chapters follow the scholars and other experts who have searched for—and "found"—Atlantis in every corner of the globe. From north America to the jungles of Brazil, from France to Israel, from the Atlantic Ocean to Sweden, the search has been long and wide. Many scientists now believe that Atlantis has been found, and that it lies buried on a submerged volcanic island in the Eastern Mediterranean, 75 miles north of Crete. Are they right? A final chapter examines the latest startling evidence in this, the greatest puzzle of the lost lands.

Contents

Chapter 1
Puzzles of the Past

A vase or gold trinket, a bronze statuette, or a piece of lively wall painting—to the archaeologists these are more astonishing than the stuff of legend. Yet often it is the legends that lead scholars to long-lost cities and civilizations. The stories of the Trojan War and King Minos and the Minotaur led to the discovery of Troy and Knossos—but raised other questions: Are there other civilizations behind the legends of antiquity? Is Plato's Atlantis waiting to be discovered? Are archaeologists and scholars on the way to fitting together the many pieces of the puzzle of the past?

The besieged inhabitants of Troy looked out from their walls one morning and saw that their attackers had gone. On the plains outside their city was a huge wooden effigy of a horse—an animal held sacred by the Trojans. This gift-offering by their Greek enemies was brought in triumph into the city. Unknown to the Trojans, the horse contained Greek warriors. Under cover of darkness the Greeks opened the city gates to their returning army and Troy was taken. According to ancient Greek legend, this famous trick brought to an end the 10-year seige of Troy and ended the conflict that began when Paris, a Trojan prince, abducted Helen, the beautiful wife of Menelaus, King of Sparta. Under the leadership of his brother King Agamemnon of Mycenae, Menelaus and many other Greek warriors set out to punish the Trojans.

The many strands of the legend have provided material for poets and dramatists from ancient times to our own day. In one epic poem, the *Iliad*, by the Greek poet Homer, who lived in the 8th century B.C., a brief period in the war is described in vivid and moving detail. Another Homeric epic, the *Odyssey,* tells of the adventures of the Greek warrior Odysseus as he returns home from Troy. Dramatists of Greece's classical age, such as Sophocles and Euripedes, wrote tragedies based on the conflict. The story of two young Trojan lovers, Troilus and Cressida, was immortalized by Chaucer and Shakespeare. And a modern play by Jean Giradoux, *Tiger at the Gates*, uses the war as its theme.

Opposite: *The Procession of the Trojan Horse into Troy* by the 18th-century Italian painter Giandomenico Tiepolo. The legend of the sacking of Troy after a 10-year siege by a confederation of Greek leaders and their armies has inspired artists, writers, and musicians for generations. Yet until the late 19th century most scholars believed that the story of Troy, part of which was immortalized by Homer in the *Iliad*, was purely imaginary.

Schliemann and the Hunt for Troy

Below: Heinrich Schliemann, the German businessman and amateur archaeologist who realized a lifelong ambition when in 1871 he discovered the remains of Homer's Troy at Hissarlik in northwestern Turkey. Not only did he make an archaeological discovery of considerable significance, but he proved that at least one of the Greek legends was based on fact.

Opposite top: the gold funeral mask of a prince. It was discovered by Schliemann at Mycenae and he firmly believed it came from the grave of Agamemnon, the king who led the Greeks at Troy and was murdered on his return home by his unfaithful queen and her lover. The mask was later proved to have belonged to a prince who lived several centuries earlier.

Opposite, bottom: the royal grave circle at Mycenae as it looked in Schliemann's day (left) and a modern view (right) showing the entrance. The graves date from 1600–1500 B.C.

The people of the ancient world accepted the story of Troy as historical fact. Alexander the Great, for instance, believed that one of the Greek heroes from the *Iliad*, Achilles, was his ancestor. After the Middle Ages, however, the story was consigned to the category of pure myth. Apart from the air of unreality created by the participation of the gods in the story, there were many inaccuracies in the text, scholars claimed. As for a city called Troy, if it had ever existed, it had long since vanished. Moreover, there was no real evidence that a Greek civilization had existed before 1200 B.C.—the time around which the war was supposed to have taken place.

One can imagine the smiles among archaeologists in the 1860s when a rich German businessman with no training in archaeology set out for the Aegean with a copy of the *Iliad* to search for Troy. As a child, Heinrich Schliemann had been captivated by these heroic tales and was convinced that they were true. His dream of finding Troy and Mycenae had stayed with him throughout years of pursuing a successful career in business, and he was now, in his mid-40s, abandoning the world of commerce to discover the lost world of Troy. All he had was his copy of Homer, plenty of money to pay a small army of workmen, and boundless determination.

Arriving in Turkey, he first explored a site near the village of Burnarbashi, where, according to tradition, Troy was buried. But the site's location and some other of its features did not tally with descriptions in Homer, and Schliemann passed it by. Some distance away at Hissarlik he found a more promising site. There, about an hour's walk from the sea, a flat-topped mound dominated the surrounding plain. He started to dig.

His faith was well rewarded. Over the next few years he discovered not one city but nine, built one on top of another. The question was, which was Homer's Troy? Schliemann thought it was either the second or the third level from the bottom, where he found traces of fire and some massive walls that he identified as those surrounding King Priam's palace. Just before he concluded his excavation of Troy Schliemann discovered, in this "palace" area, a hoard of gold jewelry— Priam's treasure. More recent studies have shown that Troy was at a higher level, and that the treasure Schliemann discovered had belonged to a much earlier king. Nevertheless, he had achieved his goal; he had found Troy. The professional archaeologists who had smiled at this legend-obsessed amateur had to acknowledge that he had made a discovery of great significance.

Schliemann went on to make more discoveries. He excavated the ruins at Mycenae and found graves containing skeletons bedecked with gold. They were not, as he supposed, the bodies of Agamemnon and his family but royalty of an earlier age. But again he had proved that Homer was not merely a spinner of tales but also an historian. Furthermore, an impressive Greek civilization based at Mycenae had existed as far back as 1450 B.C.—250 years before Troy fell.

Other Greek legends concerned the island of Crete. Here, in a labyrinth in his palace, King Minos had kept a monster, half bull and half man, called the Minotaur, to which he sacrificed youths and maidens sent by Athens as tribute. In one of the best-known

Right: two of the red pillars in a reconstruction of the stairway in the royal palace at Knossos in Crete, which dates from some time between 2200 and 1500 B.C. In 1900, British archaeologist Arthur Evans began excavations at Knossos that revealed Crete as the home of one of the most striking civilizations of the ancient world. Evans called the civilization Minoan, for the legendary King Minos of Crete.

Below: a diver recovers an ancient wine storage jar, or amphora, from the seabed off Bodrun, Turkey. The seas around our shores are often rich in archaeological treasures: submerged ports, harbors, and towns drowned when changes in sea-level altered coastlines, particularly around the Mediterranean; or sunken ships loaded with cargo, treasure, or the spoils of war. Is there also, perhaps, a whole continent of once-flourishing cities waiting to be discovered under the sea?

stories an Athenian prince, Theseus, kills the Minotaur and escapes with Minos' daughter Ariadne.

Were the stories of Crete entirely fictitious, or—as in the case of Troy and Mycenae—were they based on a real civilization? Schliemann, of course, took the latter view, and he planned to excavate on the island. Circumstances prevented his doing so; but another man, Arthur Evans, a British archaeologist, had also become fascinated with the possibility of a Cretan civilization and in 1899 he began to dig near the town of Knossos.

Almost immediately his efforts were rewarded. He discovered a magnificent royal palace—including a labyrinth that might have given rise to the legend—and abundant evidence that an advanced civilization had existed on Crete several centuries before the Trojan War took place.

Ever since Schliemann and Evans made their startling discoveries, it has been less easy to dismiss legend as a source of historical fact. In England, for example, excavators continue to search for evidence of the legendary British hero, King Arthur. Perhaps the most persistent legend of all, that of Atlantis, continues to gain supporters and inspire controversy. The source of the Atlantis legend is two of Plato's dialogues in which he describes life on an island utopia located somewhere in the Atlantic Ocean. According to the story, which Plato got from another source, Atlantis was destroyed by violent earthquakes that caused it to sink into the sea.

Many scholars dismiss the Atlantis story as impossible on various scientific grounds. This does not daunt the Atlantologists, however, who counter with their own evidence in support of its existence. Although most of them favor the view that

Atlantis was located in the Atlantic Ocean, others have suggested that it might have been a Mediterranean island, or not an island at all but a mainland state.

Certainly, the past hundred years or so have demonstrated the existence of many previously unknown civilizations. Time and again, archaeologists and travelers have discovered the remains of some unknown culture lying in a remote part of the world. Their discoveries have answered many old questions and raised almost as many new ones.

Few of these archaeological finds have been more spectacular than the Maya ruins of Mexico and Central America. Here, in thick jungle, in the 1840s, John Lloyd Stephens an American archaeologist, and the artist Frederick Catherwood, his English companion, found fantastically carved statues and temples and pyramids comparable to those of Egypt. Other explorers went on to reveal other pre-Columbian cultures, such as those of the Aztecs and Olmecs of Mexico and the Incas of Peru.

The Spanish invaders of the 16th century had discovered these civilizations, but their interest in them had been mainly predatory. They had confiscated the gold of the Aztecs and Incas and destroyed their cities. Only a few of them bothered to record what they saw, and their writings remained relatively unknown. It was not until the last century that archaeologists began to turn their attention to Central and South America and to rediscover pre-Columbian civilizations. Europeans and Americans (of both continents) who were accustomed to regard the Middle East as the original source of civilization had to revise their view of the world. Separated from Western culture by thousands of miles of ocean, the Indians of the Americas had independently created their own civilizations.

Or had they? Some people, noting resemblances between the native American cultures and those of the Old World, have suggested that some contact had occurred between the two

Cities Lost and Found

Below: a modern view of the great four-sided temple pyramid in the Mexican city state of Chichén Itzá. Known as the Castillo, or temple of Kukulcan, it was the ceremonial center from the 6th–13th century of first the Mayan and later the Toltec Empires.
Below left: the Castillo as it was when discovered by Europeans about 150 years ago. The artist Frederick Catherwood described it as "the grandest and most conspicuous object that towers above the plain. . . . It is built up, apparently solid, from the plain to a height of 75 feet." Although the pyramid as an architectural form was common to the Old and the New World, the functions of the Old and New World pyramids differed. The former were principally tombs, the latter used mainly as temples. In 1952, however, a burial crypt was discovered beneath a pyramid at Palenque, 300 miles southwest of Chichén Itzá, revealing a similarity of purpose and resurrecting speculation about links between the Old and New Worlds thousands of years ago.

Above: an aerial view of the island of Viti Levu, Fiji, in the Pacific. The island looks very like the mountain top of a sunken continent, and, indeed, there is a persistent belief in a lost continent in this area of the South Pacific. The inhabitants of the lost continent of Mu were supposed to have been the ancestors of both the ancient Egyptians and the Maya of Central America.

worlds centuries before the Spanish conquest. Also, there are Inca legends of a "white god" called Viracocha who came from across the sea and brought civilization to them. Artifacts have been found in South America that depict men with beards and narrow, beaked noses who look quite unlike Indians. Some of the people holding this "diffusionist" theory of the development of pre-Columbian culture believe that the contact was made by Egyptians or other North Africans who sailed across the Atlantic in boats made of papyrus reeds. Others believe that the visitors from over the sea were Atlanteans.

Atlantis is not the only supposed lost continent. Lemuria, a continent that once, it is said, linked southern Asia with eastern Africa, is believed by some people to have been the original home of the human species. Yet another lost continent, called Mu, is supposed to have been located in the south Pacific in the area now dotted by the islands of Polynesia. The islands are said to be the mountaintops of the former continent. According to the theory, Mu's advanced civilization produced the mysterious stone heads that stand on Easter Island.

Mysterious remains found anywhere in the world are usually interpreted by Atlantologists and other lost-continent adherents as evidence supporting their theory. There is certainly plenty of scope for speculation, for even known civilizations often present us with a mystery. About a hundred years ago, for example, the Hittites were identifiable only as an obscure tribe mentioned occasionally in the Bible. Today, thanks to archaeological detective work, we know that they were a powerful nation who once ruled a large part of the Middle East. Yet we still do not know where they came from originally, nor are we certain what happened to them after their empire collapsed.

We do know what happened to the Etruscans, those artistically gifted, pleasure-loving people who dominated ancient Italy: they were conquered and their civilization extinguished by the Romans. Their language, however, has defied countless attempts to decipher anything more than a few names and seems to be unrelated to any other language, ancient or modern. Many scholars believe that the Etruscans were emigrants to Italy and point to numerous resemblances between Etruscan culture and religion and those of eastern peoples—though as yet there is no conclusive proof of this theory.

In southern Africa, the ruins of Zimbabwe still inspire wonder and controversy. Are these stone towers and enclosures the remains of the legendary Ophir, the land from which King Solomon obtained his gold? Or are they the products of a much more recent African civilization—and, if so, what happened to the people who built them?

Now that we take myths a little more seriously than we did a few generations ago, the widespread stories of a world cataclysm are attracting some attention. The biblical account of a great flood that covered the earth and destroyed every living thing—except those on Noah's Ark—has parallels in the mythology of Babylonia, ancient Greece, India, Iceland, and many other countries. Their folklore contains harrowing stories of destruction by fire, or earthquake, or by a combination of natural forces. Of course, there are many possible explanations for these myths—the simplest being that to primitive people, a great natural disaster is viewed as an expression of divine wrath. The horror of the disaster is exaggerated with every retelling of the story. But it is just possible that these myths—like the Homeric legends—contain more truth than we suppose. Someday, perhaps, we will discover scientific evidence that some tremendous upheaval did occur in the remote past. Such evidence would make the story of Atlantis more believable than it is today.

A Sunken Continent?

One of the more fantastic variants of the Atlantis legend states that it was located on the site of the Sahara Desert—the rest of Africa, according to the theory, being covered with water. Geologists have shown, however, that the African continent has existed in its present shape for hundreds of thousands of years. If Plato's utopia was located there, it was not an island.

Yet the Sahara—one of the most inhospitable environments on earth—has yielded some surprising secrets. Tiny crocodiles live there in isolated desert pools, which they could not possibly have reached by migration. How did they get there? Ancient skeletons of elephants, giraffes, antelopes, and other animals have been found in this wasteland—thousands of miles from their present homes in the fertile parts of Africa. Human remains, too, have been discovered—not only skeletons thousands of years old but also flint tools and rock paintings and engravings. Some of the paintings show herds of cattle; others depict scenes of hunting, racing, and dancing. Obviously, at some time in its

Below: the South Pacific island of Bora-Bora. The island, and the other nearby islands, Tahiti and the Marquesas, are ancient volcanic craters with jagged peaks and ridges. They give the impression of being the tips of a mountain range of some sunken continent.

Lost Lands of the Sahara Desert

Below: The Peul girls, redrawn from a Neolithic cave fresco made between 7000 and 4000 years B.C. at Tassili-n-Ajjer (meaning "Plateau of the Rivers" in Tuareg language), South Algeria.

prehistory, the Sahara Desert was a fertile land.

Although exploration of the desert began during the last century, intensive study got underway only within the past few decades. In exploring dry canyons cut thousands of years ago by deep rivers, paleontologists have found Old Stone Age tools dating back perhaps 500,000 years. The New Stone Age is estimated to have begun in the Sahara sometime between 8000 and 6000 B.C., about the time that the climate became very rainy. At that time, too, more advanced peoples began migrating into this fertile area from all directions. Scientists believe that during this era the Sahara was the most densely populated region on earth. The communities appear to have had a fair degree of organization; there is evidence, for example, of a distinct class of craftsmen who made the tools used by the hunters and stock raisers and who also made delicate ornaments in which these people evidently delighted.

Around 2000 B.C., the Sahara began to dry up. The possible causes of this change in climate remain obscure. There may have been a disturbance in the zones of high and low pressure. But the increasing aridity of the region may also have been caused by the people who lived there, whose herds of cattle and goats must have consumed and destroyed enormous amounts of plant life. By the time the Sahara began to be mentioned by travelers it had become a dry region. In 450 B.C., Herodotus, the Greek historian comments on the large areas of the Sahara lacking any vegetation and on the sand dunes dotted with oases. The fertile Sahara had died and the Sahara we know today—desolate and unfriendly—had taken its place.

Few parts of the world have been so radically transformed as the Sahara. Yet the flowering and dying of civilizations is a worldwide phenomenon. Stone temples that once echoed to the sound of bells and chanting now sit empty and silent in the midst of encroaching jungle. Splendid columns that lined avenues through which triumphant armies marched now lie crumbling in the sand. We may know little of the people who lived in these lost lands, but their fascination endures. Contemplating fragments of their culture we are free to savor the mystery of a world that we can never know fully.

Right: part of an army of archers from a cave painting at Tassili-n-Ajjer. These two paintings and the many others found in the same area show that the Sahara once teemed with people and with the herds and wildlife that supported them. The sleek cattle, the elephants, rhinoceroses, giraffes, lions, gazelles, wild asses, and abundance of fish all point to a time when the area had a damp climate and rich pastures.

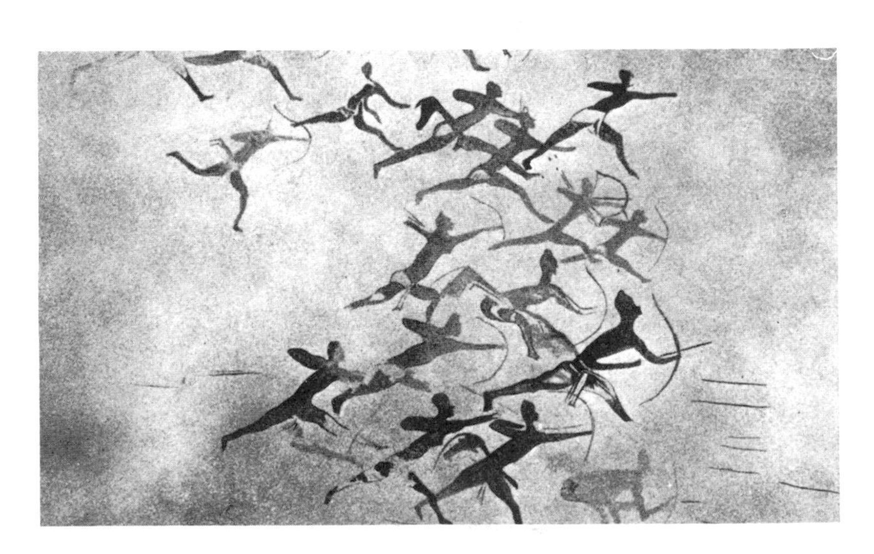

Opposite: the landscape of the Tassili region today. It is hard to believe that this wilderness of barren rock and sand, where only a few tussocks of dry grass and lizards and insects can survive, was once a land of sparkling rivers, rich pastures, thriving villages, and an abundance of wildlife.

Chapter 2
The Forgotten Hittites

To scholars of 100 years ago the Hittites appeared as just one of many small tribal peoples from the Middle East. Was it possible that they were more important than the records suggested? By the early 1900s evidence began to build up that the Hittites were the center of an empire that rivaled those of ancient Egypt and Assyria. When the Hittite royal library was found, which included a plea from a powerful queen of Egypt for a Hittite prince to share her throne, scholars knew that they had made one of the most exciting discoveries of the century—the forgotten Empire of the Hittites.

In several places in the Old Testament there are brief references to some people called Hittites. They seem to have been living in that part of Palestine where the Hebrew patriarch Abraham and his wife Sarah settled in their old age. When Sarah died, Abraham bought a burying ground from someone called Ephron the Hittite. Abraham's grandson Esau married a Hittite girl. Many generations later, King David seduced Bathsheba, the wife of Uriah the Hittite, one of David's officers. His successor King Solomon included some Hittite women among his numerous wives and concubines. The writer of the First Book of Kings goes on to list them along with Moabites, Ammonites, Edomites, Sidonians, and other "strange [foreign] women."

There is nothing in any of the Bible references to suggest that the Hittites (or *Chittim*, as they are called in the original Hebrew) were in any way a remarkable people. They appeared to pose no threat to the Israelites—unlike the powerful Egyptians and the Assyrians (a people occupying what is now mainly northern Iraq), for example. Yet one reference in the Bible long puzzled scholars. In Chapter Seven of the Second Book of Kings, a Syrian army is laying siege to the Israelite capital, Samaria, whose inhabitants are dying of a famine. During the night, God causes the Syrian soldiers to have a collective hallucination in which they hear the sound of a great army equipped with chariots and horses on the move. They say to each other, " 'Lo, the king of Israel hath hired against us the kings of the Hittites, and the

Opposite: the massive ruins of the King's Gate of the Hittite city of Hattusas, Bogazköy, Turkey. From obscure beginnings as immigrant settlers in the Anatolian plains, around 1900 B.C., the Hittites rose to be rulers of a mighty empire that reached throughout Asia Minor and Syria. Hattusas was the Hittite capital and its temples and palaces reflected the glory of its rulers. It was through the discovery of the royal library at Hattusas that scholars finally realized the significance of the ruins they were excavating.

The Hittites as Others Saw Them

kings of the Egyptians to come upon us.' " So terrifying is this prospect that the Syrians, leaving their tents, food, and possessions, flee for their lives.

Could it be, scholars wondered, that the Hittites were in fact a powerful nation? Otherwise, why would they be mentioned in the same breath with the Egyptians and cause such alarm? And if they were indeed a powerful nation, then somewhere there must be archaeological evidence of their civilization. But none had so far emerged.

Of course, there are many inexplicable statements in the Bible. Often a confusing point such as that in the Second Book of Kings turns out to be simply a mistranslation. But in 1822 the Rosetta Stone bearing Greek and Egyptian characters was deciphered and this made it possible for scholars for the first time to read Egyptian hieroglyphics. As the many Egyptian texts and inscriptions were translated, new evidence emerged regarding the Hittites that put the puzzling biblical reference in a new light. Egyptian records contained several references to the "people of Kheta," which scholars thought might be the same as the "Chittim" of the Bible. In 1300 B.C. Rameses II had fought the "abominable Kheta" and their allies at Kadesh, in Syria. A huge relief carved on the walls of an Egyptian temple shows the pharaoh and his troops inflicting injuries on their foes, who are depicted as rather unattractive long-haired people wearing heavy clothing. Later in his reign, Rameses made a peace treaty with the Kheta, and this treaty is carved on the wall of one of the temples at Karnak. For some time this was all that could be discovered about the enigmatic Hittites. Then toward the end of the 1800s more bits of evidence began to come to light that put scholars on the long path toward the eventual discovery of a forgotten empire.

The way was strewn with examples of mysterious writing. In 1812 in the Syrian city of Hamath, Johann L. Burckhardt, a young Swiss traveler, had spotted a block of basalt set into the

Below: the Abu Simbel reliefs of the Battle of Kadesh—the great battle between the Egyptian and Hittite armies. Kadesh was to be the deciding battle between the two greatest powers in the world of that time, and came in 1296 B.C. after many years of skirmishing and border fighting. It ended in stalemate. The Egyptian ruler, Pharaoh Rameses II had the battle depicted in reliefs and friezes as a great triumph for the Egyptian forces. The propaganda used in the pictures and texts was so exaggerated that for many years scholars did not realize that the pharaoh had fought the armies of a great nation. It seemed merely that Rameses II had put down a rebellious border state.

corner of a house and inscribed with hieroglyphic characters. Burckhardt described the stone in his book *Travels in Syria and the Holy Land*, noting that the characters "in no way resembled those of Egypt." Only a few years later, Burckhardt died, and his discovery of the Hamath stone—which was but one of his many discoveries—was virtually forgotten. His book was not published until 1922.

In the meantime, however, two American travelers found the same stone and several others like it when they visited Hamath in 1870. When they tried to make copies of the inscriptions, the local inhabitants warned them off. The stones, it seemed, were regarded as having miraculous powers, including the ability to cure rheumatism, and the citizens of Hamath did not want foreigners tampering with their effectiveness.

A year later, William Wright, an Irish missionary, finally succeeded in getting a good look at the stones—but only through the intervention of the Turkish governor of Syria. The governor then had the stones removed to the new archaeological museum at Constantinople, after first allowing Wright to examine them and make impressions, which the missionary gave to the British Museum.

About the same time, a stone with the same kind of writing on it was discovered in a mosque at Aleppo, about 100 miles north of Hamath. This stone, too, was credited with healing powers. When European scholars showed interest in the stone the townspeople removed it and hid it—but not before the scholars had made copies.

No one could decipher the strange hieroglyphs, but Archibald Sayce, a British archaeologist, put forward the theory that the picture writing was Hittite. About two years after Sayce proposed this idea, a British Museum team of excavators discovered the long-lost city of Carchemish. It was this city by the Euphrates River that Assyrian inscriptions dating from around 1100 B.C. had described as the capital of the "Land of Hatti" and the Hatti were yet one more candidate for the identity of the Hittites. Among the foundations of the city they found a number of inscriptions in the same indecipherable picture-writing as had been found at Hamath and Aleppo. On the evidence gathered so far it seemed that if the Hatti and Hittites were the same, then their kingdom had been located in Syria.

Then some surprising new evidence appeared. An English traveler named E. J. Davis reported seeing similar inscriptions carved into the rock in the Taurus Mountains in southern Turkey. The inscriptions themselves were next to some relief carvings that reminded scholar-detectives of other large-scale reliefs found some years earlier north of the Taurus Mountains on the Anatolian Plateau. Suddenly, it no longer seemed so certain that the Hittites' home was in Syria. Might they in fact have come from the bleak, rocky plains of Anatolia? Sayce published another paper entitled "The Hittites in Asia Minor," advancing this new theory.

As yet, however, there was no proof. No one knew for certain that the hieroglyphs were Hittite and no one had yet succeeded in deciphering them.

Then in 1887 the search for the Hittites took a new turn. An

Above: a 14th-century B.C. clay tablet found at Tell el Amarna. It is from an Egyptian provincial governor excusing himself to the Pharaoh Akhenaton for receiving an envoy from the Hittite king and is one of a large number of tablets from Akhenaton's archives known as the "Armarna Letters." Archaeologists found that not only were there the usual letters from vassal kings and governors but there was one from the Hittite king Suppiluliumas, congratulating the Pharaoh, as one equal to another, on his accession to the throne. Below: this map of the Middle East shows Hattusas and other Hittite landmarks.

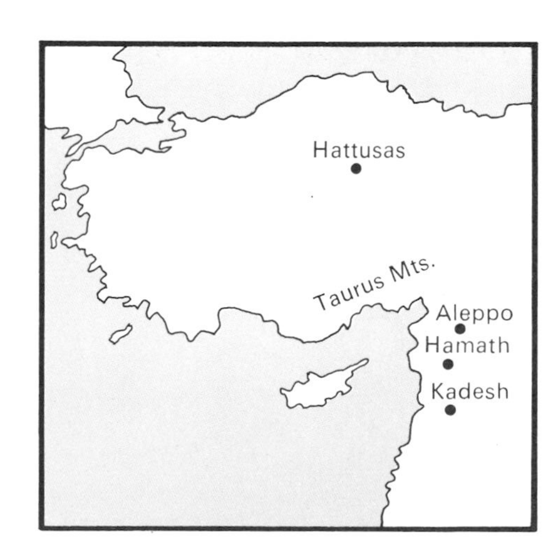

Above: Dr. William Wright of the British and Foreign Bible Society who published his book *The Empire of the Hittites, with Decipherment of the Hittite Inscriptions by Professor A. H. Sayce* in 1884. In it he put forward for the first time the idea that the then recently discovered Hittites had in fact controlled an empire—an empire, it seemed, that even the Greeks and Romans 2000 years ago had not known existed!

Egyptian peasant woman digging for fertilizer near the site of an ancient Egyptian city at Tell el Amarna found some clay tablets inscribed with the wedge-shaped script known as cuneiform writing. Realizing that such objects might be valuable, other people began to dig at the site, and within the year some 200 tablets came on the black market in Cairo. The export of antiquities was prohibited by Egyptian law, but some found their way into foreign museums. Examination revealed that they were the archives of the Pharaoh Akhenaten (reigned 1379-1361 B.C.) whose capital city stood near Tell el Amarna, where the tablets were found.

The "Amarna letters," as they came to be called, included correspondence from the leaders of the other nations of Akhenaten's time, such as Babylonia and Assyria. Most of them were written in the Akkadian (Babylonian) language and all of them in cuneiform. Among the tablets were some from the leaders of Syrian and Palestinian states loyal to Egypt, in which they referred to the military activities of the king of Hatti and complained of his aggression—more evidence that the Hittites were a military power. One letter, also written in Akkadian, was from the Hittite king himself, Suppiluliumas. Addressing the pharaoh as an equal, he congratulated him on his accession to the throne. The Hittites were beginning to emerge into the light of history.

The letters referring to the activities of the Hittite army indicated that they were moving southward into Syria and Lebanon, which suggested that the Hittite kingdom itself was located north of the Taurus Mountains.

Although all the Amarna letters were written in the Babylonian cuneiform script, two of them were in an unknown language. Scholars were able to discover only that they were addressed to the king of a place called Arzawa; and so, for want of any other identification, the language was dubbed "Arzawan." Yet another unknown people had appeared on the scene.

About 10 years after the discovery of the Amarna tablets, a few tablets written in "Arzawan" were found near the village of Bogazköy, in northern Turkey. Only recently had the bleak Anatolian plain begun to attract the attention of archaeologists. Before then, they had been fully occupied in excavating the legendary cities of Mesopotamia and the Aegean and the temples and tombs of Egypt. There were, it is true, some intriguing ruins in the area around Bogazköy but as there was no historical evidence that any very advanced civilization had existed there, there was no good reason to comb this desolate part of the world in search of an ancient civilization.

The Bogazköy ruins first came to light in the 1830s when Charles Félix-Marie Texier, a Frenchman, discovered the remains of a city "as large as Athens in its prime," encircled by a wall whose gates were adorned with carvings of lions and a sphinx. Not far away, Texier found a formation of rocks decorated with large reliefs and with hieroglyphics later found to match those discovered at Hamath and Aleppo. By the end of the 1800s, having yielded examples of both the hieroglyphic "Hittite" and the cuneiform "Arzawan," Bogazköy was becoming a place of some interest.

One of the people who found it interesting was Dr. Hugo

Winckler, an expert in cuneiform at Berlin University. Winckler was familiar with the "Arzawan" texts from Tell el Amarna, and in 1903 had gone on an expedition to Lebanon to look for more writing in this language. Although this expedition was not successful, it was to lead to a great discovery. Some months after his return to Berlin he received by mail a tablet in "Arzawan," sent to him by a Turkish museum official whom he had met on his trip. As soon as possible Winckler hurried to Constantinople, where the museum official, Macridy Bey, told him that the tablet came from Bogazköy.

The two men set out for the remote village—with Winckler, who seems to have been a cantankerous individual, complaining every step of the way of the primitive traveling conditions. The journey was, however, worthwhile. Winckler gathered 34 more cuneiform tablets before the rainy season forced him to discontinue the search.

Investigating the Hittites

Left: Photograph taken during the excavations at Bogazköy in 1907 by Dr. Hugo Winckler. It shows a view of the Lion Gate on the southwestern wall of Hattusas and, behind the party of excavators, one of the two towers with which each of the gateways was guarded. It was in and around these ruins that Winckler and his party dug for some clue as to who were the architects of this once-vast city. He was well rewarded for he found the royal archives, which marked the city as the capital of the Hittite nation.
Below: the present-day remains of the city of Hattusas at Bogazköy. The most impressive of the remains are the massive walls constructed some time during the 19th to 18th centuries B.C. and which readily caught Winckler's attention.

Above: The Meeting of the Gods, a drawing from *A Description of Asia Minor*, by a French traveler, Charles Felix-Marie Texier, and published in 1839. It was Texier who rediscovered the ruins of Bogazköy and his descriptions of them aroused wide interest among scholars. The Meeting of the Gods was redrawn from a rock shrine some three-quarters of a mile outside the main city of the Hittites.

By the following summer of 1907 he had obtained financial support for the excavation of Bogazköy, and with Macridy Bey and a German assistant he set up operations there. Villagers dug among the ruins in the haphazard way of those days, while Winckler examined and catalogued the hundreds of tablets that they unearthed. Most of the tablets, being in "Arzawan," were undecipherable. But some were in Akkadian, which Winckler could read easily. One day he was handed an Akkadian tablet that began:

"The covenant of Rameses, Beloved of Amun, Great King of the land of Egypt, hero,

"with Hattusilis, Great King, King of the land of Hatti, his brother, providing for good peace and good brotherhood in the relations of the Great Kingdom between them for ever . . ."

It was confirmation of the peace treaty made after the battle of Kadesh, the same one that was carved in Egyptian hieroglyphics on the temple wall at Karnak.

For Winckler it was an electrifying moment. He held in his hands a letter written to one king from another, a letter of such importance that the recipient would certainly have kept it safely stored in the royal archives. For that, clearly, was what Winckler had discovered: the royal archives and the capital city of the Hittites, called Hattusas.

Of the 10,000 tablets excavated by Winckler's team at Bogazköy there were enough in Akkandian to enable scholars to begin piecing together the formerly unknown Hittite history. The "Arzawan" language in which the majority of the tablets were written, was obviously the Hittites' own language. As for the hieroglyphics, there were relatively few of these, and philologists (language experts) were unable at that point to determine their relationship, if any, to the cuneiform Hittite.

The cuneiform language was by no means easy to translate. For several years, the philologists had no success, partly because they assumed that, like Akkadian and the other languages of that part of the ancient world, it was a Semitic language. Then, while examining a Hittite text, Bedřich Hrozný, a Czech scholar, suddenly saw resemblances to German words. Further study revealed grammatical similarities to other Indo-European languages and confirmed one philologist's earlier guess that the two "Arzawan" letters found at Tell el Amarna were written in an Indo-European tongue. By the 1930s most of the important Hittite texts had been translated.

Wherever the Hittites came from originally, they had evidently moved down into Anatolia by about 1900 B.C. We know this from writings left by Assyrian traders. The Assyrians then controlled the trade route leading from Anatolia to Mesopotamia and had established several trading settlements in Anatolia. They kept careful records of their dealings with the native population. Those found at Kültepe (the ancient city of Kanesh) contain a number of Hittite names among those of the Hattite people, who are now called Proto-Hittites.

Confusingly, the people we call Hittites were not, strictly speaking, entitled to the name. The true Hittites were the native Anatolian tribe whose home was the area around Hattusas, from which their own name was derived. The Indo-European invaders, whatever they originally called themselves, simply adopted the name of the original inhabitants.

It seems to have been a relatively peaceful invasion. There is no evidence of any sudden attack on Anatolia or any large-scale violence. The Indo-European migrants must have lived in Anatolia for at least 150 years before they began to build up military power and conquer the land they lived in. Their conquest was made easier by quarrels among the Hattian princes, who were intermittently at war with each other.

The first Hittite monarch to make a name for himself was Anittas, who ruled a city called Kussara and who began to conquer the lands and cities of his Proto-Hittite neighbors. One of these conquered cities, Nesa, he made his new capital; but Hattusas—for some unknown reason—he destroyed and declared accursed. "But in its place I sowed weeds," he wrote. "Whosoever becomes king after me and peoples Hattusas once more, let him be smitten by the weather-god of Heaven!" Ironically, this accursed city was to become the capital of the Hittite kingdom and empire established by Anittas' successors.

There is a documentary gap between the reign of Anittas, who died around 1750 B.C., and the next powerful ruler, who is sometimes called Labarnas in Hittite texts but who later called himself Hattusilis, the "man of Hattusas." Apparently undaunted by Anittas' curse, he moved the capital to that city, which had an easily defensible site, and then began to expand his kingdom southward and eastward. His adopted son, Mursilis I, launched an ambitious campaign of conquest down into Syria, where he subdued Aleppo, and then drove on into the Eurphrates valley. His aim was partly to capture this vital trade route, for Assyria had become a vassal of the Babylonians and was no longer an effective trading power. Mursilis and his army eventually reached the splendid city of Babylon, which they captured and looted. This seems to have been a purely aggressive act, for there is no evidence that the Babylonians posed an

More Evidence

Above: fragment of the border of a 15th-century B.C. clay vase found at Bogazköy. It is quite possible that the decorative fragment is based upon an actual Hittite city wall and watchtower, and gives scholars some idea of how to reconstruct the upper parts of the ruins of the city. The craftsman has even imitated the wooden beams projecting from the floor and roof of the tower.

The Role of the Hittite Women

Below: a panel from a small golden shrine belonging to the Pharaoh Tutankhamen. It shows the young pharaoh and his queen Ankhesenamun. After the death of her husband, Ankhesenamun wrote to Suppiliumas, the Hittite king, asking him to send one of his sons to marry her (according to Egyptian law, as the daughter of the previous pharaoh, her husband automatically became king of Egypt). After first sending a messenger to find out if the plea were a trap, the wary King Suppiluliumas eventually sent one of his sons to Egypt. It appears he was too late. By hesitating, the queen's enemies must have had time to organize themselves, and the Hittite prince was assassinated. The widowed queen was forced to marry an important palace courtier.

immediate threat to the Hittites. It served, however, to give the Hittites an instant reputation as a power to be reckoned with. On the return journey, Mursilis reinforced his reputation by conquering the Hurrians, a then-powerful people through whose kingdom—called Mitanni—he had to pass.

Mursilis had been home for only a few years when he was assassinated by one of his family. For several generations after this the Hittite kingdom was both torn from within by palace intrigues and assassinations and weakened on its borders by attacks from their neighbors, chiefly the Hurrians. Finally, one king, Telepinus (reigned 1525-1500 B.C.), managed to establish a law of succession that was generaly followed throughout subsequent Hittite history. He also succeeded in repulsing the barbarian invaders that threatened the northern and eastern frontiers of his kingdom, and he made a treaty of peace with the kingdom of Kizzuwatna to the west.

The reemergence of the Hittites as a military power began some 60 years after Telepinus' death. King Tudhaliyas II moved into Syria and destroyed the city of Aleppo, which had defected to the Hurrian camp during the period of Hittite weakness. The Hurrian king of Mitanni responded to this new threat by forming an alliance with Egypt, and once again the Hittite kingdom had to defend itself against attacks from the south.

In the year 1380 B.C., King Suppiluliumas I came to the throne. Soon after his accession he began to build an empire. He made a surprise attack on Mitanni and sacked its capital city. He then reconquered the Syrian states that had depended on Mitanni and pushed southward as far as Lebanon, acquiring several states

that had been vassals of Egypt. Fortunately for Suppiluliumas, Egypt, under Akhenaten, was preoccupied with religious reform

border states.

Suppiluliumas then set about consolidating his empire by means of a series of diplomatic marriages. Members of his family were married off to the heads of the newly conquered states. Thus ties of family loyalty strengthened the treaties between Hatti and its vassals.

The king was rather suspicious, however, when he received a marriage proposal for one of his sons from the queen of Egypt. The queen was Ankhesenamun, widow of the boy king Tutankhamen, who had succeeded Akhenaten.

"My husband has died," wrote the young queen, "and I have no sons, but of you it is said that you have many sons. If you would send me one of your sons, he could become my husband. I will on no account take one of my subjects and make him my husband. I am very much afraid."

It seems that the queen's grandfather, Ay, who already held considerable power, planned to marry the girl himself and so become pharaoh, as soon as the time allotted for embalming Tutankhamen's body was over. Suppiluliumas knew nothing of this, and he suspected a trap. He sent an envoy to Egypt to investigate. The envoy returned with another message from Ankhesenamun, chiding him for his distrust and repeating her plea for a husband. Without further delay the king dispatched his son Zannanza to Egypt. But the crafty courtier Ay had the Hittite prince assassinated on his arrival, and married the unfortunate Ankhesenamun himself.

Nearly a century later a union did take place between the two royal houses when Rameses II took as his principal wife the Hittite princess Naptera. This marriage took place 13 years after the two nations signed the peace treaty following the Battle of Kadesh—the same treaty that Winckler discovered at Bogazkôy.

Although the reliefs at Karnak represent Kadesh as an Egyptian victory, in reality neither side emerged clearly triumphant. The immediate cause of the conflict had been the defection to Egypt of a Hittite buffer state. After the battle, this state, Amurru, returned to the Hittite fold, preserving the status quo.

Although the Hittites were a warlike people, they seem to have been relatively civilized by the standards of the day. There is little evidence of their having committed atrocities against their foes, and they ruled their vassal states firmly but diplomatically, trying to win their loyalty rather than terrorizing them, as the Assyrians were to do later.

The Hittites appear to have had a strong sense of justice. Although specific information about their legal system is sparse, we do have a document instructing the king's judicial representatives in the conduct of a case. It repeatedly urges them to "do what is just" and "administer justice fairly." However, the same document also states that "if anyone oppose the judgment of the king, his house shall become a ruin. If anyone oppose the judgment of a dignitary his head shall be cut off."

The Hittites were a religious people and collected a large

Wall relief of Queen Tuwarisas, wife of King Araras, with her youngest child and a goat, made around the 8th century B.C. The position of women among the Hittites was superior to that of women in lands round about them. They were not regarded merely as the possessions of their husbands. Women who married slaves kept their status as free women. They helped choose a husband for their daughters and could disown their sons. In special cases they could even divorce their husbands. A widowed queen would retain her title and position—she was never merely the king's wife but had definite duties, mainly religious—even when her son came to the throne. His wife had to await the death of her mother-in-law before she was allowed to use the title "queen."

Above: wall painting from Abu Simbel in Egypt of the pharaoh Rameses II fighting the Hittites at the Battle of Kadesh. Although the artist has made the pharaoh appear to be cutting through his enemies like a reaper through a wheatfield, in fact Rameses nearly lost the battle and only just managed to hold the formidable Hittites to a stalemate.

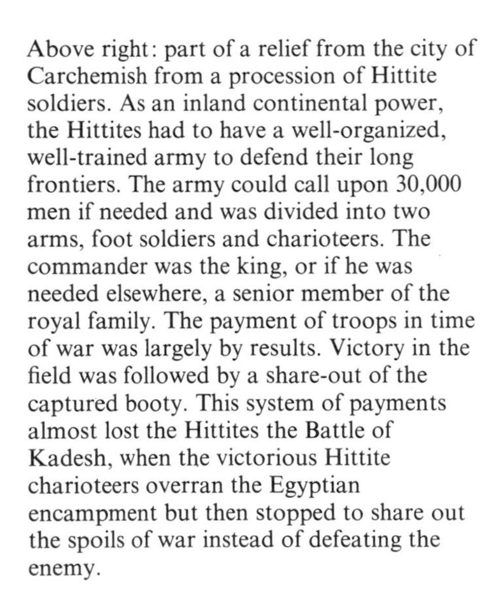

Above right: part of a relief from the city of Carchemish from a procession of Hittite soldiers. As an inland continental power, the Hittites had to have a well-organized, well-trained army to defend their long frontiers. The army could call upon 30,000 men if needed and was divided into two arms, foot soldiers and charioteers. The commander was the king, or if he was needed elsewhere, a senior member of the royal family. The payment of troops in time of war was largely by results. Victory in the field was followed by a share-out of the captured booty. This system of payments almost lost the Hittites the Battle of Kadesh, when the victorious Hittite charioteers overran the Egyptian encampment but then stopped to share out the spoils of war instead of defeating the enemy.

number of gods, including many from neighboring countries. Teshub, the all-important weather-god, for instance, they adopted from the Hurrians. In common with other ancient peoples, the Hittites also deified their kings, but only after their death. One of the king's responsibilities was to lead the most important of the Hittite religious rituals, the 38-day spring festival. Many of these festivals must have been celebrated at Yazilikaya, the beautiful rock sanctuary near Bogazköy whose walls are inscribed with reliefs depicting the Hittite gods and kings.

The Hittites do not seem to have been a very imaginative people. Their art never reached the degree of sophistication and skill shown by the Egyptians or the Assyrians, for example. Apart from a few myths, their writings consist mainly of religious texts of a tedious, ritualistic character. Of their architecture only foundations remain, giving us a clear idea of floor plans but almost no idea of Hittite structures.

It was in the arts of warfare and diplomacy that the Hittites excelled. They seem to have invented chariots with spoked wheels, which were lighter and more maneuverable than the disk-wheeled variety, and their swift chariot troops were the main strength of the Hittite army. It was a surprise attack by these charioteers that lost Rameses the initiative at Kadesh and prevented an Egyptian victory.

After Kadesh, the Hittite Empire was to last for another 100 years. Having established a balance of power with Egypt, the Hittites enjoyed fairly amicable relations with that great kingdom. The new threat came from Assyria, which was once again independent and was just beginning its rise to power. Also toward the end of the 13th century, conflicts with western Anatolian states increased, particularly with Arzawa, one of their closest neighbors to the west. To the north the Phrygians, another Indo-European people, were moving down and pressing against the northern frontier. Hittite texts also refer to a people called the Ahhiyawans, who, according to one theory may have been the Achaeans—Homer's name for the Greeks. Further excavations of Hittite sites may turn up evidence in favor of the theory—and perhaps historical support, too, for Homer's account of the war between the Achaeans and the Trojans.

The fall of Troy took place around the year 1200 B.C., about the same time that the Hittite Empire collapsed. We do not know exactly how it collapsed—detailed historical information has not been discovered. We do know, however, that throughout the Middle East and the Mediterranean lands, great upheavals were taking place. Egypt was attacked by invaders whom the Egyptians called the "Sea People." The Mycenaean civilization based in southern Greece was destroyed by Dorian invaders moving down from the north. Whatever specific events led to the final extinction of the Hittite Empire, they were part of a pattern of

Warriors and God Kings

Left: a statue of a Hittite king, carved in the Assyrian style from the end of the 8th century B.C. Hittite kings were regarded as the principal servants of the gods and spent a large proportion of their time attending to innumerable public rituals connected with the many gods. Unlike many of their neighbors, the Hittites never worshiped their kings as gods during their lifetime. When dead, however, they were frequently depicted in the pose and dress of a god, as here.

Above: a detail of a procession of gods from a carved relief at the rock shrine at Yazlikaya outside Hattusas. Their chief god was the weather god, a deity that corresponded to the Greek Zeus, whose sign in picture-writing was the lightning flash. The chief female divinity was the sun goddess, wife of the weather god. The gods would speak to their worshipers through oracles, or their wishes could be discovered by examining the livers or entrails of sacrificed animals, or by noting the flight of birds.

migration and political ferment that affected virtually all of the known world.

According to Greek writings, the Phrygians now became the dominant power in Anatolia. As to the fate of the Hittite people, this is still, to some extent a mystery. Some of them must have moved south into Syria. For here, south of the Taurus Mountains, Hittite culture reemerged in what we call the Neo-Hittite states. These were a number of more or less independent city-states, a few of which—notably Carchemish—had once been vassals of the Hittite Empire. It is probable that the passage in the Second Book of Kings about the "kings of the Hittites" is a reference to the rulers of the states, and not to the kings of the Hittite Empire. These petty kings were also the Hittites referred to by the Assyrian king Tiglath-pileser I in a document dating from around 1100 B.C.

The extent to which these Neo-Hittite states were related to the Anatolian Hittite Empire is still in doubt. From the evidence it looks as if their language was that of hieroglyphic carvings that Burckhardt and others discovered in Syria during the last century, and not that found on the cuneiform tablets at Bogazköy. Philologists had been trying to decipher the hieroglyphic writing for decades when, in 1947, a bilingual text was discovered. It was found at the ancient town of Karatepe, capital of the Hittite province of Kizzuwatna. A long hieroglyphic inscription on a palace wall was followed by another text in Phoenician. Comparison of the two texts revealed that their content was the same in both cases. Philologists have established that this writing was a dialect of an Indo-European language called Luwian, which resembled cuneiform Hittite in some respects. Although hieroglyphic Hittite was sometimes used by the scribes of Hattusas, examples of this language have more often been found in Syria. Some writers have suggested that it was the people of Kizzuwatna who moved down into Syria from their homeland in the Taurus Mountains and brought Hittite culture, and the hieroglyphic Hittite language, into this area. Unfortunately, few Hittite writings have survived from this period, and we have only the sketchiest outline of the history of these Neo-Hittite states. At Carchemish, excavators discovered hieroglyphics giving a reasonably complete genealogy of the rulers of that state; but most of the little we know of Neo-Hittite history comes from the records of other nations, mainly Assyria. Apparently the Neo-Hittite states enjoyed a certain amount of prosperity, for the increasingly powerful kings of Assyria were able to demand large amounts of gold and silver from them as tribute.

For several centuries Assyrian power waxed and waned, but by the early 9th century B.C. Assyria had become a formidable aggressor. In 876 the Assyrian king marched his armies through Syria with virtually no resistance from the Hittite rulers, who apparently made no effort to combine against him. A few years later, 12 kings of Palestine and Syria formed an alliance against Assyria, which the Assyrians ruthlessly crushed. Their king boasted that he "scattered their corpses far and wide . . . With my weapons I made their blood to flow down the valleys of the land . . . With their bodies I spanned the Orontes as with a bridge."

For a while the Neo-Hittite states enjoyed some autonomy under Assyrian rule, but in 738 Assyria began annexing these states. By the 7th century they were merely provinces of Assyria. Their language and culture were dying out. The very existence of the great empire of Hattusas, from whicq they had derived much of their civilization, was sinking into oblivion.

Today, after more than 70 years of rediscovering the Hittites,

The Religions of the Hittites

Below: King Shulumeli offering a libation to the weather god, from a stone relief of between 1050 and 850 B.C. Our information on the Hittite gods comes mainly from carvings in low relief at the many shrines and temples. None of the large images of the gods have survived, perhaps because they were made of precious metals and so disappeared when the Hittite empire faded from history around 1200 B.C.

The People of a Thousand Gods

we still have many unanswered questions about them. For one thing, some of the statements in the Old Testament referring to Hittites living in Palestine do not tally with what we have learned of Hittite history. When Abraham arrived in Palestine he found living there the "sons of Heth," whom the writer also calls Hittites. This was around 1700 B.C., when the Hittites were just beginning to achieve power in Anatolia and had not started their expansion into Syria. Even at its peak, centuries later, the Hittite Empire never reached into Palestine. It is possible that the people called Hittites in the story of Abraham were really Hattians, the Proto-Hittites who had for some reason wandered far from their Anatolian home and settled in the hills of Palestine. The confusing similarity of the names "Hattian" and "Hittite" might account for this puzzling biblical passage.

Later, in Chapter 13 of the Book of Numbers we read that when Moses led the Israelites into the "land of Canaan" they found Hittites among the tribes that lived in the mountains. Although we do not know the exact dates of the Exodus, it may have occurred as late as the mid-13th century B.C. By this time, of course, the Hittite Empire was at its zenith and embraced most of Syria. Yet Palestine was in the Egyptian—not the Hittite—sphere of influence. One Hittite text offers a possible explanation. Written in the time of Suppiluliumas, it states that the "weather-god of Hatti brought the men of Kurustamma [a northern Hittite state] into the land of Egypt"—a term meaning all the land under Egyptian rule. Exactly why they went there the writer doesn't say, but the British scholar Oliver Gurney, in his book *The Hittites*, suggests that the reference to the weather-god may mean that the move was organized or sanctioned by the Hittite state. The text goes on to say that these people and the

Below: a king and queen worshiping before the statue of a bull. The bull played an important part in Hittite religion and appeared to be synonymous with the all-powerful weather god.

Right: a Hittite battle chariot. The chariot was made of a wooden frame covered with leather and mounted on a wide axle which ended with a spoked wooden wheel—which, it is thought, was probably invented by the Hittites. The lightweight chariot was extremely maneuverable and contributed greatly to the success of the Hittite armies.

"people of Egypt" then violated an oath they had sworn to the weather-god; whereupon the Hittite king "invaded the border land of Egypt." It is possible that these people from Kurustamma settled in the hills of Palestine and that they are the Hittites referred to in Numbers and some of the other parts of the Old Testament. As yet, however, this is only a guess.

Another question that has not been answered is the whereabouts of the original home of the Hittites. It has now been established that they came from the north, but this could include almost anywhere in Europe and Asia. Philologists have pointed out one possible clue: the Hittite language belongs to the "centum" group of Indo-European languages. These are the language groups, including Greek, Italic, Celtic, and Germanic, that originally used a variant of "centum" to express the number 100. (The Romance languages still use "cent," "cento," and so on; and in English the root survives in such words as "century" and "centipede.") The eastern Indo-European languages used variants of "satem" for 100. This bit of evidence supports the theory held by many scholars that the Hittites originally came from Europe—possibly from the area of the Danube. Other scholars, however, believe that they came into Anatolia through the Caucasus Mountains and were of eastern origin.

There also remains the question of what happened to the Hittites after the collapse of their empire. Although some of them moved into Syria and helped to form the Neo-Hittite states, and some must have remained in Anatolia under the rule of the invaders, it is possible that others may have moved north. In his book *The Hittites, People of a Thousand Gods,* the German writer Johannes Lehmann offers for consideration an intriguing theory relating to this question.

In A.D. 98 the Roman historian Tacitus wrote in his *Germania* of a warlike people called the Chatti who lived between the Rhine and Weser rivers. In the course of time the name Chatti was altered to Catti, then Hassi, and finally Hessians. Their land was called Hesse. Were the Chatti of whom Tacitus wrote the descendants of the Hittites of Anatolia? The idea seems far-fetched. Yet, Lehmann observes, archaeologists have discovered signs of Hittite influence—if not of their actual presence—in Western Europe. Images of a god riding on a bull, the Hittite weather-god, have been dug up at sites all along a path leading from Syria through Anatolia and then into Europe along the Danube and the Rhine, with an offshoot leading into Italy. A few have even been found in Britain. A map showing these sites is included in a book entitled *Altanatolien* by the German scholar Theodor Bossert.

A 1500-mile migration by the Hittites is a long way from being proven, but it is not all that implausible. Other peoples, notably the American Indians, have migrated for thousands of miles. It may be that in the next few years or decades conclusive proof of a Hittite migration to Germany will come to light. The possibility that some of the Hessian mercenaries who took part in the American War of Independence may have been remote descendants of the Hittites would certainly add a strange footnote to history.

Above: a gold pendant in the form of a seated goddess. It is probably the sun goddess called, among other titles: Mother of all the Gods, Queen of the Land of Hatti, Queen of Heaven and Earth. Not only was she the wife of the chief male deity, the weather god, but she sometimes took precedence over him. Her cult extended far beyond the borders of the Hittite empire, where she was worshiped under other names.

Chapter 3
The Mysterious Etruscans

Who were the prosperous, enterprising, luxury-loving people who suddenly appeared in central Italy in the 7th century B.C.? And where did they come from? The people themselves are silent. They left few writings apart from tomb inscriptions and a few short texts, and these remain largely indecipherable. To their Greek and Roman contemporaries they were known as Etruscans or Tyrrhenians, and it is through the writings of these contemporaries that much of what we know about the Etruscans has been gathered. Meanwhile, we await the finding of a bilingual text—in Etruscan and a known language—to unravel some of the mystery surrounding these unusual people.

Before Rome became a republic it was ruled by a dynasty of Etruscan kings. Sextus, the son of one of these kings, became infatuated with a Roman matron named Lucretia. One night when Lucretia's husband was away, Sextus gained entrance to her bedroom and threatened to kill her if she did not allow him to make love to her. Lucretia declared that she would rather die than betray her husband, to which the inflamed Sextus replied that if she forced him to kill her he would place a murdered naked slave beside her body so as to give the impression that she had been killed while committing adultery. Lucretia was forced to comply.

Returning home, Lucretia's husband Collatinus found her in tears. After hearing the cause, he tried to console her, assuring her that she was not dishonored because she had been taken by force. But Lucretia did not take so lenient a view of her predicament. "It is for you to see what is due to him. As for me, though I acquit myself of guilt, from punishment I do not discharge myself; nor shall any woman survive her dishonor pleading the example of Lucretia." And she plunged a knife into her heart.

This outrage by the son of a much-hated king was all Collatinus and his friends needed to incite them to rebellion. They carried Lucretia's body to the forum, where they soon attracted a large crowd. Their grief and anger had the desired effect. The Roman people decided to banish the king, Tarquin the Proud, along with his family. When Tarquin returned to Rome from his

Opposite: sculpture of an Etruscan husband and wife from a tomb at Cerveteri dating from around 550 B.C. Much about the Etruscans remains a mystery to this day. Some scholars think that their looks—facial bone structure, sloe-eyes, the way they dressed their hair, the man's beard, their clothes—suggest an ancestry somewhere in Asia Minor. Herodotus, the 5th-century B.C. Greek historian, states categorically that they came from Lydia (in what is now western Turkey). Archaeologists and language experts still search hopefully for new clues that will unravel the mystery of these luxury-loving enigmatic people.

Above: the interior of an Etruscan tomb from the 4th century B.C. Tombs were built to represent a room in an Etruscan house with sloping ceiling, a central beam, and supporting pillars. Plaster representations of articles used in the daily life of a rich Etruscan family have been used to decorate the interior; they include a wine jug, a ladle, a wheel of cheese, and a basin on a tripod.

Below: Italy, showing the Etruscan empire at its greatest extent in the 7th century B.C.

military camp the gates were shut against him. Sextus was killed by the revolutionaries and the other sons were sent into exile.

Such, in abbreviated form, is the Roman historian Livy's account of how in 510 B.C. Rome came to shake off Etruscan rule and begin its long road to domination of the known world.

It is doubtful if the rape of Lucretia—if in fact it really happened—was the immediate cause of the Roman revolt. The story has all the earmarks of propaganda: typically licentious Etruscan assaults typically virtuous Roman lady and brings down on himself and his co-oppressors the vengeance of the outraged patriots. It is worth remembering that the story was not written until some 500 years after the city's liberation and that its author was a Roman historian motivated by a desire to present his nation's history in the most favorable light.

True or not, the story is unusual in that it describes the action of an individual Etruscan. For although we now know a great deal about the Etruscan way of life, the people themselves remain elusive. They have faces—the faces painted on the walls of their tombs and sculpted in terracotta—but no identities in any meaningful sense of the word. This is because we have no Etruscan literature. We have not discovered any Etruscan Plato, or Sophocles, or Seneca to comment on the nature of humanity from an Etruscan viewpoint or give expression to Etruscan myths and ideals; there are no accounts of Etruscan heroes or statesmen written by their compatriots. Those examples of Etruscan writing that we possess are for the most part brief tomb inscriptions identifying the deceased and the parents of the deceased, as well as a few short texts, apparently of a religious nature, the longest of which contains about 1500 words.

Not only is the written legacy meager; it is also largely incomprehensible. As yet, no one has succeeded in translating the Etruscan language. The few Etruscan words whose meanings are known are mainly proper names, including those of the Etruscan gods.

For Etruscan history, we must therefore rely on the often critical writings of their contemporaries and rivals, particularly the Greeks and Romans. We see the growth, zenith, and decline of Etruscan civilization reflected in a series of distorting mirrors.

In their art, however, the Etruscans reveal themselves with a spontaneity and vividness that makes us think we know them very well. The walls of their tombs are covered with detailed representations of Etruscan life. If a picture really were worth 10,000 words, as a Chinese proverb claims, we would need no writing to tell us their story. As it is, we can only piece together fragments and are left, still, with a mystery.

Along with their language, the big puzzle about the Etruscans is their origin. Where did they come from? The home of the Etruscan civilization, called Etruria, was west central Italy, a region that now includes the provinces of Tuscany (a name obviously derived from "Etruscan") and Umbria. This area had been inhabited for many centuries before the distinctive Etruscan culture appeared in it. The earlier inhabitants (who *may* be the ancestors of the people we call Etruscans) are called Villanovans, because the first excavations revealing their existence were made at the hamlet of Villanova, near Bologna. The Villanovans were skilled in iron-working and pottery and they usually cremated their dead. Yet the ashes of the dead were surrounded with objects presumably needed in the afterlife: jewelry and other accessories, weapons, and household implements.

Villanovan tombs dating from around the 7th century B.C. show a change both in funeral customs and in the quality of the objects. Cremation begins to be replaced by inhumation—burial of the body. Along with the obviously native-produced objects are some foreign products: vases, pots, statues, and jewelry from Greece, Egypt, Phoenicia, and other Mediterranean lands, some of them made of precious metals. Obviously, the people buried in these tombs were wealthier than their predecessors and were trading with other nations.

It was about this time—from about 750 B.C. onward—that the Greeks began colonizing the southwestern coast of Italy. Hesiod, a Greek poet of the 8th century B.C., refers in one of his poems to the "far famed Tyrrhenians" who occupied the area north of the Greek settlements in Italy. "Tyrrhenians" is the Greek name for the people we call Etruscans, which brings us to the theory that the Etruscan people originally came from somewhere else.

The first person to put this theory in writing was Herodotus, the Greek historian who lived in the 5th century B.C. He tells of how, sometime after the Trojan Wars, a great famine occurred in Lydia, a nation located in part of what is now Turkey. As the famine grew more severe, the Lydians tried to ignore their hunger by playing games and eating only every other day. Eventually the king decided that half of the population would

The Etruscan Way of Life

Above: a deep tray (or *foculus*) containing a set of domestic equipment. Formed from black clay, the pottery was produced between the 7th and early 5th centuries B.C. Such domestic utensils were obviously much prized by the Etruscans who, it would appear, had their favorite pieces placed in their tombs.

Interpreting the Future

Above: fresco from a tomb in Tarquinia painted around 520–510 B.C. Because of the subjects portrayed, it is known as the Tomb of Hunting and Fishing. The tomb is divided into two rooms and all the walls are completely covered with paintings of a high standard. In this scene a youth is killing birds with a sling while four others in a boat painted with a "lucky eye" are fishing. The sky is crowded with seabirds, probably wild duck.

have to emigrate. The group chosen by lot to leave the country were led by his son Tyrrhenos. They set out in ships and finally settled in the "land of the Umbrians"—central Italy. They no longer called themselves Lydians, according to Herodotus, but adopted the name of their prince and called themselves Tyrrhenians.

Actually, the Etruscans called themselves Rasena—a word found in various dialects of Asia Minor—but the Greeks persisted in calling them Tyrrhenians, and the part of the Mediterranean that adjoins the west coast of Italy is still called the Tyrrhenian Sea. Although the Romans accepted the theory of their Lydian origin and often called them Lydians, they also called them Tusci, or Etrusci, from which their modern name is derived.

Most of their contemporaries accepted the theory of the Etruscans' Eastern origin. An opposing view was put forward by Dionysius of Halicarnassus, a Greek historian living in Rome in the 1st century B.C. He observed that the "Tyrrhenians . . . do not have the same language as the Lydians. . . . They do not worship the same gods as the Lydians; they do not have the same laws. . . . It thus seems to me that those who say that the Etruscans are not a people who came from abroad, but are an indigenous race, are right; to me this seems to follow from the fact that they are a very ancient people which does not resemble any other either in its language or in its customs."

In the light of modern discoveries neither Herodotus nor Dionysius has an airtight case. If, as Herodotus states, the emigration from Lydia took place around the time of the Trojan Wars (around the beginning of the 12th century B.C.) this would mean that the "Tyrrhenians" were settled in Italy at least 500 years before the civilization we call Etruscan makes its appearance. As it stands, Herodotus' story is roughly analogous to some modern historian's claiming that English settlers colonized North America in the Middle Ages—despite the fact that there is no evidence of their colonization before the early 17th century. It may be that the Lydian source from which Herodotus took his information had given the wrong date. Or it may be that the Lydian emigrants settled somewhere else—which would create a whole new mystery for some enterprising archaeologist.

Despite the confusing matter of the dates, the basic theory that the Etruscans were an Eastern people is quite plausible. Dionysius' claim that their customs did not resemble those of any foreign people was based on inadequate knowledge. Equipped with detailed studies of the customs, laws, and religions of ancient peoples, the modern historian can see resemblances unknown to a man living in Dionysius' time. The fact is that the Etruscans did resemble some Oriental peoples in many aspects of their civilization.

One of the most striking similarities was the emphasis in their religion on foretelling the future. The Etruscan religion—in fact every aspect of Etruscan life—was dominated by the pronouncements of the *haruspices*, the priests who studied various natural phenomena and interpreted their significance for the future. They claimed they could tell from the direction and duration of

Left: a bronze model of a liver divided into areas for divination. It was used to teach student priests how to read the omens from the real liver of a sacrificial victim. Each section has the name of a god engraved upon it. A deeply religious people, the Etruscans lived by a book of sacred laws that gave detailed instructions for finding out the will of the gods. Examination of the liver of sacrificial sheep was one of the ways of finding out what the gods had in store for their human worshipers. Hardly any important decision was taken among the Etruscans without first divining the omens.

thunder and lightning, for example, which of the gods was sending a message and what sort of message it was. The birth of a deformed child or animal was also regarded as significant. But it was the art of hepatoscopy, the examination of the liver of a sacrificed animal, that was the keystone of Etruscan divination—as it was for the people of Babylonia and other parts of Asia Minor. In fact the practice of telling fortunes from the livers of animals seems to have originated around 2000 B.C. in Babylonia, one of the most ancient civilizations. Excavations in that part of the world have unearthed many terracotta models of livers engraved with prophecies based on the physical characteristics represented on the model. Etruscan art contains many pictures of priests divining the future from the livers of sacrificed animals. Some of the complexity of the art can be inferred from a bronze model of a liver found at Piacenza in 1877, which was probably used as a teaching model. Its surface is divided into 40 sections, each inscribed with the name of a god or goddess and each corresponding to a division of the sky. The liver of an animal dedicated and sacrificed to the gods was believed to be an image of the Universe and so capable of revealing its aspects at that moment.

This peculiar practice and the overriding importance it assumed both in the ancient Near East and in Etruria is one bit of evidence supporting the theory of the Etruscans' Eastern origin. Among Western peoples divination had no such importance. The Greeks, for example, might consult an oracle for advice on an important matter, but not in the course of conducting the ordinary business of life. Among the Greeks there was nothing corresponding to the *Disciplina Etrusca*, a detailed book of ritual, mostly concerned with divination. The practice of liver divination was virtually unknown. The Romans, whose civilization was influenced by the Etruscans, adopted these divination practices somewhat half-heartedly, leaving the actual performing of the rites to the expert Etruscan priests. No other people in the Western world were so adept at rites as the Etruscans or so dominated by their religion.

There were, to be sure, some resemblances between Etruscan religion and those of the Greeks and Romans. Some of their gods and goddesses were the same. The three supreme Etruscan

Above: engraved bronze mirror of the early 5th century B.C. The figure is an Etruscan priest examining a liver. The name written on the mirror has been translated as Calchas, the diviner who accompanied the Greek armies to Troy. The priest would hold the liver in his left hand and run his fingers over the surface to find any imperfections. As every part of the liver was assigned to a different god or goddess, some benevolent, some harmful, a defect in the area of a kindly god would be a good omen, one in that of a malevolent god, a bad omen.

Gods and Women

Below: an early Etruscan bronze statue of the goddess Menrva from the 5th century B.C.

Below center: Minerva, the Roman form of the Etruscan Menrva.

Below right (above): the Etruscan god Aplu, who became the Greek and Roman Apollo, the ideal of manly youth and beauty. Known as the Apollo of Veii, this Greek-influenced terracotta statue of the 5th century B.C. is recognized as a masterpiece of Etruscan art.

Below right (bottom): the Roman version of the god Apollo. Originally the god's name meant "destroyer," which has given rise to the theory that he was once a folk-hero, who rid the earth of monsters and evils.

deities, Tinia (the most powerful), Uni, and Menrva, who were worshiped as a trinity in sanctuaries with three halls, were adopted by the Romans as Jupiter, Juno, and Minerva. On the other hand the Etruscans adopted some of the Greek gods, such as Poseidon (called Neptune by the Romans and Nethuns by the Etruscans) and Apollo (Aplu in Etruscan). But the Etruscans' attitude toward their gods differed sharply from that of the Greeks and Romans. The Greeks, especially, regarded their gods as beings more or less like humans but equipped with supernatural powers. They invented stories dramatizing the gods' weaknesses and defects. These same myths were often pictured in Etruscan painting—which was strongly influenced by the Greeks in both style and content—but the Etruscans clearly regarded these gods as powerful and mysterious beings who demanded constant devotion.

Another way in which the Etruscan differed from their neighbors was in the status enjoyed by their women. The Greeks and the early Romans kept their women out of sight. Only courtesans attended their banquets; respectable women remained at home with the servants, pursuing useful occupations such as spinning or weaving. Etruscan society was more enlightened in this respect. It was considered perfectly natural for women to accompany their husbands to games, chariot races,

Above: the tomb of the Etruscan noblewoman Larthia, wife of Svenia. The care and lavish detail shown on the tomb, or sarcophagus, which was erected sometime between 217 and 147 B.C., is an indication of the position and respect accorded to women in Etruscan society.

and banquets. This custom of dining together was completely misunderstood by the Greeks and the Romans. Theopompus, a Greek writer of the 4th century B.C., noted for malicious scandal-mongering, described in authoritative detail the lax behavior of the Etruscans:

"The Tyrrhenians possess their women in common; these take great care of their bodies and exercise naked, often along with men. . . . They sit down to table not beside their husbands but beside any of the guests, and they even drink to the health of anyone they please. Moreover they are great wine-bibbers and very beautiful to behold. The Tyrrhenians bring up together all those children that are born to them, heedless of who their father may be. These children live in the same manner as their protectors, passing most of their time in drinking and having commerce with all the women indifferently." And so on.

Other writers presented a more restrained picture of Etruscan life; but it is difficult to evaluate their accounts in the absence of any comment from the Etruscans themselves. We must turn to the images in Etruscan tombs. There, in the frescoes, we find ample evidence of sensuality, though nothing to support the wilder assertions of Theopompus. Certainly there are signs that the Etruscan woman was considered a worthwhile person. Her sculpted image reclines beside that of her husband on a sarcophagus; tomb inscriptions give the names of both the father and the mother of the deceased. By contrast, among the Greeks and Romans only the father's name was normally given. Among the tombs at Caere (now Cerveteri) is one built solely for a woman and furnished with more than 100 objects—gold ornaments, perfume bottles, and a dinner service—for her use in the afterlife. Such objects are sometimes engraved "I belong to Larthia" (for

example) indicating that women had possessions of their own.

None of these marks of status seems remarkable from a modern viewpoint, but to the Greeks and Romans they must have seemed eccentric, to say the least. Yet in the earlier civilizations of Crete and Mycenae women also attended public games and enjoyed a degree of equality. And in Lydia, the Etruscans' supposed homeland, the mother's name sometimes appears on tomb inscriptions as it does in Etruria.

Perhaps the most persuasive evidence in favor of the migration theory is the Etruscan language. Although its alphabet is similar to the Greek, the language itself does not resemble any of those within the family of languages known as Indo-European, to which Greek and nearly all other ancient and modern European languages belong. It is hard to believe that if the Etruscans had lived in Italy since time immemorial they would have developed a language so radically different from those spoken by their neighbors.

As Dionysius observed, however, their language is not the same as that of the Lydians, another Indo-European tongue, nor does it even resemble it. The same can be said of other languages of Asia Minor. If the Etruscans were emigrants from another land, then there ought to be another group of ancient people—those who remained at home—who spoke the same language. Unless, of course, the population had died and their civilization been extinguished.

Wherever and however the Etruscans were living before about 700 B.C., from that time onward they enjoyed a life of great prosperity. Their land was fruitful and rich in minerals, particularly tin, copper, and iron. It was the mining of these much-sought-after metals that gave the Etruscans the wealth to buy

Above: a golden ornament of 400–250 B.C. The Etruscans were skilled at producing extraordinarily fine jewelry and developed the technique of granulation—decoration of the surface with thousands of tiny gold beads—seen here, to a degree unrivaled in the ancient world.

Right (top): a gold wreath of 37 ivy leaves from the 3rd century B.C.

Right (bottom): a breast pendant heavy with granulation. The formula of the solder used to secure the beads disappeared when the Etruscan civilization came to an end.

Artists and Gold Workers

Left: the Franèois Vase, named for its discoverer, was imported into Etruria from Athens and bears the names of its Greek potter and painter. The seafaring Etruscans imported large quantities of Greek goods, with the result that their arts and crafts were influenced by Greek styles and the subjects of many of their paintings and decorations were taken from the Greek myths.

and fashion into exquisite ornaments the gold, silver, and ivory of lands to the east and south. The Etruscans had mastered the subtler techniques of jewelry making very early in their history. Their skill in the technique of granulation—decorating the surface of gold jewelry with thousands of tiny gold beads—exceeded that of any other goldsmiths of the ancient world. The formula of the solder they used in this process died with their civilization and has never been rediscovered.

Of course, we are not one hundred percent sure that it was the Etruscans themselves who did this work. Many of the vases once thought to be Etruscan have since been proved to be of Greek origin. The confusion was caused by the fact that Etruscan potters, from about 700 B.C. onward, copied Greek styles. Greek craftsmen lived and worked in Etruria and had a strong influence on Etruscan taste. But the Etruscans also borrowed themes from the art of Egypt, Mesopotamia, and Syria. The result is an art full of fabulous beasts—winged horses, sphinxes, and the chimera, a creature incorporating a lion, a goat, and a snake.

The Etruscans were not only skilled craftsmen but also aggressive traders and mariners. Any ideas the Greeks may have had about controlling the western Mediterranean were checked by the Etruscan navy, which quickly gained dominance of the Tyrrhenian Sea and expanded their trade all along the coast of

Right: the famous bronze Chimera of Arezzo. This Etruscan sculpture of the late 5th century B.C. is typical of the Etruscan love of mythical beasts and monsters which are well represented in their art. It is also typical of their borrowing from Greek myths. In Greek mythology, the chimera—part lion, part goat, part serpent—was slain by the hero Bellerophon.

Below: a bronze statue of an Etruscan warrior of the 5th century B.C. There was, in fact, no Etruscan national army, only armed bands led by warrior princes. When threatened by the Romans or the barbarians the city states had to hire mercenaries and slaves to defend them. Every citizen called to the defense of the state was required to name another also and so the hastily gathered armies of mercenaries, conscripts, and slaves were often crushingly defeated.

southern Europe and North Africa. They soon came into conflict with the Greeks who had established colonies in France and Spain as well as in Italy. Greek writers of the 6th and 7th centuries B.C. refer bitterly to the "piratical Tyrrhenians." Carthage, too, had ambitions in the Mediterranean, and a three-sided contest began, in which Carthage was ultimately the victor.

On land, the Etruscans extended their sphere of influence to include a large section of the Italian peninsula from the Po valley in the north to Campania in the south. Yet the Etruscans never formed a unified nation. Etruria consisted of a number of independent city-states that were bound by ties of custom, language, and religion. They joined forces temporarily for military purposes—for example, to fight off invading Celts—but their essential disunity later made them vulnerable to the highly organized and disciplined Romans. The Etruscan states were governed first by priest-kings and later by magistrates elected by the ruling class. The only regular occasion on which the heads of states met together was the annual festival of the god Voltumna. Sometimes this religious occasion also served a political purpose; it gave the representatives of the various states an opportunity to discuss matters of general concern and settle any differences between them. The festival was apparently held in some kind of sacred grove in the area around Volsinii (now Bolsena).

If there was a temple there in honor of Voltumna, it has disappeared, along with nearly every other above-ground Etruscan building. This is because the Etruscans built mainly in wood and bricks, using stone only for the foundation. From those foundations that remain we can see the floor plans of their temples and houses. Our ideas of what the structures looked like are derived mainly from their tomb interiors, which they built to resemble homes, and from terracotta decorative elements such as friezes and statues that adorned their temples. The few remaining arches and city walls show Etruscan building techniques applied to the planning of cities.

Like most other aspects of Etruscan life, the foundation of a new city was pervaded with ritual. As always, the omens had first to be read by the priest. These would determine the orientation of the city. Then the founder, equipped with a bronze plowshare and with part of his toga draped over his head, for reasons that are not clear, would plow a furrow marking the boundary of the city. According to the Romans, who adopted these foundation rites, there were also rules for the orderly geometrical layout of streets and placements of gates and temples. Yet archaeologists have found little evidence in the sites of Etruscan towns of such Roman-style regularity. Here again, the written information about Etruscan customs is secondhand and at least partially misleading. The Etruscan ritual books for the founding of cities have disappeared.

Ironically, it was the Etruscans who made Rome—originally just a group of villages—into an important city, ringed with fortifications and endowed with fine buildings. The Etruscans were noted for their skill in hydraulics, and one of the achievements of the Tarquins was the draining of the forum and the

Etruscan Art and Architecture

Above: model of an Etruscan temple. The wood or brick superstructure was often covered with decorated plaster.

Left: the interior of an Etruscan tomb. Funerary art has been an invaluable aid to scholars in showing what Etruscan architecture was like. Houses, palaces, villas, and temples have all disappeared above ground mainly because the superstructures were made of wood and bricks. Tombs, however, were fashioned after the houses of the living with rooms, doors, windows, pillars, decorated ceilings, even wooden beams, all carved from the volcanic rock in which the tombs were situated.

construction of a sewer system. Livy tells how the hated Tarquin the Proud "caused to be constructed, despite the protestations of the people who found this labor very trying, a great subterranean sewer intended to receive all the filth of the city, a work which our modern magnificence found hard to equal." This was the famous Cloaca Maxima, which empties into the Tiber and is still in use today.

The legacy of Etruscan rule in Rome included not only engineering techniques, which the Romans were to develop with impressive results, but also certain customs we now think of as typically Roman. One was the triumphal procession, in which the king was preceded by officials bearing the *fasces,* the rods and ax that were the symbols of unlimited power. Another custom was the gladiatorial combat. Although these gladiatorial fights to the death did not take place on the scale found in the later Roman Empire, they were certainly a well-established Etruscan custom. They grew out of the practice of sacrificing prisoners of war in honor of the Etruscan dead; this custom was then modified so that the prisoners fought each other.

Even after the Romans won independence from the Etruscans it still took them more than 200 years to defeat their former masters. This gradual, piecemeal conquest was aided by the Etruscans' disunity, their over-reliance on omens—even in conducting a war—and their misfortune in having occasionally to fight off the Celts to the north as well as the Romans to the south. Eventually, however, the last Etruscan stronghold, Volsinii, fell in 280 B.C. It came about through a rebellion of the city's slaves—the people who made possible the luxurious life of the Etruscan aristocrats. Some citizens who managed to escape

Above: brick arches in Rome that lead to an opening of the Cloaca Maxima. As soon as a city had been dedicated by the priest, the city engineers moved in to make the place clean and comfortable for the citizens. They were especially skilled at tunneling and excavating and, it is said, it was the Etruscans who taught the early Romans how to construct the arch.

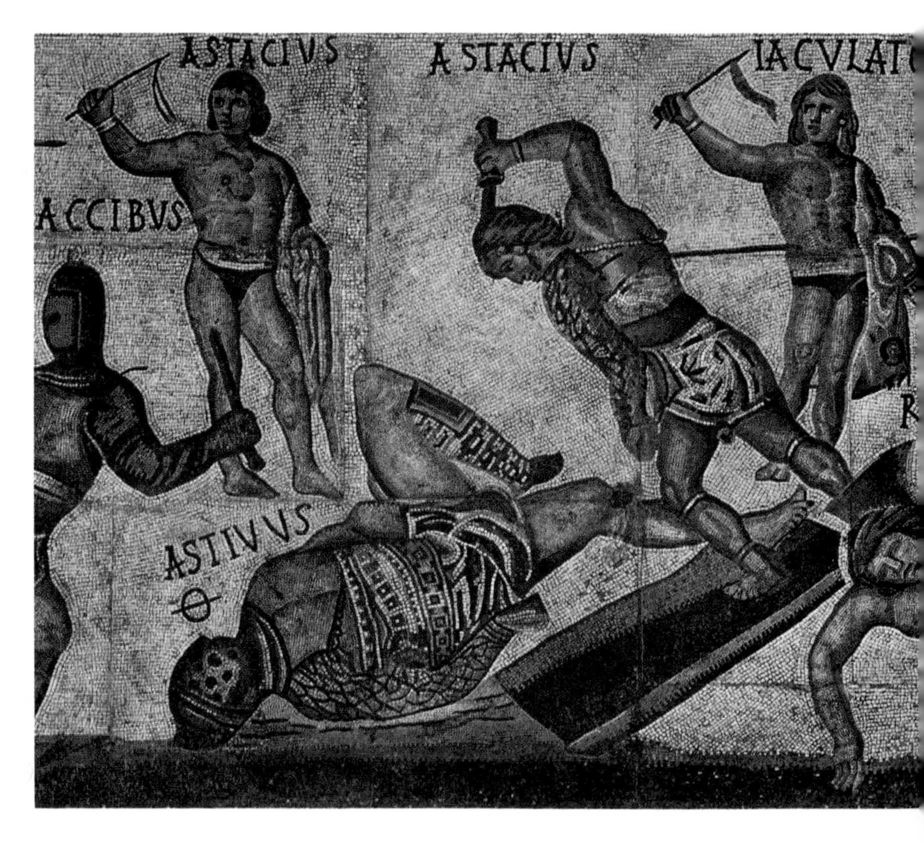

Right: another Etruscan legacy to Rome, though a more dubious one, was the gladiatorial combat seen here on a Roman mosaic. In Etruria the combats were part of a funeral rite for soldiers who had died in battle, but this religious aspect was soon lost when the Romans adopted and expanded the combats into the cruel, bloody spectacles of the arena.

from the violence in their city appealed to the Roman army for help. The Romans obligingly killed the slaves, offered the surviving aristocrats hospitality, and razed Volsinii to the ground.

Etruscan civilization did not disappear at once. For another 200 years Etruscan arts and crafts were practiced, though not on the high level of earlier times. Some of the city-states enjoyed a degree of autonomy. Etruscan religious beliefs and practices survived until the fall of the Roman Empire. Every year delegates still gathered to honor Voltumna at his festival. Officially, the Etruscan language had been replaced with Latin, but it continued to be spoken for a few hundred years after the Roman conquest. Some Etruscan cities were deserted and allowed to decay; others were rebuilt by the Romans. Under the earth outside the Etruscan cities lay the cities of the dead, which were soon forgotten.

Throughout the Middle Ages the Etruscans remained a shadowy people, known only to a few scholars who could read what the Greeks and Romans had written about them. In the Renaissance curiosity about these people began to revive. A Dominican friar, Giovanni Nanni, caused a certain amount of excitement in 1498 when he published a collection of fragments attributed to various obscure writers of antiquity. His book included some Etruscan inscriptions which he claimed to have copied off the walls of tombs near his native city of Viterbo (originally an Etruscan town). Although Nanni has long been regarded as a hoaxer, it seems likely that the book's Etruscan fragments are genuine. His translations, which were based on the traditional assumption that all languages were derived from Hebrew, are less reliable.

Interest in Etruscan civilization was further stimulated by the

Rome's Debt to the Etruscans

Left: a funerary dance, depicted as a relief on an Etruscan vase of around 500 B.C. Music accompanied nearly every aspect of Etruscan life—and death. Trumpets, lyres, and especially flutes appear in many frescoes and carvings. Contemporary Greek and Roman writers remark on how the double flute was used at religious ceremonies and also as an accompaniment to various activities of the Etruscans' private lives—from bread making to wrestling matches.

"Etruscomania!"

writings of Thomas Dempster, an exceptionally pugnacious Scotsman who—when he was not engaged in brawls—taught and studied at some of Europe's major universities. His massive work *Seven Books Concerning the Kingdom of Etruria*, included all the existing knowledge of the Etruscans, drawn from classical sources, and Dempster's own interpretations and conclusions. Although Dempster's scholarship was impressive, the book lacked any firsthand investigation of Etruscan remains. At the time Dempster was writing, the early 1600s, archaeology did not exist.

It was not until the 18th century that excavations began at Volterra, some 40 miles southwest of Florence. One of the most

Above: the tomb of the Cardinal, Tarquinia, a picture from a book on the Etruscan tombs by the British artist James Byres, published in 1842. When the tombs were discovered in the 18th century widespread looting occurred as these repositories of a nation's history were ransacked for gold, silver, and jewelry. Many artistic treasures, especially the wall paintings, were allowed to deteriorate or were deliberately destroyed in an effort to remove treasure in the form of precious metals from the tombs.

important Etruscan cities, it had a wall five miles in circumference, parts of which are still standing. Outside the wall, the excavators discovered thousands of tombs filled with treasures, which soon found their way into museums and private collections throughout Europe. The Guarnacci Museum at Volterra, founded shortly after the excavations began, houses one of the largest and finest collections of Etruscan art in the world.

As more and more tombs were opened at other sites and more riches were discovered, a new word, "Etruscomania," was coined to describe the passion for Etruscan art that was sweeping through Europe. At the same time, travelers and scholars were also beginning to discover the art and ruins of ancient Greece, and a certain amount of confusion resulted from the mixture of Greek and native Etruscan artefacts found in Tuscany. A spirited dispute broke out between Giovanni Batista Piranesi, Italian architect and engraver, whose book on Roman architecture claimed that it owed everything to the Etruscans and nothing to the Greeks, and Pierre Jean Mariette, a French connoisseur who replied that the Etruscans were originally Greek and had learned architecture from their forebears. National pride, artistic prejudices, and fragmentary understanding of ancient history combined to make the new field of Etruscology a fertile area for speculation and error.

The haphazard and often destructive approach of the excavators added to the confusion. Some people were interested only in the profitable aspects and salvaged only the items of obvious commercial value. No one bothered to make a careful inventory of the objects found in a tomb, and often humble objects that might have yielded worthwhile information about Etruscan life were thoughtlessly destroyed. Snatched from their context, with no notes of what was found with them, the valuable pieces lost much of their archaeological significance. Many of the wall paintings that reveal so much of Etruscan life were damaged by the smoke of the excavators' torches or simply left to deteriorate.

While the looting continued into the 19th century (one of the arch-looters was Napoleon's brother Lucien, whose estate included the tombs of Vulci), interest grew in the Etruscans themselves. George Dennis, an English explorer, spent six years traveling from one Etruscan site to another, making notes and sketches of what he found. His observations were published in 1848 in two volumes entitled *Cities and Cemeteries of Etruria.* Dennis's achievement was mainly to describe in vivid detail the many sites that had already been discovered, but he also discovered several new Etruscan burial sites. Today, Etruscan remains are still unearthed from time to time. Unfortunately, though, most Etruscan cities lie beneath modern towns, where the density of building rules out much archaeological work. Had serious archaeologists been on the scene in George Dennis's day, before so much urbanization had taken place, we would certainly know more about the Etruscans than we do now.

The person who arguably did more than anyone else to open people's eyes to the beauty of Etruscan art was D. H. Lawrence, the English novelist. His book *Etruscan Places*, published in

Above: George Dennis (1814–1898) has been called the "founder of Etruscology." Self taught in Greek and Latin, he also mastered French, Spanish, Portuguese, Italian, Modern Greek, Turkish, and Arabic. He acquainted himself with the latest discoveries in history, anthropology, and archaeology. In the mid-19th century Tuscany, where old Etruria was situated, was almost deserted outside the cities and provincial towns, and it was here that Dennis visited the tombs and remains of the vanished Etruscans.

Left: the "Valley of Tombs, Castel d'Asso," a plate from George Dennis' *Cities and Cemeteries of Etruria*, published in 1848. Dennis' book remains one of the most comprehensive textbooks on the ruins of Etruria.

D. H. Lawrence and the Etruscans

Above: the English author D. H. Lawrence (1885-1930). Lawrence's *Etruscan Places*, posthumously published in 1932, did more to popularize the civilization of the Etruscans than any other writer—including George Dennis. Lawrence's sensitive observations of the tomb paintings and funerary art made the ancient Etruscan come alive for people as he pointed out the freshness and gaiety, the liveliness and humor of the people depicted in many of the murals and sculptures.

1932, two years after his death, overflows with praise for the lively, sensuous paintings on the walls of the tombs and for the unfettered way of life they depict.

"The naked slaves joyfully stoop to the wine-jars. Their nakedness is its own clothing, more easy than drapery. The curves of their limbs show pure pleasure in life, a pleasure that goes deeper still in the limbs of the dancers, in the big, long hands thrown out and dancing to the very ends of the fingers, a dance that surges from within, like a current in the sea."

Lawrence's boundless enthusiasm takes us to the other extreme from those classical writers who could find nothing good to say about the Etruscans. Certainly the paintings surge with life, and the Etruscans obviously delighted in music and dance and sport and in their own bodies. (Although whether slaves did their work "joyfully" is open to question.) What Lawrence ignored or discounted was the rigid, hierarchical structure of Etruscan society, its occasional cruelty, and the all-pervading demands of the Etruscan religion. To be sure, that religion made few moral demands on the faithful, but having to consult the gods on every occasion must have taken some of the spontaneity out of life.

The Etruscans were, quite literally, a god-fearing people. Paintings in the later tombs depict frightful demons punishing the dead. Aita, a corruption of Hades, the Greek god of the Underworld wears a wolf's skin over his head. The figure of Charun, who carries the dead into the underworld, is not the placid ferryman of the Greeks but a hideous grimacing figure with bluish flesh that reminds the onlooker of bodily decomposition. He carries a club to smash the skulls of the dying in order to

Right: detail of a fresco from the Tomb of the Lionesses of around 520 B.C. The dancers, the blond-haired naked youth and the black-haired girl, are engaged in a dance for the dead. The girl plays the castanets in the lowered hand while the left hand has two fingers forked in a ritual gesture. Other parts of the frieze depict musicians and banqueters. Above them are the two lionesses from which the Tomb gets its name.

Above: Etruscan musicians and a servant at a feast. Detail from the Tomb of the Leopards of around 480–470 B.C. The servant, musicians, and on another wall the banqueters all wear myrtle wreaths and are clothed in brightly colored mantles with large borders. The whole painting is reminiscent of Greek styles of painting.

finish them off. He is accompanied by Tuchulcha, a repellent creature with the face of a vulture and the ears of a donkey, who clutches snakes in his hand ready to strike.

It may be significant that at the time most of these grisly scenes were painted Etruria was bit by bit falling into the hands of the Romans. In many religions, particularly those of eastern lands, priests were inclined to attribute political setbacks to inadequate piety on the part of the people and exhort their flock to mend their ways in order to forestall disaster. The frightful demons represented in the paintings may reflect a "revivalist" phase in the Etruscan religion; or they may simply give visible expression to an increasing pessimism concerning life in this world and the next.

In the faces of some of the later portrait statues one can see traces of an apparent resignation or perhaps world-weariness that presents a sharp contrast to the carefree, smiling faces in earlier tombs. The paintings and statues suggest that a change was occurring in the Etruscan world view—a change that would be natural enough in circumstances of decline and defeat.

Of course, it is possible to interpret the situation the other way around. Perhaps the decline in Etruscan power and the collapse of the city-states before the Roman offensive were originally caused in part by the mentality reflected in the late Etruscan art. Did the fatalism of their religion undermine the initiative and

Above: part of a fresco from the Tomb of Orcus, painted in the 2nd century B.C. Orcus, or Aita, the god of the Underworld, is seen wearing a wolf helmet and grasping a snake, next to him his wife Persephone with snake-entwined hair. Facing them is an armed warrior with three heads, probably the monster Geryon, who was slain by Hercules. There appears to have been no heaven for the souls of the Etruscan dead—only a gloomy Underworld and a dreadful Hell.

Above right: the demon Tuchulcha, one of the fearsome monsters with which the Etruscans populated their Underworld. By the 2nd century B.C., when this and the picture above were painted, the Etruscans began to take an increasingly gloomy view of life—and death. One by one the city-states were falling to the Romans or being overrun by the barbarians, while their priests blamed these catastrophes on the lack of piety among the people.

energy shown by the Etruscans in their early days? Or did their life of pleasure begin to cloy, and lead them to a preoccupation with suffering and a passivity in the face of danger?

Endless psychological games can be played on the causes of the Etruscans' decline without ever being able to prove whether the insights are even remotely correct.

One of the frustrations facing scholars is that although, according to Roman writers, the Etruscans did have a literature, that literature has disappeared. Many scholars doubt whether Etruria ever produced much, if any, imaginative writing, but certainly they did write some history and perhaps some religious poetry. Marcus Terrentius Varro, a Roman writer of the first century B.C., included some Etruscan texts in his book *The Divine Antiquities*, which dealt with the history, geography, and anthropology of early Italy. This book was still in existence as late as 1320, when Petrarch reported having seen it. Since then it has vanished.

The longest piece of Etruscan writing to have been discovered is a 1500-word text on a piece of linen used to wrap an Egyptian mummy of a young woman. The wrapped mummy was donated to a museum in Zagreb, Croatia, in the mid-1800s and the wrappings removed and displayed separately. Not until 1891 was the mysterious writing identified as Etruscan. Although scholars have still not succeeded in reading it, they are fairly sure that it is a ritual calendar of some sort. It consists of several sections, each of which seems to begin with a date (though this is by no means certain). Also, there are frequent references to "gods"—one of the few known Etruscan words—and many repetitions, suggesting a kind of ritual response.

Why an Egyptian mummy should be wrapped in an Etruscan manuscript has naturally puzzled the experts. Some have suggested that the young woman was an Etruscan—one of those who fled to Egypt after the Roman conquest—and that the writing had some significance for her. A more likely explanation perhaps is that the embalmer simply used any linen he could lay his hands on, even if it was covered with writing. The text could have reached Alexandria when Etruscans were migrating from their Eastern homeland (if they did make such a journey) or when some of them left Etruria after the conquest. The fact that the linen was torn into strips, breaking the sequence of the lines, and wrapped with the writing inside suggests that its use was accidental.

The seemingly endless task of trying to translate the Etruscan language has engaged the efforts of hundreds of scholars and codebreakers, both amateur and professional. They have approached the task in two basic ways: by comparing it with other languages and by examining a text as one would an encoded message, trying to find clues within the language itself. Neither of these methods has yielded any significant results. The problems can be illustrated with reference to a pair of dice found in an Etruscan tomb at Toscanella more than 100 years ago. Each face of the dice is marked with a word: *Maχ*, *ci*, *zal*, *śa*, *θu*, and *huθ*. We know that in ancient times dice were marked with the num-

The Etruscan Way of Death

Below: The Banquet of Velthur Velcha, from the Tomb of the Shields in Tarquinia. What strikes the visitor to the tomb most about the portraits of these and other members of the family around the walls, is the look of melancholy on the faces of the banqueters.

The Enigmatic Alphabet

bers 1 through 6, just as they are today, so it seems likely that these six words represent the first six numbers. The words used for numbers in one language are often very similar to those used in a related language. For example: "une, dos, tres" in Spanish and "uno, due, tre" in Italian. If a language could be found having similar words for the first six numbers, it might supply meaningful translations for other Etruscan words. But if the words on the Toscanella dice do represent numbers, no one has yet succeeded in finding a language whose number names correspond to them.

Pursuing the possibility that the words are not those of numbers but rather a sentence of some kind, other people have suggested an enormous variety of translations, based on various borrowed words from both Greek and Gothic to produce: "May these sacred dice fall double sixes."

The search for a key to the Etruscan language has for many people become an obsession. They may decide, on the basis of a few similarities, that Etruscan is related to Egyptian, or Basque, or Gaelic, for example; and then, using the chosen language as a key, offer translations of the few existing Etruscan texts. The translations are usually somewhat forced and often meaningless, and each tends to meet with a certain amount of derision from those holding different theories.

What the scholars keep hoping to find is an Etruscan "Rosetta Stone"—a text that is repeated in another, known language. Such a hope is not unreasonable. When Rome began ruling Etruria the government must have sometimes had occasion to issue statements not only in the official language but also in the language of the Etruscan people. A bi-lingual text of even a few

Right: two of the three gold tablets found on the site of the temple of Uni (the Roman goddess Juno) near the Italian port of Santa Severa. The tablet on the left is in Punic, the other Etruscan. They caused considerable interest when they were found, for, if the Punic and Etruscan tablets were literal translations of each other, as scholars hoped, scholars would have had the key to the Etruscan language they had searched so long for. They were disappointed, however. Although the texts contained the same information, neither was a literal translation of the other—so the Etruscan language remains an enigma.

Etruscan	𐌀	𐌁	𐌂	𐌃	𐌄	𐌅	𐌆	𐌇	𐌈	𐌉	𐌊	𐌋	𐌌	𐌍
Greek	A	B	Γ	Δ	E	ꟻ	Z	(H)	Θ	I	K	Λ	M	N
English	A	B	C	D	E	V	Z	H	Th	I	K	L	M	N

Etruscan	𐌎	O	𐌐	𐌑	𐌒	𐌓	𐌔	𐌕	𐌖	𐌗	𐌘	𐌙	8 archaic	
Greek		O	Π			P	Σ	T	Y	X	Φ			
English	(S)	O	P	Ś	Q	R	S	T	U	Ṡ	(Ph)	(Ch)	F	

Above: the letters of the Etruscan alphabet arranged with their Greek and English equivalents. Whereas the alphabet can be deciphered and a pronunciation for each letter worked out (it is also known that Etruscans wrote from right to left), the *sense* of most of their words still has to be worked out by scholars. Efforts to link the language with Albanian, Basque, Greek, Hebrew, Latin, Sanskrit, and many others have so far failed.

hundred words would give us not only the meanings of those Etruscan words in that particular text but also clues, through roots, prefixes, and suffixes, to many other Etruscan words and to the structure of its grammar.

A certain amount of excitement followed the discovery, in 1964, of three gold tablets, one inscribed in Punic—the language of the Carthaginians—and the other two in Etruscan. The three tablets were found lying together between the sites of two Etruscan temples at Santa Severa on the Tyrrhenian Sea. Professor Massimo Pallottino, the leader of the excavation, and his associates set to work on the three texts, which together contained about 90 words. The Punic text consisted of the dedication of a temple to the goddess Astarte offered by the king of the Etruscan city of Cisra, which had stood on that site. It raises a number of questions about the relationship between the Etruscans and their occasional allies the Carthaginians and about the role of Astarte, chief goddess of the Carthaginians, in Etruscan religion. It is worth noting that Astarte, the goddess of fertility, was also worshiped in Lydia and that in that country her cult, noted for its orgiastic rites, also involved prostitution. One of the charges brought against the Etruscans by the Greeks and Romans was that their young women acquired their dowries by prostituting themselves. Was the dedication of a temple to Astarte a kind of ecumenical-diplomatic gesture made by the Etruscan king to the Carthaginians? Had he simply been converted to her cult? Or did his action have deeper roots, to be found in an Eastern homeland?

As for the Etruscan texts, they were disappointing. Although they do seem to contain information similar to that on the Punic tablet, careful examination has shown that neither is a literal translation. Once again the Etruscans have proved inscrutable.

Still, the archaeologists, scholars, and codebreakers keep on digging and pouring over Etruscan texts, hoping to find a key that will unlock the mystery of this baffling language and perhaps reveal the origins of these fascinating people.

Chapter 4
Ghost Cities of the Desert

Many once-proud cities have been discovered lying buried under the sands and arid plains of the Middle East. Two of the most romantic of these are Petra and Palmyra—one hidden and secret; the other rising up out of the desert like the skeleton of some vast stranded monster. In both, their splendid ruins speak eloquently of the wealth and power of their long-dead citizens. Where did the wealth come from that enabled them to live lives of such luxury that even Rome cast covetous eyes on them? The silent cities are being coaxed to give up their long-held secrets.

In the Jordanian desert, lying in a valley that runs from the Gulf of Aqaba to the Red Sea, stands the massive mountain of Petra. To the traveler it seems at first sight impenetrable, but there is a crevice in the rock face leading into a narrow passage known as the Siq. For about a mile this narrow passageway turns and twists slightly downhill, getting narrower as it goes. Then, just as the rock seems to bear down menacingly on the traveler, blocking out the sun, imposing Corinthian columns and part of an elaborate cornice are glimpsed between the Siq's walls. Suddenly the traveler emerges into the light, and stands before a huge façade carved into the rock. It looks at first like something out of 17th century Rome: basically classical but with an exuberance that characterizes baroque architecture. Its spectacular color, which varies from peach in the sunlight to rose-red in the shadows, gives it the appearance of an elaborate stage-setting. Yet, here it stands in the hollow of a mountain mass in an isolated valley in Jordan, seemingly out of place and out of its time.

This fantastic building, a preview of the splendors to come, was probably one of the temples of this extraordinary city of Petra, and was built sometime in the 1st or early 2nd century B.C. It is now known as the Khasneh, or Treasury, because of a sculptured urn that stands on top and is supposedly filled with gold. In fact, so powerful is the belief in the treasure that the urn is pock-marked with bullet holes from the many people that have

Opposite: the traveler's first glimpse of the city of Petra, the home, some think, of the Edomites of the Bible, and later capital of the Nabataeans. Lying some 180 miles from Amman, the capital of Jordan, the mountain of Petra rises from an arid plain and seems at first impenetrable. A narrow crack in the rock leads, after about a mile, into the red, pink, and peach-colored city.

The Earliest Explorers

fired muskets at it to break it open and release the treasure.

Past the Khasneh the gorge narrows again and leads on to the main part of Petra, where hundreds of temples and tombs—some very plain, others decorated with obelisks, pillars, and cornices in a variety of styles—project from the rock. Over the centuries the wind has blurred much of the detail of their decorations. But the loss of detail is amply compensated for by the vivid colors. At a distance they look pinkish, or gold, or mauve. Seen up close they appear, in the words of Aubrey Menen, a British writer, "to have been painted over by inebriated theatrical scene-painters, drawing great brushes dripping with colour across the carved pillars and lintels."

Petra had been a ghost town for 1000 years—unknown except to the Bedouin tribesmen who passed that way—until it was rediscovered in 1812 by Johann Burckhardt, a Swiss-born explorer. He set out alone on a journey through the Mediterranean lands in 1809, having first learned to speak Arabic. Partly to facilitate travel through lands suspicious of the "infidel" and partly because he was genuinely attracted to Moslem culture, Burckhardt disguised himself as an Arab and took an assumed name—Ibrahim ibn Abdallah. Having acquired a very good knowledge of all the Moslem rites, his behavior and appearance raised no suspicion. When, occasionally, someone would remark on his accent he would explain by saying that his native tongue was Hindustani. As a sample of Hindustani, he would rattle off some Swiss-German, which seemed to satisfy his hearers.

Above: Johann Ludwig Burckhardt, the Swiss-born explorer who discovered Petra. Burckhardt, who was born in 1784, had decided early to become an explorer and after studies in Germany joined the London African Association. He studied Arabic in England and at the age of 28 was traveling through Jordan to join a caravan across the Sahara when he became the first European to discover the ancient city of Petra in 1812.

Burckhardt spent about two years in Syria, visiting some of its ancient cities and ruins before heading south toward Cairo. While passing through southern Palestine he heard stories of an amazing ancient city hidden among the hills. Although intrigued, Burckhardt knew he could not simply ask to see the place. The natives would be sure to regard this as an attempt to discover the treasure that they believed to be buried all around the place. So he declared his intention of making a sacrifice at the tomb of the Prophet Aaron, which he knew was near the site of the ruins. His guide grumbled a bit, but agreed to lead him to the place. Making their way past an encampment of suspicious Bedouins, the guide, Burckhardt, and the sacrificial goat entered the Siq.

Burckhardt's astonishment and delight on seeing the splendors of Petra must have been very difficult to hide. To the increasing irritation of his guide, he paused to examine several of the monuments, covertly making notes and sketches in a notebook concealed in the folds of his robe. He knew that if the natives were to discover this notebook they would confiscate it in the belief that it contained magic spells for obtaining the supposed treasure. It was not even necessary to be found carrying the treasure; a magician, they believed, could simply spirit it away by remote control.

By the time Burckhardt and the guide reached the foot of the mountain on which the prophet's tomb was located it was growing dark, and so the goat was sacrificed without making the climb. Burckhardt and his guide returned to their camp without incident.

The book in which Burckhardt reported his discovery was not

published until 1822, five years after he had died of dysentery in Egypt. Yet even before the publication of *Travels in Syria and the Holy Land*, word had reached Europe that the legendary city of Petra had been found. Two English naval officers furtively explored it in 1818, and later in 1826 Léon de Laborde, a French scholar and aristocrat, visited it and recorded his impressions in a series of extremely accurate drawings that evoke all the romance of the ruined city.

Petra appealed both to lovers of the romantic and mysterious and to serious scholars. The romantics reveled in its craggy, enclosed, and somewhat forbidding setting and in the profusion of tombs. Travelers gained an added excitement by spending the night in one of these tombs, which is what a Mr. W. H. Bartlett did in the 1840s. In his book *Forty Days in the Desert* he described the tomb in which he and his Arab guides passed the night: "It was indeed a very comfortable abode, the funeral chamber was large enough for the reception of a goodly company, and had evidently been used by former travellers; the rock was blackened with smoke. . . ." A lamb was slaughtered and roasted, and "the satisfaction of having fully attained an object long desired, with all appliances and means to restore the fatigue of sight-seeing and clambering, made this evening among the desolations of Petra pass away with a sort of wild gaiety."

Architectural historians found Petra a fascinating puzzle, filled as it is with buildings showing how the influences of Assyria, Egypt, Greece, and Rome, have been adapted and transformed by the people who built Petra, the Nabataeans. Archaeologists began working in the area in 1929. Since 1958 a team of British excavators has been doing more intensive work in Petra itself. Gradually the team is bringing to light some of the

Below: Petra as it was when it was rediscovered by two French travelers, the scholar and aristocrat Leon de Laborde, and Maurice Linaut, an engineer. The two Frenchmen, after their initial astonishment at the splendors of Petra, set to work to draw plans of the city's layout and to sketch the main monuments—drawings which were so accurate they have been described as photographic.

Above: a general view of the rock tombs of the Nabataeans, who discovered the building potential of the cliffs that surrounded their settlements. At first shepherds, the Nabataeans gradually developed a talent for caravan trading, especially in the "riches of the East" such as incense, myrrh, and the precious aromatic herbs that were much sought after throughout the Roman and Greek world. Safe within their rock-fortress home, the Nabataeans gradually controlled an empire that stretched from present day Saudi Arabia to Damascus, Syria.

Right: early tombs of the Nabataeans. Nearly all the carvings in the face of the cliffs are tombs or temples. In its heyday Petra had many houses crowded together below the carved facades of the tombs, the city itself containing as many as 20,000 people. These early tombs are carved in a more austere style than the flamboyant styles of those carved at the height of the empire.

culture and history of the people who inhabited that extraordinary city-state.

Long before the Nabataeans built Petra, the area was occupied by people known as Edomites. This tribe lived in a state of continual hostility with the Jews, their neighbors to the west, and they are mentioned frequently and unfavorably in the Old Testament. They apparently mined copper and iron in the mountains that border the Wadi Araba, a riverbed extending from the Dead Sea to the Gulf of Aqaba. Whether or not the Edomites lived on the actual site of Petra is doubtful, but they did live nearby, at the point where another river, the Wadi Musa, cuts through the mountains on the eastern side of the valley and goes on to join the Wadi Araba. This point became the crossroads of several important trade routes, and the Edomites, having gained control of this area, were in a position to profit from the caravans that passed their way.

Rivalry for the control of the trade routes was one of the main causes of the hostility between the Edomites and the Jews. Under King Solomon the Edomites were defeated and Solomon gained control of the trade routes.

Jewish control of the area ended 200 years later in 587 B.C. when the Babylonians conquered the Jews and took them into captivity. Most of the Edomites moved down into the lands from which the Jews had been expelled. A few remained in Edom, which in its turn was being invaded—but gradually and peacefully—by a nomadic tribe, the Nabataeans. Of Arabian origin, they had lived by keeping sheep and raiding caravans. However, they seem to have integrated fairly easily with the Edomites and to have adjusted to a more settled way of life. They may have learned the craft of pottery, at which they later excelled, from the native people, who were themselves fairly skilled in this craft.

Sometime after settling in Edom the Nabataeans began to occupy the site of Petra. The exact date is unknown, but archaeologists have turned up evidence, including the remains of a wall, suggesting that some kind of urban settlement existed there by about 300 B.C. About that time the Nabataeans also seem to have discovered the building potential of the cliffs surrounding them, for they began to carve tombs into the rock. The earliest of these had no façades as such; they were simply doorways, decorated in a severe style called rectilinear, leading to the interior. Later, they began to cut façades from the rock, using and adapting Assyrian styles. About half of the remaining monuments in Petra show this Assyrian influence.

The Petra we see today consists mainly of tombs and temples carved into the rock. But of course when it was a living city it contained many houses, flat-roofed dwellings built around courtyards in the traditional style of Arabia and Palestine and rather crowded together. At the peak of its prosperity, around the 1st century B.C., Petra contained perhaps as many as 20,000 people; an additional 10,000 people lived in its suburbs. They were governed by a king, from about 168 B.C., who, according to the Greek writer Strabo, was a "democratic" one. "He often . . . submits his accounts to the people, and sometimes also the conduct of his own personal life is enquired into." Some modern

Petra Revealed!

Below: the color-streaked cliff face of Petra honeycombed with carved temples and tombs. Of the free-standing buildings between the cliffs, little remains today.

David Roberts R.A.

writers, however, have suggested that such practices were mainly or entirely ceremonial. Like most ancient peoples the Nabataeans apparently had a mystical regard for their kings; at least one of them, named Obodas, was deified.

Water—not surprisingly—was especially prized, and one of the principal Nabataean deities, Al Uzza, was the goddess of springs and water. On a practical level the Nabateans used the water they had with great ingenuity, constructing sophisticated irrigation systems that enabled them to farm the desert and they developed techniques of conserving water that made Petra an oasis even at dry times of the year.

The Nabataean language—of which only a few examples have been discovered—was a Semitic language similar to Aramaic, the language spoken all over ancient Syria and some neighboring lands. Occasional inscriptions on tombs, which give us a sketchy idea of Nabataean religion, are about the only Nabataean writings that remain.

Although they produced beautiful pottery and splendid architecture, the Nabataeans seem not to have had much aptitude for painting or sculpture. Like the Edomites and the Jews they did not make representations of their gods; a squared-off block of stone, or sometimes an obelisk, represented Al Uzza, Dusares—the chief god—and the other Nabataean gods. Later in their history, the influence of Greek and Roman culture led to some figure-carving, but the surviving examples are undistinguished.

It was in architecture that Greek and Roman influence transformed Petra. This transformation began in the 1st century B.C. Continual wars between Egypt and Syria resulted in more and more trade shifting away from these areas and into the peaceful domains of the Nabataeans. As the Nabataeans became richer and more powerful they enlarged their territory, which eventually reached as far north as Damascus. They began to build on a grand scale, influenced no doubt by the Greek architecture that had followed the conquests of Alexander the Great through the Middle East some 350 years before.

The first thoroughly classical monument in Petra was the Khasneh. Iain Browning, a British author and authority on Petra, thinks that the people who built it must have been Greek. In his book *Petra* he observes that "there was no build-up to the creation of this uniquely beautiful monument and as all its characteristics are totally foreign to the native tradition, one must believe that it was designed by an architect from outside the Nabataean orbit."

The Nabataeans soon began copying the new style, though with varying degrees of success. Some of the tombs in the style now called Nabataean Classical are fussy and awkward-looking. Others, however, achieve both grandeur and elegance of proportion; and in the one called the Deir, or Monastery, the Nabataeans produced a masterpiece. This vast façade, 150 feet wide and 138 feet high, is cut deeply into the rock, and uses classical forms boldly and majestically. The inside of the Deir is relatively small, the chamber itself measures only 38 by 33 feet, and may have been a sanctuary. It seems likely that the great rituals connected with the Nabataean religion were enacted in front of the building, where a large area has been leveled.

The Amazing Architecture

Opposite: picture from *Travels in the Holy Land* by the English traveler D. H. Roberts, published in 1842. It depicts the most famous of the Petra monuments, the Khazneh. It dates from a time during the 1st century B.C. when the Nabataeans began building on a grand scale, influenced, it is believed, by the Greek architecture that followed in the wake of Alexander the Great's conquests of 336–323 B.C.

Below: the Monastery, Ed Deir, a temple reached by a steep rocky track. It is probable that elaborate rituals were carried out on the level ground in front of the temple, which acted as a magnificent backdrop.

The Influence of the Romans

Against such a background the rituals must have been an impressive sight.

Many of the buildings in Petra date from the period after A.D. 196, when the city, and the Nabataean kingdom, became a Roman province. With the expansion of the Roman Empire through the Middle East, it was inevitable that this rich little kingdom should have come under Roman rule. The Nabataeans had made handsome profits on Roman overland trade with India and Arabia. By annexing Petra, which now became part of the province of Arabia, Rome controlled this trade herself, at a great saving.

Although the Nabataeans continued building in their own style, the Roman administration in Petra conducted a building program that gave it the hallmarks of a Roman provincial city. An amphitheater, with room for some 3000 to 4000 spectators, was hewn out of the rock between the Khasneh and the main part of the city. Time and the wind have softened the edges of its tiers so that they fade here and there into a blur of cream and mauve rock. In the heart of Petra the Romans built an imposing colonnaded street and a new gate leading to the Temenos, the sacred enclosure in front of the Kasr el Bint—a temple that, unlike the others in Petra, is a free-standing structure.

This area was the heart of Petra, and it was here that the market was located. In her book *Pleasure of Ruins* the English writer Rose Macaulay paints a vivid picture of this place during Petra's prosperity: "Here the caravans of merchants from east and west brought and sold their rich bales, their spices, ivory and amber . . . crowding in the market places of the rock city, looked down on by steep rainbow heights wherein were carved something like a thousand sepulchres."

Petra continued to be an important trade center for at least another two centuries. But slowly, almost imperceptibly, its importance waned. Other cities, such as Jerash and Palmyra to

Right: the Roman amphitheater in Petra. The enormous wealth of the Nabataeans was bound sooner or later to attract the attention of the acquisitive Roman emperors. By A.D. 200 Petra and its lands had become a province of Rome and soon acquired that status symbol of a Roman province, the amphitheater.

Above: remains of Petra's Roman period, the Ksr el Bint and the Temenos Gate, as seen from a cave in Petra. The Ksr el Bint was a free-standing temple, perhaps the only one not carved from the rock face. This was the heart of Petra and all around it the great markets, that were the source of Petra's wealth, took place. In front of it was a colonnaded sacred enclosure, the Temenos, built by the Romans.

the north, attracted more trade, and as Petra gained in grandeur it lost the original base of its prosperity. The merchants left, and then so did the Roman legions whose duty it had been to protect the trade routes.

With the adoption of Christianity by the Roman Empire in the 4th century Petra acquired a bishop, and a few of its tombs and temples were consecrated as churches. But the city was no longer of any political or economic significance to the weakening Empire—then ruled from Byzantium—and it was left to its own devices.

In the 7th century Moslem rule extended throughout the territory around Petra, but it is unlikely that this affected Petra, as the city had probably ceased to exist. Archaeological and geological examination of the Petra area have shown that it was severely damaged around that time, probably by an earthquake. The destroyed buildings fell into a layer of river mud that had collected there over a period of some 200 years. Long before this natural disaster, however, and probably before the Moslems conquered the area, the last few inhabitants of Petra had departed.

In the Middle Ages the Crusaders built a fort on top of one of the hills overlooking Petra, and they may well have taken some of the stones for its construction from the ruined city. What they thought of its opulent tombs is unknown, for they left no record of it.

The absence of any Nabataean written history makes it difficult—and perhaps ultimately impossible—to understand fully some of Petra's remains. For example, there is the Columbarium, whose name is the Latin word for dovecote and also for a place holding cremation urns. Yet the niches carved into its walls are much too small to hold either a dove or a funerary urn. So far, no clues to the purpose of this strange place have been discovered.

Above: the circular pool on the Hill of Sacrifice at Petra. It was on this rocky peak that, scholars believe, important religious rites were carried out. Remains of a temple and an altar, obviously used for animal sacrifice, have been found.

Below: a view of the northeast rock wall of Petra. It was the French traveler Laborde who described such a sight as "The most extraordinary spectacle, the most magical picture of nature in its grandiose creation . . ."

Another mystery is the great Couloir (passageway) that leads to the top of Umm el Biyara, the rocky peak that towers over Petra. The first part of the ascent up this steep hill is by way of an extremely uneven rocky path. Then suddenly the path is replaced by a wide, smooth ramp flanked by a high stone wall. The size of this passageway and its careful construction suggest that it must have been used for important processions. The peak was probably an important sanctuary, for among the ruins on the top are some that may have been a temple. It is possible that the ramp was used for animals to be led along to be sacrificed.

Like most ancient peoples the Nabataeans offered animal sacrifices to their gods. Did they also practice human sacrifice? Some writers maintain that they did not. On the other hand, an inscription has been found at another Nabataean town that reads: "Abd-Wadd, priest of Wadd, and his son Salim, and Zayd-Wadd, have consecrated the young man Salim to be immolated to Dhu Gabat. Their double happiness." Some Byzantine writings (admittedly prejudiced) refer to an annual sacrifice of a youth among the Nabataeans. There is a place at Petra obviously used for sacrifice of some kind. Located on a rocky plateau some 600 feet above the valley, it consists of a courtyard approximately 48 feet by 21 feet, with an altar at the western end where the sacrifices were performed. Basins and drains carved into the altar clearly indicate its purpose.

The idea of ritual sacrifices taking place high above the splendid classical monuments of Petra creates a strange contrast in the mind's eye between a yearning for the spiritual while pursuing material ends. Similar contrasts can be found in any culture including our own. But something in the atmosphere of Petra, the haunting quality of a world in which the works of man are fused into the works of nature, gives the place a heightened sense of mystery.

Second of the Ghost Cities

Left: the ruins of the once-majestic city of Palmyra. Rising from the desert some 140 miles east of Damascus, the columns and colonnades of many of the now vanished buildings still stand sentinel against the driving sand. In the foreground the rising tiers of seats of a Roman amphitheater, and in the background an Arab castle sits perched atop a hill.

Below: this map of the Middle East shows the sites of both Petra and Palmyra, the two "ghost cities" whose history and rediscovery is the subject of this chapter.

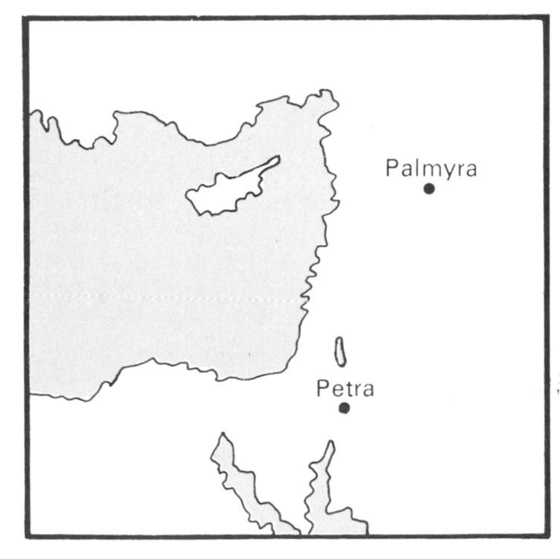

Some 300 or more miles to the north of Petra lies the ruined city of Palmyra which, in contrast to Petra's seclusion, rises up out of the open desert, and is visible for miles around. "It looks," writes Aubrey Menen, "like the skeleton of some unimaginably vast monster, its bones sticking up through the sand."

Earlier visitors to Palmyra portrayed it in more lyrical terms. A Dr. Kelman, who visited the site around the turn of the century, wrote: "In a square mile or so of fawn-coloured earth, lay the city in all its beauty and in all its sadness. Over the whole expanse, broken masonry of white or orange limestone was scattered in endless confusion—a tumultuous sea of stone fragments." The Comte de Volney, an impressionable Frenchman, visited Palmyra about 100 years earlier and found it a melancholy reminder of the transitory nature of worldly pomp and power. Rose Macaulay relates how Volney, sitting on a height overlooking the city, became overcome with emotion: "covering his head with his cloak, he gave himself up to sombre meditations on human affairs. Presently there arrived to him a phantom, and conversed with him on the condition of man in the universe and the philosophy of human history. Other beings, shadowy but eloquent, arrived to take part in a long conversation

Above: a detail from the Triumphal Arch (right) at Palmyra, gives some idea of the magnificence of the city in its prime. Founded around a large oasis with springs and fertile soil, it served as an important trading center between the empires of Rome and Parthia. Traders from Persia, India, and China came through the city from the East, those from Phoenicia from the West. Taxes levied on the ivory, spices, silks, gold, and jewels soon made the city and its citizens among the most prosperous in the Middle East.

on life: in fact, by the time he descended again into Palmyra, his book [on the Ruins of Empire] was practically written."

Westerners are not the only people to have found Palmyra overwhelming. A few years ago, an Arab sheik made a visit to the city and was conducted around Palmyra by Polish archaeologists at work on the site. They explained its origins and history, but the visitor would have none of such ordinary explanations. He insisted that structures of such vast dimensions could not possibly have been created by humans, they could only have been created by spirits, or jinns, favorably disposed to King Solomon (who, according to Arab tradition, built the city—and who figures in several stories about lost cities).

Most of Palmyra's magnificence dates from the 2nd century A.D. when it was at the peak of its prosperity as a trading center. But its history goes back nearly 2000 years B.C. In Cappadocia (part of Turkey) excavators found clay tablets of that early period which had been used by traders and that mentioned an oasis called Tadmor, the original name of Palmyra. (It acquired the name Palmyra sometime in the 1st century A.D. from the Romans, who apparently confused "tadmor" with another Semitic word "tamar," which means date palm.) At Palmyra itself there is evidence of human settlement reaching back perhaps as far as the Stone Age. At some point, a group of Arabian nomads began moving into the area and—like the Nabataeans at Petra—adopting a settled way of life. In time they also adopted the language of the Aramaeans, another Semitic people whose civilization consisted of a number of small states in Syria. But they always retained a trace of their nomad origins; every Palmyrene added, after his own name, the name of the tribe to which his people had belonged.

For many centuries Palmyra must have been a modest-looking place, with buildings of no special distinction or permanence. The earliest buildings found so far on the site date from around the 1st century B.C. It was the much later influences of Greece and Rome that brought grandeur to this oasis town. But Palmyra must have been reasonably prosperous even in its earlier days. With the growth of long-distance trade, made possible in the desert by the domesticating of the camel, it began to attract traders from Persia, India, and China to the east and from Phoenicia to the west. Traders could thus do their business at a mutually convenient place, at a great saving of time and money. Caravans laden with ivory, spices, silks, gold, and jewels came to Palmyra. The Palmyrenes levied a tax on all the trading carried on in their city. In return they offered a marketplace in which to do business and, of course, fresh water and accommodation for the traders. The Palmyrene merchants prospered. In fact Palmyra was first and foremost a "nation of shopkeepers"—or caravan leaders. Statues of merchants adorned public streets and squares, along with those of soldiers and statesmen.

Some idea of the wealth the city acquired in its heyday can be gathered from the portrait statues of Palmyrene women. They are richly bedecked with jewels, and their hair is elegantly coiffured. Further evidence of Palmyra's prosperity is seen in the way the Palmyrenes lavished their wealth on the tombs of their dead. At the southern approaches to the city lies a necropolis, a group of tower-shaped tombs that include some of the oldest buildings in Palmyra. They are rather grim-looking buildings, most consisting of several stories, as well as underground chambers. One of them is large enough to have held up to 400 bodies. The tombs are decorated with carvings, including portrait statues of the deceased, and paintings—some of them

The Splendor of Palmyra

Below: Palmyra as it looked in the 18th century, from *Ruins of Palmyra* by the English traveler Robert Wood, published in London in 1753. Among the ruins are the remains of Turkish fortification—B marks a Turkish tower built on the portico of the Temple of the Sun—a mosque and minaret (marked F); and mud enclosures around land cultivated for corn and olives by the Arabs (D).

Above: this portrait bust of a Palmyrene woman of the 3rd century A.D. gives some idea of the wealth of the inhabitants of the city of that time.

very elaborate. They clearly belonged to the rich. The poor citizens of Palmyra were buried in desert graves marked with simple headstones.

Flanking the city's main thoroughfare is the Great Colonnade, the most imposing feature of Palmyra. When it was built, sometime during the 2nd century A.D., it consisted of more than 700 columns. Most of these have now crumbled into the sand, but enough remain to give a fair idea of the avenue's former magnificence. Measuring around 29 feet in height, they are crowned with intricate Corinthian capitals, most of which are now badly worn by the wind. At one time this avenue was lined with shops and trading offices, but now only a few foundations remain.

Near the end of the colonnade stand the ruins of the great Temple of Bel, dedicated to the supreme deity of Palmyra. Here the Palmyrene priests sacrificed animals to Bel and to the other gods. After the sacrifice they would serve ritual feasts to a select congregation of prominent citizens. We don't know much about Palmyrene religion, apart from its sacrifices and feasts, but astrology may have played some part in it. One of the niches that originally contained statues of the gods is decorated with the signs of the zodiac.

The Roman Empire cast covetous eyes on wealthy Palmyra. Once, when Rome's finances were in a bad way, Mark Anthony sent its creditors to Palmyra to pillage the city. He justified the action by declaring that Palmyra favored Parthia over Rome in its trade. But the Palmyrenes got wind of the plan, and they evacuated the city, taking their valuables with them to a place miles away. The creditors, finding a deserted city, returned to Rome empty-handed.

Later relations between Rome and Palmyra were more diplomatic. The extension of Roman overlordship through Syria inevitably made Palmyra dependent, to some extent, on the Empire. By the reign of Vespasian (A.D. 70-79) a Roman "ob-

Below: the great temple of Bel in Palmyra. It stands at the end of a long colonnade and is built after the style of the temples of Greece and Rome. Within the columns is part of a fort built by Arabs.

Palmyra in its Heyday

server" was stationed in the city to arbitrate disputes over customs and to send confidential reports back to Rome. Palmyrene archers—famous throughout the ancient world—served in the Roman army. For a long time, however, Palmyra retained a large measure of independence. In 129 the Emperor Hadrian visited the city and conferred on it the status of a free city within the Empire—now to be called Hadriana Palmyra. Exactly how much freedom the city enjoyed is not known. Certainly it continued to thrive.

It was during the 2nd century A.D. that most of its magnificent buildings were erected. The city became renowned for the quality of its art, which is still apparent in the ornately carved

Above: the street of the colonnades with the Triumphal Arch in the background. When the majestic colonnaded street, Palmyra's most imposing feature, was erected some time during the 2nd century A.D. it consisted of more than 200 columns. About halfway up each column is a small ledge on which once stood a statue, all now lost, of one of Palmyra's famous citizens.

statues and reliefs that have withstood the ravages of the wind. Skilled goldsmiths and silversmiths catered to the Palmyrene taste for luxury and to that of foreign buyers as well.

Palmyra's prosperity depended on the uninterrupted flow of trade—and that, in turn, depended on peace. By the 3rd century the peace that had existed for so long in the area was becoming more and more fragile. The growing power of Persia threatened all of Syria, including Palmyra, which had been made a Roman province sometime early in the century. Little help could be expected from Rome, which was pouring its resources into wars with the barbarians north of the Alps and which was also weakened by a series of assassinations leading to a virtual collapse of government. In the middle of the century the Persians invaded Syria and even succeeded in capturing the Roman Emperor, Valerian, whose plague-ridden troops were no match for the Persians. The Roman Emperor died in captivity.

The successful Persians blocked Palmyra's trade routes, so that the Palmyrenes had to either come to terms with the enemy or defeat them without Roman help. At this point emerged a man

Zenobia, the Tragic Queen

Right: Zenobia, queen of Palmyra, by a 19th-century artist. Zenobia was, in fact, as romantic a figure as the artist tried to make her. Not only was she extremely beautiful, according to contemporary accounts, but she was also highly intelligent, and a clever politician. When her husband died in 268, Zenobia ruled for her infant son. Within a few years, taking advantage of Rome's preoccupation with domestic problems, an empty treasury, and barbarian invaders, Zenobia began a program of conquest that was to give her an empire from Antioch through Egypt to the Nile.

who was capable of dealing with the crisis: Odenathus, a Senator of Palmyra and regarded as its leading citizen. At first he tried to buy Persia's friendship; but the Persian king, Shapur, threw his gifts into the Euphrates. Odenathus then set about raising an army from all over Syria. Recruits flocked to the cause, and somehow Odenathus fashioned them into a disciplined army. Then he took on the Persians and defeated them.

With Odenathus' help Rome regained some of its strength in the Middle East. For his services he was granted the title of prince by the emperor, but he had already declared himself king in Palmyra. Rome recognized Palmyra's independence.

Odenathus was assassinated in 268 and was succeeded by his widow Zenobia, who reigned for their infant son Vaballathus. She was an extraordinary woman, who has often been compared to Cleopatra, and in fact she, too, was descended from the Ptolemies. According to the historians of antiquity she was not only very beautiful, but also very intelligent and enjoyed intellectual discussions with her chief advisor, the philosopher Longinus. She was an expert horsewoman, and while her husband was alive she loved to go hunting with him. She was also extremely ambitious.

Seeing that Rome was preoccupied with its German borders and with internal problems, Queen Zenobia resolved to win absolute independence for Palmyra and also to build an empire. In 271 she led her army to Antioch and captured this important Mediterranean port. Next, the Queen sent her army to Egypt where it was again victorious. Soon Palmyra ruled an empire that reached from Cappadocia to the Nile. Zenobia gave her son the title Augustus, a title that until then had been borne only by the Roman Emperor, and started minting her own currency.

Unfortunately for Zenobia, Rome had a new Emperor—one more capable than his immediate predecessors. After bringing the German situation under control the Emperor Aurelian marched his army into Syria. Near Antioch he engaged the Palmyrene army and succeeded in largely destroying its cavalry. Zenobia and the rest of her army started back toward Palmyra. At a town 80 miles from Palmyra Aurelian's forces again defeated them. Zenobia and her generals hastily withdrew to Palmyra. Some of the city's tombs were torn down to provide stones to reinforce the city walls, and when Aurelian finally reached Palmyra, after a seven days' march during which his army was continually attacked and raided by Arabs, he found the city well defended.

Zenobia had appealed for help from Persia, but it never came. Aurelian, encamped in a hostile desert and himself wounded by a Palmyrene lance, viewed the prospect of a long siege with apprehension. He offered peace, but Zenobia rejected his terms, which included her exile from Palmyra. The siege dragged on. Aurelian's army were now receiving supplies, but the Palmyrenes were starving. In this desperate situation Zenobia decided to escape. Riding a dromedary she sped through the desert, but on reaching the Euphrates she was overtaken by Aurelian's cavalry.

While Zenobia was taken into captivity, the citizens of Palmyra surrendered. Aurelian entered the city, had some of the rebels put to death, and then brought Zenobia to trial. Fearing for her own life, she proceeded to blame the rebellion on her advisors and to provide Aurelian with their names. They were executed and Zenobia and her son saved.

What happened to her after that is disputed. Aurelian planned to take her back to Rome and force her to walk in his triumphal processions. Some writers maintain that, unable to face such humiliation, she committed suicide. Others claim that she did walk in the procession, loaded with the royal jewels—now the property of Rome—and complaining of their weight. "Her feet were bound with shackles of gold," reported a Roman historian, "and even on her neck she wore a chain of gold, the weight of which was borne by a Persian buffoon." Aurelian had her married to a senator, according to this report, and she lived

Above: the head of Zenobia on a coin minted at Alexandria (about four times life size). It is the only authentic portrait that exists of Zenobia. It was removing the Roman emperor's head from Palmyra's coins and substituting her own or that of her son, and giving her son the Roman imperial title of Augustus, that jolted Rome into putting down the "rebellion" of the former state within the empire. The emperor Aurelian defeated her and her troops at Antioch and then again at Palmyra, and Queen Zenobia quietly disappeared from history.

Below: this carved relief of a tree and produce, together with contemporary accounts, points to Palmyra's fertility during its heyday. The Roman scholar Pliny the Elder (23–79 A.D.) wrote of its rich soil, agreeable springs, and fields.

comfortably with her family on an estate at Tibur.

The Palmyrenes made another attempt to win independence, but this too was quickly suppressed by Rome. This time Aurelian had the city sacked. But Aurelian's defeat of the Palmyrene army backfired on him. Palmyra was no longer able to defend itself or its trade routes, and as a result, Roman trade with the East suffered badly. Rome later decided that Palmyra did have some strategic importance, and Roman legions were stationed there. The city walls and ramparts were repaired and some new buildings were constructed. But Palmyra's economic decline and loss of population continued.

In the 7th century the Moslems easily conquered the city. They regarded its splendid buildings as raw material for their own constructions. The Temple of Bel was enclosed in fortifications.

Fall of a Once-Proud City

Left: all that remains of the glory that was Palmyra. After Zenobia's defeat the city gradually declined. In the 7th century the Moslems conquered the city and used its still magnificent buildings as the raw materials for their own fortifications. Slowly everyone left, and time, sand, and wind took over.

But gradually Palmyra ceased to be of any importance to them, and it continued quietly to decline. Its gold and bronze ornaments were removed by looters. In fact, all scraps of metal were considered worth taking, as they could be melted down and used for arms, and it was the removal of the metal clamps used to hold blocks of stone together that wrought most of the destruction in Palmyra. Time and the wind and sand did the rest.

When Western travelers began coming to Palmyra in the 17th century they found a small tribe of Arabs living among the ruins. A mosque had been constructed inside the Temple of Bel (it was still there as late as 1929), and mud huts filled the temple courtyard. Today the huts have gone. The only inhabitants of Palmyra are archaeologists, who are gradually reclaiming from the sand the fragments of a once-proud city.

Chapter 5
The Vanished Khmers

Thousands of slaves labored year after year at Angkor to erect one temple after another for the god-kings who ruled one of the greatest empires in Southeast Asia. The temples they built were colossal in size—one temple alone is larger than the Vatican in Rome. Yet, between the 15th century and their rediscovery in 1858, the structures had lain abandoned in the Cambodian jungle. What happened to the civilization responsible for them? The Khmers themselves have left no written history, only inscriptions. Between the few outside sources and the sifting of the archaeological evidence, scholars are now attempting to reconstruct the story.

Henri Mouhot, a French naturalist, stood in astonishment at the sight before him. Rising up through the thick vegetation of the Cambodian jungle, amid tree-trunks, wild orchids, and scampering monkeys, and festooned with vines and lichen, stood a magnificent temple. It is easy to imagine Mouhot's astonishment, for the temple he had accidentally discovered that day in 1858 was Angkor Wat, the largest religious building in the world. "Grander than anything left to us by Greece or Rome," he later wrote of it. The natives seemed to be as awestruck as he was. When he asked them who had built this enormous temple, they replied, "It is the work of giants," or "It built itself."

What Mouhot had discovered while looking for the tributaries of the Mekong River was more than one temple, however. He had come upon a whole city of temples. Literally hundreds of them lie imprisoned in the dense, encroaching forest that has grown over them, unchecked, for five centuries. Some of their walls have collapsed, and some of their details have eroded. Even so, the temples of Angkor are among the most astonishing sights the world has to offer. The breathtaking extravagance of these buildings, their seemingly innumerable towers and maze-like corridors, encrusted with elaborate sculptures seem to overwhelm the visitor.

Angkor Wat is the best-preserved of the temples and covers an area larger than Vatican City. This colossal structure is crowned by five towers, each in the shape of a huge lotus-bud. Its corridors

Above: the root-entwined head of a Khmer god at Angkor. Since its rediscovery, the city of temples deep in Cambodia has gradually been reclaimed from the jungle that hid and preserved it for centuries.

Opposite: a tower in the shape of a lotus-bud from the temple of Angkor Wat.

The French Arrive

Above: Henri Mouhot, the French naturalist who first brought the news of the incredible city of Angkor to the West in 1858. He published an account of his discoveries in 1864.

are lined with literally miles of beautifully carved panels, depicting scenes from Hindu mythology and from the history of the people who built Angkor. Some 2000 statues of temple dancers adorn the walls of Angkor Wat. Their curvaceous bodies and sensuous, yet enigmatic smiles recur throughout Angkor, helping to give a human aspect to this deserted city.

Mouhot was not in fact the first European to set eyes on Angkor. A Portuguese missionary had discovered it in the mid-16th century and had written of the "forest of huge and terrifying ruins of palaces, halls and temples"—and of a size, he declared, which would be unbelievable if he had not seen them. "Unbelievable," in fact, summed up the general reaction to his story (although one man not only believed in the existence of the ruins but also wrote a short book in which he suggested that they might be the remains of the lost continent of Atlantis). During the 17th century several more firsthand reports of the lost city were produced by European missionaries, but again without much response.

Mouhot's account, in his book *Voyages dans l'Indo-Chine, Cambodge et Laos*, was so vivid and detailed that his readers were convinced. Moreover, as the French were at that time beginning to colonize that area of Southeast Asia, known as Indochina, they took a special interest in his discovery, Several expeditions to Angkor were organized, and when Cambodia became a French protectorate in 1863, the daunting task of restoration was begun. Sadly, Henri Mouhot died of a tropical fever before any of this was accomplished and before the history of Angkor could be revealed. He had spent the last two years of his life exploring these ruins, which, he wrote, were "the only remaining signs, alas, of a lost race, whose very name, like those of the great men, rulers, and artists who adorned it, seems

Right: the ruins of Ta Prohm temple at Angkor. Ta Prohm has been left uncleared of jungle to show the condition of many of the temples before their restoration by the French.

destined to remain forever hidden among the rubbish and dust. . . ."

From the evidence gathered by archaeologists and other scholars we now know that Angkor was the capital of an empire ruled by a people who called themselves Khmers—a name that is preferred by modern Cambodians. The Khmer empire lasted from about the 9th century A.D. to the 15th, and at the height of its power included all of modern Cambodia, eastern Thailand, Vietnam, and Laos. In 1431 the Thais invaded Angkor and sacked it. The defeated Khmers abandoned their city, and their civilization vanished.

The history of the Khmers has been pieced together from the inscriptions on their temples, and from the writings of foreign historians—mainly Chinese. Khmer documents and letters were written on palm leaves and animal skins and have not survived. We have no trouble visualizing what those Khmers looked like. They are physically very real to us and smile down from the many temple walls. Yet at the same time they are remote, because they have left virtually no record of their ideas.

The foundations of the Khmer Empire were laid sometime during the 1st century A.D. when Indian traders and missionaries began colonizing Southeast Asia. The Indians not only estab-

Above: a sculpture from Angkor being transported across a marsh by French archaeologists in the 19th century. Statues of kings, gods, lions, elephants, and dragons, and smaller, movable sculptures were taken to France and shown in an exhibition of Khmer art, the first ever seen in the West. It created enormous interest among the public and in artistic circles in Paris.

The Origins of the Khmers

Below: map of Indochina showing the Mekon River and the city of Angkor. To the northwest lay Thailand and in the southeast, in what was later South Vietnam, lived the Chams. Both Thais and Chams played an important part in the history of the ancient Khmers.

lished ports along the coast but also introduced their language, Sanskrit, their religions, Hinduism and Buddhism, and their art and literature to the people of this area. Several kingdoms incorporating both Indian and native cultures grew up along the coast. One of these kingdoms, located around the Mekong delta, was called Funan by the Chinese. According to one tradition its ruling family was descended from a young Indian sailor named Kaundinya who was blown off course and driven toward the coast of Indochina, where he encountered the beautiful Queen Willowleaf, ruler of the country, sailing toward him in a canoe. He foiled her attempt to seize his boat and, using his magical powers, sank her canoe. Although it was an inauspicious start, their relationship later developed into love, and they married and founded the dynasty of Funan.

Most of what we know about Funan comes from the reports of Chinese diplomats. They found it a prosperous nation, fertile,

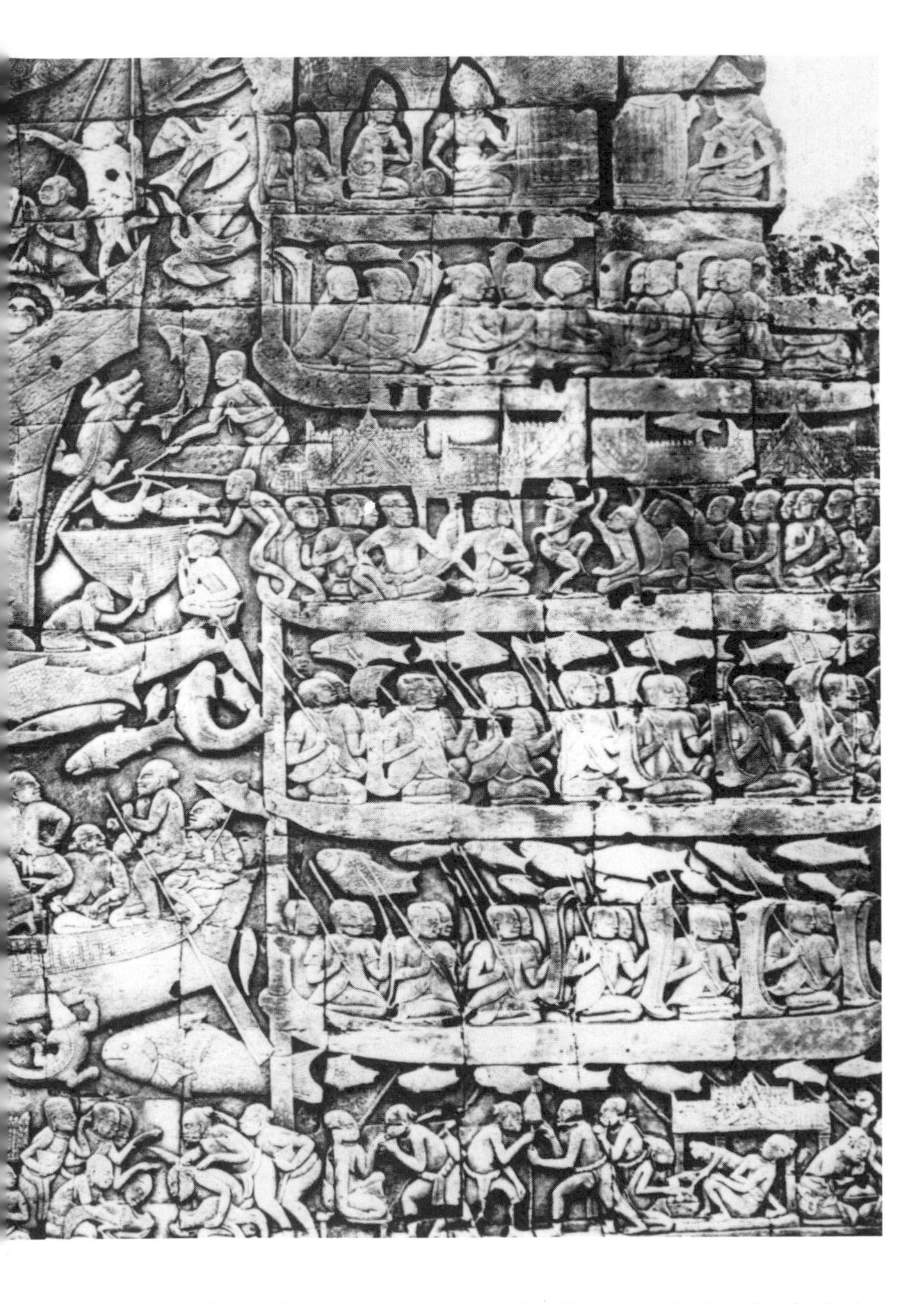

Left: a carved relief of around A.D. 1200 from the Bayon temple in Angkor Thom. Although a gloomy and forbidding place, the sculptures of the Bayon temple give a better picture than any others of the life of the ordinary citizens of Angkor. So accurate, in fact, are the carvings that experts have been able to identify all the species still found in the lakes today.

and enjoying a thriving foreign trade. The population included a large number of Indian craftsmen, who built and decorated the temples that the people of Funan dedicated to the Hindu gods and to Buddha. Early in Funan's history, the worship of Shiva, the Hindu god of destruction and reproduction whose symbol was the *linga*, or phallus, became the official religion.

The rulers of Funan extended their jurisdiction over neighboring states, and by the middle of the 3rd century their empire reached from the Indian Ocean to the South China Sea. One of their northern tributary states was Chenla (as the Chinese called it), home of the Khmers. They called their land Kambujadeśa (Cambodia), meaning the land of the descendants of Kambu, a mythical priest who founded a royal house. During the 6th century the king of Chenla decided to take advantage of the growing decadence of Funan and attack it. After a series of terrible floods had left Funan extremely vulnerable, the Khmers

Mount Meru–Center of the Universe

easily conquered it. They took over not only Funan itself but also most of its empire.

From the mid-500s to the end of the 700s was, for the most part, a time of internal and external conflicts for the Chenla empire. There were frequent wars with the Chams, who lived in what is now South Vietnam; and eventually, for some time during the latter part of the 7th century Chenla became a satellite of the powerful kingdom of Java.

The first of the great Khmer kings probably owed his position to the support of Java, which had deposed his predecessor. Soon after attaining the throne, Jayavarman II declared—and won—his country's independence from Java. He established a strong central government, unifying the country, and moved the capital inland, where it would be less vulnerable to attack. The site he chose was a mountain near the Great Lake in the area called Angkor. The lake was teeming with fish, which would provide food for the large Khmer army as well as for the great numbers of slaves and other workers who were to build his city. The forests were full of game, and the high rainfall and the periodic flooding of the land made it very fertile. Another natural asset was the extensive deposits of sandstone, which Jayavarman and his descendants would use to construct great temples to the greater glory of their gods—which they identified with themselves.

The most significant aspect of Khmer life and culture was the cult of the god-king. This cult—called *devaraja* in Sanskrit—was established by Jayavarman II at the same time that he proclaimed his country's independence. A learned brahman performed a ritual in which he declared that the Khmers were freed from Javanese overlordship because their king was divine. He was endowed with the creative energy of Shiva. Therefore the linga, which had long been worshiped as the symbol of Shiva, was now to be equally worshiped as the symbol of the king.

The devaraja cult met with some resistance among orthodox Hindus, but Jayavarman suppressed it with a combination of strong-arm tactics against his opponents and clever propaganda that convinced the masses that their own wellbeing depended on their faithfully following the cult. His methods were successful. Not only he, but each of his successors as well, was accepted as a god.

Of course, the Khmers were not the only people to deify their monarchs. Many ancient peoples believed their kings to be divine. What set the Khmer devaraja cult apart was that it identified the king with an existing god—usually Shiva, but sometimes Vishnu, the protector god. The other god of the Hindu trinity, Brahma, was less highly venerated. Among the Khmers the worship of the god-king assumed an overriding importance. An army of priests devoted themselves to the worship of the royal linga. Naturally, this venerated object had to be suitably housed, and so began the custom of each king building a temple in his own honor. The temple also served as the king's tomb after his death.

The temple that housed the royal linga was regarded by the Khmers as the center of the world. For them, each new royal temple became Mount Meru, which, according to Hindu mythology, stood at the center of the Universe and united the

Opposite: Angkor Wat from the air. It is the largest of the Angkor temples and the largest religious edifice in the world. Built for King Suryavarman II, the temple symbolizes Mount Meru, the center of the universe and dwelling place of the gods. Each Khmer god built his own temple-tomb, which became Mount Meru for him and for his people during his lifetime—hence the large number of temples at Angkor.

Above: "The Churning of the Sea of Milk," one of the favorite themes of sculptors at Angkor. The carving illustrates the Hindu legend which tells how the god Vishnu in the guise of a tortoise (center bottom of panel) descends to the bottom of the cosmic Sea of Milk and supports a mountain on his back. A giant many-headed snake is coiled around the mountain and pulled backward and forward by a team of gods and a team of demons, one on either side of the sea. The churning produces ambrosia—food of the gods and symbol of all that is desired by the world.

earth with the heavens. A French writer on Angkor, George Cœdès, explains the connection between the mythical mountain and the temple: "Just as Mount Meru was supposed to penetrate to the celestial vault and to carry the lowest layer of the heavens on its peak, in the same way the central temple of the city established the liaison between men and gods through the mediation of the god on earth, who was the king."

Some of the Khmer temples were built on mountains; others were built in the form of stepped pyramids to suggest mountains; still others, such as Angkor Wat, had a raised central section crowned with towers representing peaks. The word "phnom," which appears in the names of many temples and in the name of Cambodia's capital, Phnom Penh, means "mountain" in the Khmer language.

Scholarship appears to have been highly regarded at Angkor and learned men often held debates there. Unfortunately, though, their words and thoughts have vanished and it is to Khmer art that present-day scholars turn to get some idea of Khmer beliefs. The carved panels in the temples are a rich pictorial source of Khmer theology and mythology. One of the favorite themes of the sculptors is the Churning of the Sea of Milk. This curious legend, which is of Indian origin, tells how Vishnu, in the form of a tortoise, descends to the bottom of the cosmic Sea of Milk and supports a mountain on his back. A giant snake, or *naga*, is coiled around the mountain and pulled forward and backward by a team of gods on one side of the sea, a team of demons on the other. The churning action produced ambrosia, the food of the gods and a symbol of all that is good in life—health, wealth, and happiness.

In one of the outer corridors of Angkor Wat there is a series of carved panels showing 32 different kinds of hell awaiting those who have sinned in various ways. There is, for example, a Hell of Broken Bones for those who have damaged property, a Hell of Boiling in a Kettle for those who embezzle the king's money or steal from priests, and an extremely unpleasant Hell of Worms

Khmer Beliefs

Left: a Khmer view of Heaven and Hell, one of the panels from a public gallery in the temple of Angkor Wat. The tortures of the damned (who are being beaten with clubs, picked up bodily and clawed in head and feet, and, bottom left, having their tongues torn out) are contrasted with the serenity of the blessed as they sit forever in their gilded pavilions in the top panel. The prospect of the blessed has not captured the imagination of the sculptor, however, who wryly depicts boredom and monotony on some of the faces.

Who Built Angkor?

Right: King Suryavarman II, who reigned from 1113 to around 1150. He is regarded as one of the greatest of the Khmer kings. He ascended the throne after a period of civil unrest and quickly restored order and peace. After some military adventures against the rival kingdom of the Chams, in latter-day South Vietnam, Suryavarman turned to building the great temple of Angkor Wat, the supreme masterpiece of Khmer creation. He is depicted here on an elaborate throne holding court.

for those who offend parents, friends, priests, or gods. The obvious corrective intent of these carved reliefs suggests that this part of the temple was open to the public. Only priests and royalty could enter the more sacred parts of Khmer temples.

The great Jayavarman II moved his capital several times before settling at a place he called Hariharalaya. It was the first of several cities that would be built in the Angkor area over the next 400 years. Very little remains of the secular buildings erected in the reign of Jayavarman II, who died in 850. In fact, apart from the numerous temples and some bridges and roads, no buildings remain even from the later days of Angkor, for the simple reason that all buildings other than temples were made of wood. Even the royal palace was a wooden building, admittedly a richly decorated one. Archaeological work has revealed traces of four palaces, built between 1000 and 1350.

The king who built Angkor Wat was Suryavarman II, who reigned from 1113 to around 1150, and who is regarded as one of the greatest of the Khmer kings. Suryavarman seized the throne from the previous, weak ruler, and he soon showed that he was made of stronger stuff. His military conquests are celebrated in lavish detail on the walls of Angkor Wat. Hundreds of foot soldiers and officers mounted on horses and elephants and accompanied by musicians are carved parading past the king. Another relief vividly depicts a battle between the Khmers and the Chams.

Toward the end of his reign Suryavarman was less successful in battle, but his building program accelerated, transforming the capital, Yasodharapura, into a city of great splendor. Temples

were erected one after another, not only by the king but also by members of the aristocracy, who vied with each other in their extravagance. Quantity was matched by quality. The reign of Suryavarman saw the flowering of Khmer art—above all in his temple of Angkor Wat, in which he was worshiped as Vishnu. In this masterpiece, says the Czech writer Miloslav Krása, "the art of the Khmers crystalized into its purest form, majestic in its vastness, exquisite in its minutest detail. . . ."

A British writer on Khmer art, Geoffrey Gorer, has suggested that the tranquil sensuality found in many of the reliefs can be traced to the effects of opium. Drug-taking was common among the Khmers of all classes—opium mainly among the court, and various other narcotics among the rest of the population. In the beautiful carvings of temple dancers at Angkor Gorer sees evidence of the state of mind of the opium-taker: "These . . . flower-garlanded sylphs re-appear endlessly on every wall of nearly every temple; smiling enigmatically . . . seen with such sensual admiration but with no desire . . . in hieratic dancing poses, kindly and formal and inhuman."

Where did the wealth come from to support all this magnificence? Much of it resulted from the great fertility of the land, which was increased by a more important—if less imposing—building program, that of an irrigation system. Cambodia's rainy season lasts from November to May. By storing the excess water in great reservoirs, called *barays*, and then systematically flooding the rice fields during the dry season the Khmers were able to get three harvests a year from the same land—more than enough to feed the population. There were several of these

Above: wall relief of the Khmer army on the march. The wealth and fertility of the Khmer kingdom attracted the attention of neighboring states such as the Javanese, Thais, and Chams, and in consequence the state had to maintain a large army for its defense—and for the ambitions of its rulers.

Below: relief from a pillar in the Bayon temple of celestial dancing girls—*Apsaras*—who were said to have been born from the flying spray of ocean waves. Their hand gestures are used in present-day Cambodian ballet.

barays, one of which was over five miles long and a mile across.
The land produced other crops besides rice. One was cotton, which the Khmers wove into fine cloth, some of which they exported. There was also a rich supply of minerals. Chinese travelers in Cambodia wrote of the country's gold, silver, copper, and tin; some of these may have been obtained through trade, however. The network of rivers that crossed the country and the excellent system of roads built by some of the Khmer kings facilitated trade and helped to make Cambodia the richest nation in Southeast Asia.

The construction of the temples and the roads and irrigation system could be accomplished relatively cheaply as most of the heavy work was done by slave labor. Some of the workers were members of the poorest class who were conscripted for the job; others were drawn from the huge population of slaves.

For all its prosperity and magnificence, the Khmer empire was seldom very secure. A few years after the death of Suryavarman II the peasants and slaves in the provinces revolted. The revolt began with the murder of a few tax collectors, then quickly spread and within a few weeks the rebels had reached the capital. The rebellion was put down with ferocity. The army swept through the country massacring slaves and peasants by the thousands, until the government—alarmed at the reduction of the work force—brought the reprisals to a close with a public execution in which the ring-leaders were buried alive.

Several years after the revolt, civil war broke out and a usurper seized the throne. With Angkor in a weak, divided state, its old enemies, the Chams, invaded. But they failed to take the capital and were forced to flee by the Khmers' formidable Royal Regiment of Elephants. A few years later, in 1177, the Chams tried again, this time with a surprise attack by ship. They caught the Khmers unprepared and swarmed into the city where they indulged in an orgy of looting, destruction, rape, and murder. After a few days most of them departed, leaving an occupation force in the devastated city.

Then the Chams made a serious mistake. Living in exile in Champa at the time was Suryavarman II's son who had left Angkor on his father's death rather than contest the claim of a usurper. The exile, Jayavarman, was a Buddhist. Although Buddhism had been tolerated throughout the history of Angkor, its teachings against bloodshed were directly opposed to official policy. Jayavarman would not use force to gain the throne, but he now saw an opportunity to gain it peacefully. The Chams, no doubt believing that he would serve admirably as a puppet, allowed him to return to his country.

The intended puppet turned out to be the greatest ruler in Khmer history, Jayavarman VII. The suffix "-varman," borne by all Khmer kings, is Sanskrit for "protector." Jayavarman was more than a protector; he was his country's avenger. On returning to his ruined country he immediately took steps to restore its prosperity and its military strength. Whatever pacifist scruples he may have had as a Buddhist he now put aside. He raised a huge army and navy and drove the Chams out of the country. A few years later his army invaded Champa—pillaging, burning, and butchering as the Chams had done at Angkor. It

The Evidence in the Carvings

Opposite: sculpture of a *devata*, or heavenly being, as a guardian spirit on the walls of the Banteay Srei (Citadel of the Women) temple. Cambodian ballet dancers still use the same patterns of jewelry, necklaces, and bracelets today.

Below: King Jayavarman VII, who returned from exile to be crowned king in 1181 when he was already over 50 years old. Although a Buddhist and opposed to bloodshed (he had voluntarily gone into exile rather than fight against relatives for his throne) he was roused to wrath by the destruction caused when the Khmer's old enemy the Chams invaded his country. He raised a huge army and navy and soundly defeated them. Later he led his army into Champa to avenge the devastation of Angkor.

Above: the towers of the Bayon temple in Angkor Thom. After defeating the Chams and reducing their kingdom to the status of a province in his empire, Jayavarman VII began a feverish building campaign, not only restoring Angkor Wat after the ravages done to it by the Chams, but building himself a new capital, Angkor Thom. The new capital was dominated by the temple of the Bayon with its towers decorated with the faintly smiling face of the Buddha. Next to the temple was the royal palace and the whole new city was enclosed by high walls, magnificent gateways, and a moat, all of which still survive.

took several years of fighting to subdue Champa completely, but eventually it was reduced to the status of a province within the Khmer empire.

Able-bodied Chams were brought back to Angkor, where they were forced to repair the damaged temples and to build Jayavarman's new city, Angkor Thom.

If the reign of Suryavarman II was the high point of Khmer culture, that of Jayavarman VII was by far its most extravagant. The new king was obsessed with building. For 40 years the Khmers and the foreign slaves worked feverishly to satisfy the king's insatiable demand for more temples, more libraries, more monasteries. Thousands of them died in the process. The French writer John Audric speculates that Jayavarman "never completely recovered from the shock of seeing his flattened capital and after that only by the construction of more and more buildings, more massive and sacred than ever, could he efface it from his memory."

Although a Buddhist, he eagerly adopted the god-king status established by his Hindu predecessors, declaring that he was the living Buddha. At the center of Angkor Thom he built the great

The Builder King

temple of the Bayon, the god-king's spiritual home. It is an overwhelming building, dark and forbidding. In the days of the Khmers the moat surrounding it was filled—as was the custom—with crocodiles. Today the crocodiles have gone, but the visitor is still made uneasy by the constant sensation of being watched. Pierre Loti, a Frenchman who visited Angkor early in this century, described the experience: "I stared up at the tree-covered towers which dwarfed me, when suddenly by blood curdled, for I saw an enormous face looking down on me, and then another face over on another wall, then three, then five, then ten, appearing from every direction, and all had the same faint smile."

There are, in fact, some 200 of these faces on the towers of the Bayon, each eight feet high. They represent Jayavarman VII as the Buddha.

Despite his megalomania, Jayavarman seems to have had the rudiments of a social conscience. He had no pity for the mainly foreign workers who died while constructing his buildings, but he did have some compassion for the sick. He built 102 hospitals,

Left: one of the towers from Angkor Thom. The smiling face of the Buddha looking down from every side creates an eerie effect on visitors to the site of Jayavarman's capital. The faces are, of course, Jayavarman's. He adopted the practice of his Hindu forebears and declared himself god-king—only in his case he became Buddha in place of their Shiva.

The Daily Life of the Khmers

Right: carved stone panel from the Bayon temple depicting scenes of daily life among the Khmers. On the lowest level, under a tent in the fresh air, some cooks are making pâtés, which are in the process of being taken from their molds, others are plunging a wild boar into a pot, and yet others are grilling meats or fish on skewers—much as they are still served in Indochinese street markets. In the central band under an open-sided tent people are eating their meals with their fingers according to local custom. Only the Vietnamese and Chinese help themselves with chopsticks. At the very top a king (only very lightly sculptured for some reason) gives an audience to his subjects.

locating them throughout the country. They were linked by a new network of roads that radiated out from Angkor Thom. The roads were built of stone and raised above the ground to offer safe travel in times of flood. At intervals along the roads Jayavarman built rest houses—121 of them—for the convenience of travelers. Both rest houses and hospitals were attached to temples or small shrines, and in the foundation stones of the religious buildings archaeologists have found inscriptions detailing the organization of the secular building alongside. For example, one hospital employed 32 staff, including two doctors, two cooks, six water-heaters and medicine-grinders, and two storekeepers who distributed the medicines. Ingredients used included nutmeg, cardoman, sesame, and vinegar.

Details such as these go a small way toward giving us a picture of daily life among the Khmers. Unexpectedly, it is the walls of the gloomy Bayon that give us such a lively view of life among the ordinary Khmers. Whereas the reliefs that decorated earlier Khmer temples depicted religious or mythological subjects or the triumphs of the god-king, most of the Bayon

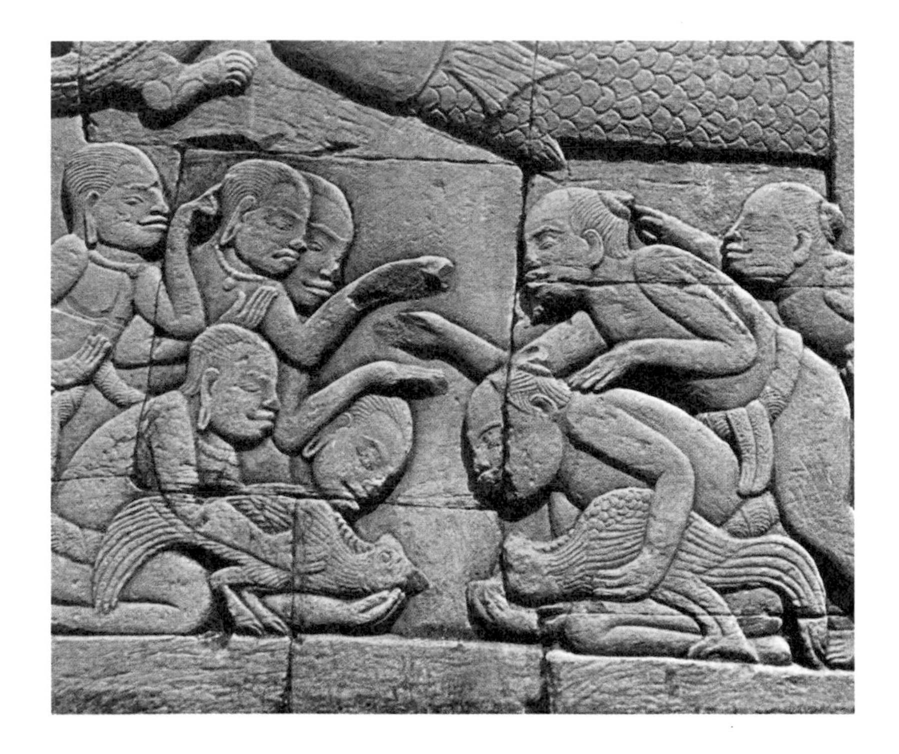

Left: a detail of a cockfight from a carved panel in the Bayon temple. It is another vivid scene from the life of the Khmers as lived in the middle of the 12th century. Other friezes depict scenes of hunters attacking wild beasts and fishermen on the Great Lake with nets full of fish. Other panels show temples being built, with slaves quarrying stones and making bricks. Religious processions wind their way through other friezes.

reliefs are devoted to scenes of ordinary life. They show men and women at work: fishing, cooking meals, planting, and taking their produce to market. People are shown playing games, dancing, and betting on fighting cocks. A woman is shown about to give birth, with the midwife standing by. Inevitably, there are also numerous battle scenes, but these are rendered more attractive by the backgrounds of graceful foliage and by the fish that swim among the fighting galley ships.

Unfortunately, the great frenzy of building under Jayavarman VII seems to have left the Khmers literally exhausted. There is evidence of haste and carelessness in the construction of many of the temples. Many are in a poorer condition than earlier structures. Many were left unfinished. The civilization of the Khmers was to last for another two centuries following the death of Jayavarman VII in 1218, but they were never again to build on a scale even remotely approaching that of the Buddha-king—or, indeed, of his predecessors.

A vivid picture of life in Angkor in the late 13th century has come down to us from Chou Ta-kuan, the Chinese envoy from Peking. Chou Ta-kuan lived in Angkor for a year, observing and reporting to his emperor on conditions in the Khmer capital. Although he regarded its inhabitants as barbarians—not being Chinese—he found certain things to admire, and his report, entitled *Memoirs of the Customs of Cambodia*, is probably fairly accurate. He describes Angkor Thom in great detail and seems impressed by its luxury. The golden towers about the city, he notes, are probably what strike foreign visitors most, and help prompt the title "rich and noble Cambodia." One such golden tower was over the private apartment of the royal residence. The great lake about a mile and a quarter from the walled town contained a stone tower in its center in which a stone Buddha reclined with water flowing continuously from his navel.

He also describes Khmer festivals and pageantry, including a splendid procession of the king and his retinue through the streets of Angkor in which the procession, led by cavalry was followed by hundreds of standards and pennants. A massed procession of musicians came next and there were more bands at the intervals along the route. Behind the musicians large numbers of dancing girls glided by, each wearing flowers in her hair and carrying tall, lighted candles. After them came palace maidens in their hundreds, carrying gold and silver vessels, trays of precious stones, ropes of pearls, and splendid ornaments.

Behind them marched the king's bodyguard, composed exclusively of women, described by Chou Ta-kuan as tall and good looking Amazons. After these came the nobility, riding on elephants and shaded by red parasols, then the king's wives and concubines—some riding on elephants, some in chariots, and some on litters protected with gilded sunshades. Finally—the king himself, riding on an elephant with gilded tusks. He stood upright under a red and gold canopy and was adorned with jewels. In his hand he carried the sacred golden sword, the symbol of his divine authority.

Above: a woman sells fish from her market stall in this relief from the Bayon temple in Angkor Thom. Khmer women obviously had more freedom than did Chinese women. In 1296 the Mongol Emperor of China sent an embassy to the Khmers and it is from one of its members that a description of Khmer customs, manners, and religious practices has come down to us.

Differences in status among Khmer officials were marked by variations in their trappings. The highest dignitaries in the land had gold shafts to their palanquins and four parasols with gold handles, reports Chou Ta-kuan. Those immediately below them in office had the same palanquin, but only one or two parasols. Lesser dignitaries had silver shafts on their palanquins, or simply a silver-handled parasol. The parasols, with long fringes hanging down to the ground, were made of red Chinese taffeta.

The aristocracy lived in houses with tiled roofs. The middle and lower classes were not allowed to use tiles; their roofs were thatched. Clothing—of which the Khmers wore very little—was also strictly regulated according to class, with bright and intricate patterns being worn only by the upper classes. The common people possessed no furniture, and they cooked their meals with one clay pot, a clay pan for the sauce, and halved coconut shells for ladles.

Even the lower classes, however, owned slaves. Middle class families might have 10 to 20, and only the poorest of the poor had none. They were held in the greatest contempt, and it was forbidden to have sexual intercourse with them. A foreign guest who did so was ostracized.

Chou Ta-kuan has much to say about the sexual customs of the Khmers, some of it disapproving. Young girls were deflowered between the ages of seven and 11 by a priest, who performed the service by hand, following—in the case of rich families—an elaborate banquet. After the ritual, the girl was free to do as she wished. Wives reserved the right to be unfaithful to their husbands if the husband went away for more than 10 days or so. As in most cultures, there was prostitution. Groups of women loitered in the main square, and Chou Ta-kuan observes that their main targets were Chinese men, because they were generous.

But Khmer women engaged in other business as well. It was they, Chou Ta-kuan noted with amazement, who did the trading in the marketplace. The Chinese, themselves, when they took a wife on settling in Angkor, looked on her business aptitude as one of her more desirable qualities. Some women also held political offices, and some enjoyed high reputations as scholars.

At the time Chou Ta-kuan was living in Angkor the country was still producing three, or even four rice harvests a year. The economy was prosperous. Evidently the irrigation system, which had been allowed to deteriorate in the years following the death of Jayavarman VII, was once again in good working order.

There were, however, other signs of decline. Warfare, particularly against the Thais, was demanding a disproportionate part of the nation's resources. During Chou Ta-kuan's stay he reported rumors that every able-bodied man was being forced to fight in the war against Thailand.

Another sign—although Chou Ta-kuan does not mention it—was that no new temples were being constructed. None had been built since the great burst of building acitivity under Jayavarman VII, and in a civilization that had delighted in extravagant architecture, the change was significant.

One possible cause of the lack of building was the spread of Hinayana Buddhism. Jayavarman VII and his followers practiced Mahayana Buddhism, an elaborate and ritualistic form of the religion that a worldly, luxurious court could accept. Hinayana Buddhism, with its simplicity, humility, and renunciation of earthly desires, was opposed to such a pleasure-centered life. In his report Chou Ta-kuan observed that there were, in the streets of Angkor, thousands of Buddhist monks carrying their begging bowls. This form of Buddhism had not appeared in Angkor until the end of the 13th century, when Chou Ta-kuan was writing. It appealed strongly to the common people, offering them a way to become resigned to suffering and to achieve inner peace. At the same time, it undermined the allegiance of the people to the cult of the god-king, even though he identified himself with the Buddha. The new religion taught

The Place of Khmer Women

Below: princesses in the royal apartments, from a relief at Angkor Wat. There were some 5000 girls living in the palace of the god-king of the Khmers and they fulfilled most of the positions about the king—servants, guards (the king's bodyguard was an entirely female regiment of lance and shield-bearing lithe young Amazons), handmaidens, and concubines. Next to the king himself ranked his five official wives and their children.

The Legacy of the Khmers

that the Buddha himself had never claimed to be a god. Kings should give up their riches, as the royal prince Buddha had done, and live simply. By the end of the 14th century, Hinayana Buddhism had become the religion of nearly the entire population, including some of the aristocracy. Once this situation had come to pass, the whole force behind the Khmer civilization, the power and authority of the god-king, simply withered away.

It is impossible to reconstruct exactly the course of the Khmers' downfall, though some factors that contributed to it have been pieced together. For example, we know that around the beginning of the 15th century there were power struggles within the royal family and that several times the ruling king was deposed for another member of his family. Such events had occurred many times in the past, but now there was no strong leader to command allegiance—let alone the worship accorded earlier kings.

Possibly because of ineffective leadership and possibly because the new religion undermined the will to produce, the Khmers let their irrigation system deteriorate. The rice harvests declined sharply, and without this economic base, the country faced ruin.

It may be that a great flood precipitated the fall of Angkor. A Buddhist legend tells of a flood that supposedly occurred because the king drowned his chaplain's son in the Great Lake for having offended his own son. The naga-king, or snake-god, then caused the lake to overflow the surrounding countryside and destroy Angkor Thom. Apart from the fanciful cause, the story may be true. Even today, the flooding of the Mekong River and its tributaries forces the water level of the Great Lake, which is part of the Mekong River system, to rise and overflow the land. In the 15th century the shore of the lake may have been much nearer

Above: Banteay Samre temple, built around 1100, was one of a succession of smaller shrines and temples built at Angkor that were the forerunners of the larger temple structures culminating in the grandeur of Angkor Wat. The Buddhist monks pictured here are visitors to the historic monument.

Right: two dancers from the Cambodian Royal Ballet. They are enacting one of the ancient Khmer dramas and as such are direct cultural descendants of the ancient Khmers depicted on the carvings of the temple walls. Those ancient dancers performed half-naked, however, while modern Cambodian dancers are completely clothed from head to foot. This, too, is historical; when Angkor was captured by the Thais 500 years ago they took the Royal Ballet to entertain their own monarch, who ordered the flimsily clad dancers to be arrayed in the splendid dress of his own court. When the Ballet was restored to the Khmer kingdom many years later, they retained the dress of their one-time captors.

Angkor and a flooding of the lake potentially more harmful.

The death blow to Angkor was delivered by the Thais. Eastern Thailand had once been under Khmer domination, but as the Khmers declined they had gained in power and had started invading Cambodia's northern and eastern provinces. In the late 1200s they were already formidable foes, requiring a massive expenditure of Khmer manpower. From 1350 onward the Thais and the Khmers were almost continuously at war. In 1388 the Thais succeeded in taking Angkor Thom. They were aided by conspirators within the government who wanted to bring an end to the *devaraja* cult, which the king and his closest supporters were attempting to revive. The victorious Thais installed a puppet king on the throne and then made the mistake of withdrawing their forces too soon. Within a short time the Thai puppet king had been assassinated and a Khmer king installed in his place.

The internal strife and the weakened economy had left Angkor extremely vulnerable. In 1431 the Thai armies attacked Angkor again. In contrast to their previous restrained behavior, they now rampaged through the city, looting and destroying. Some of the invaders had a genuine respect for Khmer culture, however, and they took back to their own country many of its ideas the customs, as well as artists who were required to lend their skills to the building of the Thai capital, Ayudhya. They also took with them the beautiful temple dancers, who enjoyed great popularity in Thailand after having been more adequately clothed, in accordance with Thai custom. The tradition of Khmer dancing has survived the centuries, preserved for many years by the Thai conquerors, and modern Cambodian dancers wear the elaborate costumes imposed on them long ago by an alien culture.

Sometime after the destruction of Angkor Thom by the Thais, the Khmers abandoned the city. Exactly what happened has long been a subject for speculation. Records are extremely sparse. However, recent scholarship has discovered that the exodus was a gradual one, and that the king and court remained in the city for a year or two after most of the population had fled. Apparently they made some attempts to get the irrigation system working again, but they lacked the resources for such a daunting task. Malaria swept through the country, and there may have been more floods. Seeing the ineffectiveness of the ruling class, the slaves once again revolted and swarmed through Angkor, looting and burning what was left of it. The government managed to pull itself together in order to deal with the slaves in the customary manner. But the situation was hopeless. Finally, the king ordered the evacuation of Angkor and retreated into the hills.

From that time until the French arrived in the 1800s Cambodia's history was a succession of civil wars, assassinations, and foreign invasions. The Khmer kings ruled from several places in their stripped-down country, desperately trying to keep their thrones and to keep their neighbors at bay. The nation that had once been the richest and most powerful in Southeast Asia had lost all semblance of glory, or even of self-respect. And while it struggled to survive, the ruined capital of Angkor stood in the jungle, overgrown with weeds, and forgotten.

Above: the incredible Khmer legacy, Angkor Wat, viewed from across a moat once filled with crocodiles. Animals at pasture on the once-royal lawns add a rural footnote to the exotic buildings.

Chapter 6
The Enigma of Zimbabwe

The spur to Portuguese conquests along the east coast of Africa in the 1500s was the gold that was mined in a fabulous kingdom somewhere in the interior. Most of the gold eluded the Portuguese and by the 19th century the great kingdom, whose ruler bore the chilling title "Ravager of the Lands," appeared to have been swept away on the tide of history. Or had it? Is the sprawling stone complex in southeastern Rhodesia the remains of the Ravager's capital? If the Africans, who were not known to have built in stone, did not build it, who did? Archaeologists are still unraveling the mystery.

On a high plateau in southwestern Rhodesia, Africa, lies a sprawling stone complex covering some 60 acres that for many years has been the subject of mystery and romance. Speculation about the origins of the giant stone walls and roofless buildings has ranged from the possibility that they were once in the land of Ophir—the land that provided the gold for King Solomon's Temple in Jerusalem, to the possibility that it was once the city of the legendary Prester John—the priest-King who was supposed to have ruled somewhere in Africa or Asia in the 12th century.

The first Europeans to hear of the imposing stone buildings—known as Zimbabwe or Symbaoe—were the Portuguese, who, by the end of the 1400s, had established a chain of trading posts along Africa's east coast. Their ambitions in Africa had been kindled by Arab stories of gold. But although some gold had been mined and traded for goods from the Orient, the amount that passed through Portuguese hands was much less than they had been led to expect. The land from which the gold came was a confederacy of states ruled by a leader called the Mwene Mutapa (or Benemotapa, in Portuguese writings), which meant "Ravager of the Lands" or "Master Pillager." Stories abounded of the Mwene Mutapa's wealth and power and of some great buildings made of stone that were located in the southern part of his territories. A description of these buildings and of the mines in the surrounding areas was included in a book written

Opposite: the Elliptical Building at Great Zimbabwe. The building was almost certainly a royal residence. In the heyday of its prosperity Great Zimbabwe would not have appeared so overgrown as it now does.

Above: southern Africa showing the site of Zimbabwe. The shaded area indicates the extent of ancient mine workings found nearby, and the broken line the extent of ancient ruins.

The Legendary Kings and Queens

Right: a 17th-century French portrait of Zimbabwe's king, the Mwene Mutapa. Portrayed here in completely European terms based on a description of him by the 16th-century Portuguese historian Joao de Banos, Mwene Mutapa was the ruler of a wealthy confederacy of states that occupied an area stretching from the Kalahari Desert to the Indian Ocean. Portuguese reports spoke of his fortress palace as a stone building held together without mortar.

by a Portuguese, Joao de Barros, and published in 1552.

In the midst of a plain, he wrote, "is a square fortress, masonry within and without, built of stones of marvellous size, and there appears to be no mortar joining them. The wall is more than twenty-five spans in width, and the height is not so great considering the width. . . . This edifice is almost surrounded by hills, upon which are others resembling it in the fashioning of stone and the absence of mortar, and one of them is a tower more than twelve fathoms high.

"The natives of the country call all these edifices Symbaoe, which according to their language signifies court, for every place where the Benemotapa may be is so called . . . .

"In the opinion of the Moors who saw it, it is very ancient and was built there to keep possession of the mines . . . .

"Considering the facts of the matter, it would seem that some prince who had possession of the mines ordered it to be built as a sign thereof . . . and as these edifices are very similar to some which are found in the land of Prester John at a place called Acaxumo, which was a municipal city of the Queen of Sheba, which Ptolemy calls Axuma, it would seem that the prince who was lord of that state also owned these mines and therefore ordered these edifices to be raised there . . . ."

Neither de Barros nor any other Portuguese colonist ever saw "Symbaoe." His account is based on reports by the Swahili traders and, like many secondhand reports, it contains some factual errors: the main building, for example, is elliptical, not square. It does, however, offer a correct translation of the name. Although "Zimbabwe," comes from words in the Mashona language that could mean "houses of stone," it is more probably derived from those meaning "venerated houses"—that is, those occupied by the chief. The complex of buildings described by de Barros is the largest of many "zimbabwes" in southern Africa.

It was de Barros' report that helped to perpetuate the legend that the buildings were ancient—dating back to Old Testament times—and that they had been built by a foreign people. The story persisted, accepted as fact, for the next 400 years.

Because the natives who came in contact with the Portuguese lived in simple mud huts, the idea that the buildings might have been built by the local inhabitants was quickly dismissed. The local population seemed to have no idea when, or by whom, the buildings were constructed. "The walls were built when stones were soft," they told a later explorer. So both the Christian Portuguese and the Moslem Swahili traders linked Zimbabwe with their own familiar legends of lost kingdoms. Joao dos Santos, a Portuguese missionary, wrote in a book published in 1609:

"The natives of these lands, especially some aged Moors [Swahilis], assert that they have a tradition from their ancestors that these houses [Zimbabwe] were anciently a factory of the Queen of Sheba, and that from this place a great quantity of gold was brought to her. . . . Others say that these are the ruins of the factory of Solomon, where he had his factors who procured a

Below: the queen of Sheba visits Solomon at Jerusalem. The treasures of gold brought to Solomon by the queen were said to have been mined at Zimbabwe, which was a possession of the queen. A Portuguese missionary declared that the gold had indeed gone to Solomon, but not through the queen of Sheba. He thought Zimbabwe was the region of Ophir, mentioned in the Bible, to which Hiram, king of Tyre, came and transported "four hundred and twenty talents" of gold to King Solomon.

Above: the outer wall of the Elliptical Building. It is 800 feet long and in parts is 17 feet thick and 32 feet high. The wall was obviously built over a long period starting at the northwest end, with only half the height and width that it reaches at its eastern end. The eastern end shows the most careful workmanship—neatly fitted stones and a frieze of two lines of chevron pattern. Other names of the Elliptical Building, "the house of the great woman," as it was called by Karanga people living there in the 1800s, and "the temple," are more romantic names and, indeed, may come near to the Building's original purpose.

great quantity of gold from these lands . . . not deciding this question, I state that the mountain of Fura or Afura may be the region of Ophir, whence gold was brought to Jerusalem . . . ."

The First Book of Kings in the Bible tells how Solomon arranged with Hiram, King of Tyre, to have gold and other riches brought to him from Ophir. Hiram's navy "came to Ophir, and fetched from thence gold, four hundred and twenty talents, and brought it to King Solomon."

The Portuguese believed that they had at last located the mysterious land of Ophir. Other Europeans were quick to take up the idea. Books, by Italian, French, Dutch, and English geographers perpetuated the ideas of de Barros and dos Santos. Milton's *Paradise Lost* refers to Sofala (an Arab African port) as "Sofala thought Ophir." The Dutch, who settled around the Cape of Good Hope in 1652, made several attempts to find the

The Amazing Wall of Zimbabwe

stone buildings of "Ophir" but without success.

Not until the late 19th century did a European set eyes on Zimbabwe. Adam Renders, a German-American hunter, reached it in 1868, having heard of the ruins from a man who had never succeeded in finding them, a German missionary named Merensky. Renders left no record of his discoveries, but a few years later he showed the ruins to Carl Mauch, a German geologist, who wrote detailed descriptions of what he found there.

What Mauch found was a group of ruins extending over some 60 acres of a valley and a nearby hill, constructed of blocks of granite fitted together without mortar. The largest of these ruins, called the Elliptical Building—sometimes the Temple—is a huge enclosure whose outer wall measures more than 800 feet in circumference. This wall is, in places, 14 feet thick and up to 32 feet high, and its upper edge is decorated with a chevron-patterned frieze. Within the enclosure are several smaller enclosures and passageways and a solid round tower, 18 feet in diameter and 30 feet high, known as the Conical Tower.

Above: the outer wall of the Elliptical Building as it appeared to members of the British South Africa Company forces on their march to occupy Mashonaland in 1890. The settlers, under Cecil Rhodes, had come to Mashonaland because they believed there was gold to be found there. The sight of the great stone structures of Zimbabwe convinced them that here indeed was the Land of Ophir of the Bible.

Overlooking the valley is a 300-foot-high hill whose summit is crowned by the Hill Ruins. The walls of these ruins curve in and out among the great boulders to form a pattern of natural and man-made structures in which one seems to grow out of the other. In fact, the granite blocks used to construct Zimbabwe did, in a sense "grow out" of the hills. Years of alternate heating and cooling of the rocks caused their surfaces to split and shed thin layers of rock some three to seven inches thick, which would then slide down the hillside to collect at the bottom as scree. The builders of Zimbabwe collected and cut these slabs into manageable pieces and fitted them tightly together. The quality of the masonry varies, but the best work is regularly coursed and is wider at the base than at the top, which makes these walls very strong.

Between the Hill Ruins and the Elliptical Building are a number of smaller enclosures known as the Valley Ruins. Many of the walls in these ruins have large gaps that were once filled with circular dwellings made of *daga*, a kind of gravelly clay that was also used to pave the enclosures. Traces of daga still exist in most of the Zimbabwe ruins, though none of the huts have survived.

Following the discovery of Zimbabwe many attempts were made to compare its buildings with other buildings in Mediterranean and Middle Eastern lands that might have influenced its construction. The Elliptical Building, for example, was compared to the temple of Haram Bilqis ("Sacred enclosure of the Queen of Sheba") in a part of the Yemen that traditionally belonged to the biblical queen. The temple does have an irregular elliptical courtyard, but the temple itself is rectangular and symmetrical—whereas there are no straight lines anywhere in Zimbabwe.

Mauch and those who followed him were convinced that the ruins were ancient and that the work was of a foreign culture. In a doorway of the Elliptical Building he found some wood that he identified—wrongly—as cedar and which he claimed could not have come from anywhere else but the Lebanon. Mauch gave a further boost to the Solomon and Sheba theory in an article that was published in a geographical magazine.

Below: a photograph from *The Occupation of Mashonaland* showing Mashona Africans among the Hill Ruins of Zimbabwe. Rhodes thought the stone buildings could not possibly have been made by Africans—the Mashona themselves did not know how they came to be there—and on a visit to the ruins he told the local chiefs that he had come to see the ancient temple that once upon a time belonged to white men.

Enter the Explorers

Left: the village of the Karanga Chief Mugabe among the Hill Ruins at Zimbabwe, a photograph taken by the British South Africa Company's official photographer Lieutenant Ellerton Fry, at the time of the European occupation in 1890.

Below: another photograph by Ellerton Fry of civilian visitors to the overgrown Hill Ruins.

By 1890, after Mauch's visit to the Ruins, the whole area occupied by the Mashona, or Shona, people—and which included the Zimbabwe ruins—began to be settled by the British South Africa Company, whose director was Cecil Rhodes. The Company's primary interest was the area's gold deposits, but the ruins of Zimbabwe soon attracted considerable attention. In his book *Great Zimbabwe* the Rhodesian archaeologist and author Peter Garlake observes that the ruins "quickly became a symbol of the essential rightness and justice of colonization and gave the subservience of the Shona an age-old precedent if not biblical sanction. Thus, on Rhodes' first visit to the Ruins, the local Karanga chiefs were told that 'the Great Master' had come 'to see the ancient temple which once upon a time belonged to white men.' "

Rhodes appointed Theodore Bent, a British traveler and antiquarian, to make a thorough investigation of the ruins. Being particularly interested in Mediterranean culture, Bent looked first of all for signs of it at Zimbabwe, but he soon rejected the idea that the ruins had a Phoenician origin: "from my own personal experience of Phoenician ruins I cannot say that the Zimbabwe ruins bear the slightest resemblance whatsoever." He was disappointed to find, in excavating the site, that nearly all the objects dug up were African, and that the few pieces of imported glass and porcelain were only a few hundred years old. At one point, he confided to a guide, "I have not much faith in the antiquity of these ruins, I think they are native . . . ." Yet he continued to search for signs of an ancient foreign culture, and when he discovered some soapstone monoliths

Bent, the First Archaeologist

carved in the shape of birds in one of the Hill Ruin enclosures, he believed he had found the sign he was looking for. Nothing resembling these had ever been found in Africa south of the Sahara, but they did bear slight resemblances to objects in some Middle Eastern civilizations. Bent also found some similarities between Zimbabwe architecture and that of Arabia, but he never established any clear connection between the two cultures. In the course of his work he visited some of the other stone ruins in Rhodesia, but without any more success. Nevertheless, his book *The Ruined Cities of Mashonaland,* published in 1892, greatly stimulated interest in these mysterious structures.

In the meantime, the lust for gold was threatening to destroy them. A company called Rhodesia Ancient Ruins Limited was formed with the express purpose of digging for buried treasure among the country's ruins. Although Zimbabwe itself was exempted, at Rhodes' request, a certain amount of unauthorized digging nevertheless went on there. Other sites were badly damaged. In 1901 legislation was passed protecting the sites, and the Rhodesia Ancient Ruins Company was closed down.

The protection was short-lived, however. More damage was soon to be inflicted, this time in the name of scientific inquiry. A journalist named Richard Hall, who had written a book entitled *Ancient Ruins of Rhodesia,* was, in 1902, appointed Curator of the Zimbabwe ruins. Although his stated responsibility was "the

Right: the British traveler and antiquarian Theodore Bent. Within a year of the occupation of Mashonaland, the speculation aroused by the Zimbabwe ruins prompted Cecil Rhodes to appoint Bent as an investigator into the origins and history of the mysterious stone structures. Widely traveled in the eastern Mediterranean and the Persian Gulf, Bent's specialty was the origin of the Phoenicians, so he was able quite early in his research to rule out a Phoenician background for the ruins. As his excavations continued Bent remarked that he hadn't much faith in the antiquity of the ruins and that he thought they were native. Nevertheless, in his final report he put forward his opinion that the ruins were of high antiquity.

Above: the famous Conical Tower in the Elliptical Building at Zimbabwe, an illustration from Theodore Bent's *The Ruined Cities of Mashonaland*, published in 1892. The drawing is by his wife. The area around the tower was, from the evidence collected by Bent, a place where rituals were carried out.

preservation of the building," Hall began to excavate the site in search of material supporting the ancient origin theory.

He went at his task with enthusiasm, removing stones, undergrowth and even trees within the enclosures, and digging up layer upon layer of archaeological deposits—which in places were 12 feet deep. Much of this material he dismissed as "the filth and decadence of the Kaffir occupation." So thoroughly did Hall do his work that later excavators of Zimbabwe have had difficulty finding undisturbed deposits to examine.

Untrained in archaeology, Hall had no idea of how to classify his finds according to the techniques of stratigraphy—the method of carefully examining layers of earth and debris to establish the comparative dates of the objects found in them. He had already classified the ruins into four types and periods: (1) Sabaean (Arabian) of between 2000 and 1100 B.C.; (2) Phoenician, dating up to the beginning of the Christian era; (3) a transition period; and (4) a "decadent period," which he attributed to the native population. The objects he turned up while excavating he assigned to these various periods simply on the basis of quality of workmanship.

Hall's work at Zimbabwe drew sharp criticism from archaeologists outside the country, and after two years he was dismissed. However, he had made extensive notes on his discoveries, and in 1905 he published another book, incorporating this material, entitled *Great Zimbabwe*.

Within a year the assumptions of Hall, Bent, Rhodes, and others were to be sharply challenged. The British Association for the Advancement of Science appointed a young archaeologist named David Randall MacIver—a pupil of Sir Flinders Petrie,

Above: Richard Hall's excavations at Zimbabwe. Hall, a freelance journalist, was appointed Curator of the Ruins in 1902 with instructions to clear the ruins and make them accessible to the tourists the British South Africa Company expected would come to the country once peace had been concluded in South Africa. Hall interpreted his instructions very widely and removed not only all the trees and undergrowth, but also went on to remove earth deposits within the ruins to a depth of between three and five feet—deeper in some places. Hall uncovered many gold ornaments, as well as soapstone dishes, phallic symbols, iron tools and weapons, copper ornaments, and foreign porcelain and glass.

the famous English Egyptologist—to examine and report on Zimbabwe and other Rhodesian ruins at the Association's next meeting that same year. The title of the book MacIver produced, *Mediaeval Rhodesia*, gave away his thesis: that the ruins were not ancient but only a few centuries old. In his Conclusions, MacIver tersely summed up his findings. In "not one" of the seven sites he investigated "has any object been obtained by myself or by others before me which can be shown to be more ancient than the fourteenth or fifteenth century A.D. In the architecture . . . there is not one trace of Oriental or European style of any period whatever." Putting it positively he stated: "(1) That imported articles, of which the date is well known in the country of their origin, are contemporary with the Rhodesian buildings in which they are found, and that these buildings are therefore mediaeval and post-mediaeval. (2) That the character of the dwellings contained within the stone ruins, and forming an integral part of them, is unmistakably African. (3) That the arts and manufactures exemplified by objects found within these dwellings are typically African, except when the objects are imports of well-known mediaeval or post-mediaeval date."

In the short time available MacIver could not make a thorough examination of the sites. However, he did study in detail some of

Hall's excavations in the Elliptical Building. In enclosure 15, for example, he found that the objects in the lowest layer, beneath a stone and cement floor, were virtually identical to those in the upper layers. The bits of pottery found in the trench were exactly like modern native pottery.

At the time MacIver was working, the technique of radiocarbon dating had not yet been invented, so he had to rely on foreign objects whose dates could be established by referring to known stylistic periods. MacIver himself did not find any imported objects within the Elliptical Building that could be so dated, so he relied on Hall's recorded finds of what he wrongly termed "Nankin" china and Arabian glass and on his own discoveries of similar wares at other sites. The Elliptical Building, he concluded, was not earlier than the 14th or 15th century.

Not surprisingly, MacIver's report was greeted with approval by his fellow archaeologists and roundly condemned by the white settlers of southern Africa. Hall, who MacIver had sharply criticized, replied in 1909 with a book entitled *Prehistoric Rhodesia*, in which he vehemently reiterated his original arguments and in turn criticized MacIver.

The controversy continued for some years without any fresh evidence. Then in 1929 the British Association again sponsored

Destructive Excavation

Left: two workers carrying out debris from the Elliptical Building during Hall's disastrous excavations at Zimbabwe. Without proper training in archaeology Hall dug up and removed layer upon layer of archaeological deposits, so that trained archaeologists who later excavated the site had great difficulty finding undisturbed deposits to examine.

The Mystery of the Walls

a study of the ruins. The archaeologist appointed was Gertrude Caton-Thompson. Over a period of six months Miss Caton-Thompson made an intensive study of one of the Valley Ruins and also examined other buildings at Zimbabwe and at other sites. Her report, published in book form under the title *Zimbabwe Culture*, provided the most detailed information yet obtained. In essence it confirmed MacIver's findings; but like MacIver, Miss Caton-Thompson was hampered by a lack of datable foreign objects with which to date the buildings. Under the floor of the Maund Ruin, in the valley, she found some tiny glass beads. An expert was able to demonstrate that they did not come from any pre-Roman Middle Eastern culture but could not positively identify them, apart from an educated guess that they dated from the 9th to 10th century A.D. Miss Caton-Thompson cautiously suggested that Zimbabwe might have been built several centuries before MacIver's dates, but sNe concluded that "examination of all the existing evidence . . . still can produce not one single item that is not in accordance with the claim of

Right: part of the great outer wall of the Elliptical building. Here at the northeastern end of the wall the workmanship is of the finest quality. The granite blocks are all carefully selected, matched, and then laid in long regular courses. Each of the courses is set slightly back from the one beneath making the wall slope upward. The wall is stained in parts by a growth of yellow lichen

Bantu origin and mediaeval date." As for the Portuguese statements that the Africans disclaimed any knowledge of the building of the ruins, this "does no more than show how little the native's mistrust of questions has changed from that day to this."

By the time the next serious examination of the ruins took place, in 1958, archaeological knowledge had greatly increased and techniques had improved. Most significant, perhaps, was the development of radiocarbon dating, which now made it possible to determine the age of objects containing organic substances (allowing a certain margin of error). In 1950, for example, radiocarbon dating of two pieces of wood found in a doorway of the Ellpitical Building established dates of A.D. 590 (plus or minus 120 years) and A.D. 710 (plus or minus 80 years) for the samples. This meant that the building must have been constructed sometime after A.D. 470; but it did not provide a latest date for its construction. For one thing, the wood—an exceptionally durable species—might have already been used in a previous building.

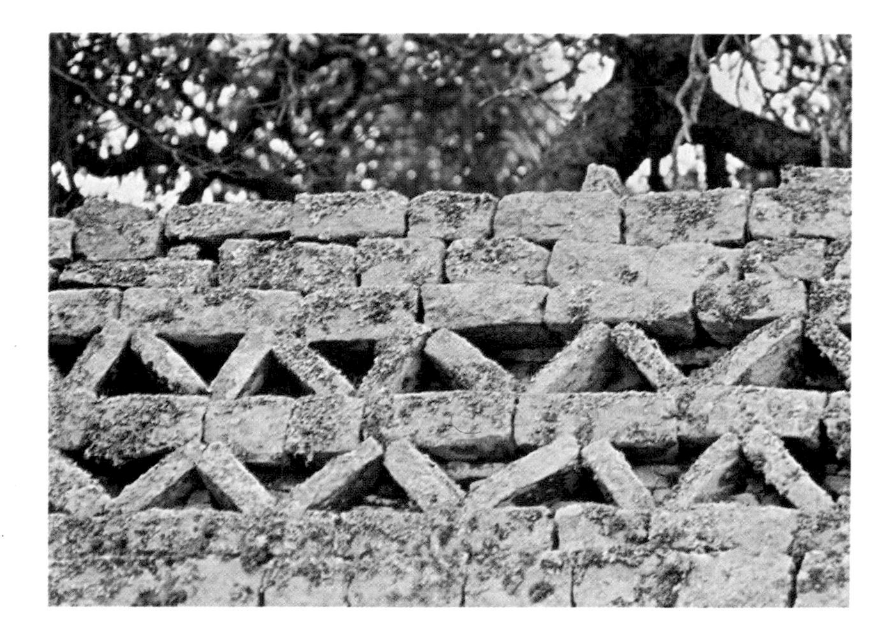

Left: a detail of the chevron-patterned frieze at the top of the great outer wall of the Elliptical Building. No clue has been found that points to the significance of the chevron pattern. Such a simple basic pattern is, of course, widespread, and this has led to theories that there was a link between Zimbabwe and various other distant chevron-pattern-using civilizations

The 1958 excavation was directed toward establishing a "ceramic sequence" at Zimbabwe and was conducted by the Rhodesian Inspector of Monuments, Keith Robinson, and later by a fellow archaeologist Roger Summers. Analysis of organic material found among layers of pottery in the Hill Ruins and the Elliptical Building produced dates ranging from around A.D. 320 to around A.D. 1380.

Today, the various theories of an "ancient" Zimbabwe have been effectively demolished, though they continue to have a romantic appeal for some people. Apart from their assumption of racial superiority, theories that the Phoenicians or the Arabs built Zimbabwe have a more understandable feature of offering a link with the known. Until recently native African history was passed down from generation to generation by word of mouth—a method by its very nature prone to error. The history of the

The Evidence of Brick and Stone

people who built and lived in Zimbabwe may be just as full of drama as that of the Phoenicians, but we shall probably never know it. Without a written language, the history has been largely lost. Attempts to reconstruct it are like putting together a jigsaw puzzle in which some of the pieces seem to come from different puzzles and some are completely missing. Artefacts, native legends, and the writings of explorers must be assembled and moved around in varying combinations until a recognizable picture emerges. Even then, the picture will contain many gaps.

The first people to live in the area around Zimbabwe were Late Stone Age hunters. The exact date is unknown but they had firmly settled in by the time a new group of people moved into the area in the 3rd or 4th century A.D. The newcomers were an Iron Age tribe, who may have been a Bantu-speaking people originally from central Africa. Their migration into the Zimbabwe area was part of a large population movement that took place about this time.

Apparently the Stone Age hunters and the Iron Age peasant farmers managed to live together fairly peacefully. Fragments of pottery produced by the newcomers have been found among Stone Age deposits and Stone Age eggshell ornaments among Iron Age deposits, which may indicate that trade was taking place between the two groups. Most Iron Age sites in southern Africa contain glass beads and seashells, indicating that the people also traded with the people on the coast.

Soon after settling in Rhodesia the Iron Age people discovered gold. Some of the gold lay on the surface and could be obtained easily by panning for it in the rivers; later, having discovered its value in trade, the people began to mine the hills for it. Skeletons of accident victims found in old mine shafts show that the miners

Above: the Conical Tower in the Elliptical Building. This tower, 18 feet in diameter and 30 feet high, was built after the great outer wall was erected and there is evidence that part of the old inner wall was demolished to make room for it. Apart from being an architectural feature it had no known function. Suggestions are that it symbolized a grain bin—grain being a form of tribute often paid to African rulers.

Right: the Hill Ruins that overlook the Elliptical Building on the plain below. It was named the "Acropolis" by excavators. The walls here were erected first, probably because of its defensive position.

Opposite: inside the Hill Ruins. The walls have been built to incorporate the massive granite boulders that litter the hilltop. The site contained many large stone monoliths, some of which were topped with carved birds. These monoliths, together with an echoing cave beneath the floors at the eastern end (sounds from it can be heard in the valley below), have suggested to some scholars that the "Acropolis" might well have served as an oracle.

A Ruined Complex

Below: a view of the north entrance of the Elliptical Building showing the gracefully curved stone steps that are a typical architectural feature of the ruins. Everywhere the builders have used gradually changing curves to soften abrupt changes of alignment between walls or over uneven ground.

were women and girls, whose smaller size enabled them to negotiate the narrow passageways. Some of them have Bushman characteristics, another indication of close contact between the two peoples.

The early farmers and miners did not build Zimbabwe. So far as can be seen they did not build in stone at all but lived in huts made of poles and daga. Their occupation of the site of Zimbabwe seems to have been fairly brief, perhaps a century or less. A Hill Ruins section dug by Keith Robinson in 1958 revealed the existence, above a layer of early Iron Age pottery, of a thick layer of sand and quartz fragments that must have been washed down by rainfall over several centuries.

Sometime around A.D. 1000 new groups of people moved into the Zimbabwe area. Black and plain pottery, quite unlike the red and decorated pottery of the former inhabitants, and the bones of cattle suddenly make their appearance. Clay models of cattle—an indication that the new people regarded animals highly—have also been found in the Zimbabwe area. Most significant, some of the new people began building in stone. The first of these stone buildings has not yet been identified but among the many ruins remaining in Mashonaland, several have sections of poorly coursed wall similar to those found in parts of Zimbabwe, which suggests that they were built at roughly the same time. Further to the west, the people of what is called the Leopard's Kopje ("hill") culture also built in stone, but in a different style, consisting mainly of stone terraces, rather than walled enclosures.

The people who built Zimbabwe have not, so far, been positively identified. In *Great Zimbabwe*, Peter Garlake suggests that they may have been the Mbire. According to African tradition the Mbire were the first of the Mashona people, and it was they—again according to tradition—who introduced into Zimbabwe the worship of Mwari, the Mashona supreme god. Some scholars believe that the Mbire arrived at Zimbabwe early in the 14th century. By that time, however, Zimbabwe was already established. Garlake points out that as no "basic cultural change" can be seen in Zimbabwe's development at this time, it seems likely that the Mbire arrived earlier, perhaps in the 11th century.

In any case, sometime around the late 12th or early 13th century, the community living around Zimbabwe—like other communities in the region—began developing into specialized classes—roughly equivalent to peasant, artisan, and governing elite. The elite were able to command the services of the labor force in the construction of stone buildings. It is possible that the first building took place on the Hill—at any rate the Hill Ruins include the oldest walls remaining in Zimbabwe. One of the enclosures on the Hill contained living quarters, an estimated 14 daga huts. Another enclosure appears to have been used for rituals; it has remains of some platforms and had yielded a number of soapstone monoliths, eight of them carved in the shape of birds. Some experts have suggested that these birds represent dead chiefs who, in the Mashonaland religion, intercede with Mwari on behalf of his worshipers.

The hilltop site had a potential defensive advantage, but this may not have influenced the builders. Few other Mashonaland ruins are built on hills, and the later Zimbabwe buildings lie in the valley. Only the Elliptical Building is large enough to have served as a fortress, and it lacks any of the features common to fortified buildings in other cultures, such as battlements and protected entrances.

The stone buildings of Zimbabwe and of the other sites housed only a small fraction of the total population: the ruling class. Garlake estimates that the enclosures at Zimbabwe may have housed between 100 and 200 adults. Hundreds more would have lived in open daga huts outside. These were the farmers, stonemasons, and other craftsmen who supported the aristocracy.

Building in the valley must have begun around the late 13th and early 14th century. At this time gold production increased, in response to increased demand from the Arab coastal towns and from markets across the Indian Ocean. The expansion of trade brought great affluence to the Arab towns and to Zimbabwe. Its location—near the rich gold deposits of Matabeleland and in a river valley that gave relatively easy access to the coast—facilitated its rise to prominence. Excavations in the Valley Ruins and in the Elliptical Building have produced many luxury objects, including ornaments of gold, copper, and bronze produced by native craftsmen, as well as imported items—glass beads and ceramics. During R. N. Hall's two years of excavating at Zimbabwe he found some £4000 worth of gold objects. The wealth must have been concentrated among the ruling elite, but at least their wealth provided work for the rest of the population. The crafts of spinning and weaving were introduced, probably through contact with the coastal towns. Building techniques were refined.

The construction of the Elliptical Building was begun sometime during the 14th century and finished in the early 15th century, when Zimbabwe's power was at its zenith. A noticeable improvement in building technique can be traced in it. Some of the walls are made of irregular blocks of stone placed with little attempt at coursing; in other places—particularly the Conical Tower and the eastern end of the outer wall—the stones are well matched and placed in regular courses.

The building evidently served as the chief's palace. It is by far the largest of the Rhodesian ruins and clearly indicates the importance of the Zimbabwe ruler. Its most striking feature, the Conical Tower, may symbolize a grain bin—grain being a common form of tribute paid to some African chiefs—and so also symbolize the Zimbabwe ruler's authority over lesser chieftains.

The decline of Zimbabwe set in soon after it had reached the peak of its prosperity. Tradition tells of a salt shortage at the Mbire capital (which we can assume was Zimbabwe) sometime around the mid-15th century. As Garlake points out, such a shortage of an essential part of diet which was extensively traded can be seen "as symbolic of both a depletion of food supplied and a disruption of trade." It is possible that the land around Zimbabwe had become exhausted after several centuries of intensive farming. Perhaps there was also some interruption in trade, or a dispute of some kind between Zimbabwe and one of its subject communities. In any case, something more than a shortage of salt would certainly have been required to induce the

Above: the only surviving doorway from the Zimbabwe ruins. It is in the Western Enclosure, two curved 30-foot-high walls; the overriding wall here is seen carried across the doorway on a stone lintel.

Above: a Rhodesian Government travel poster of 1938. Although the results of at least two of the latest investigations at that time into the ruins had ruled out an ancient origin—or a foreign one—the government was still suggesting links between the queen of Sheba and Zimbabwe. Here a black slave kneels offering golden tribute to the exotic biblical queen. The truth about the medieval architects of the imposing and mysterious buildings, and their history, was far more fascinating in its unraveling than the fictions of Ophir or Sheba, and it is a story that is still being pieced together.

ruler and his people to leave Zimbabwe—which is what happened.

According to tradition, the Mbire ruler, whose name was Nyatsimba Mutota, sent emissaries north in search of salt. They finally found salt deposits some 300 miles north, in the valley of the Zambezi River. Mutota then moved into this area, conquered its Karanga inhabitants, and established a new seat of government. After this act of conquest Mutoba adopted the title Mwene Mutapa "Ravager of the Lands" or "Master Pillager." From his new capital, in what is called the Dande area, Mutota established new trade routes to the east. He extended his domains to include part of Matabeleland, called Guruhuswa, over which he placed one of his relatives named Changamire. His other southern province, Mbire—which included Zimbabwe—he placed under another relative, Torwa. Part of de Barros' secondhand description of "Symbaoe" states that some of the Mwene Mutapa's wives lived there, cared for by a court official. However, as Zimbabwe and the new capital were some 300 miles apart, this seems unlikely—unless the wives had outlived their usefulness.

Although Portuguese and Arab accounts of the Mwene Mutapa's capital describe his living in splendor in "sumptuous apartments," it is unlikely that his buildings were anything like as fine as those at Zimbabwe. No one seems certain exactly where his capital was (though one Portuguese report mentions an unidentifiable place called "Zunbanhy"); it may be that he moved from one "zimbabwe" to another. In the Dande area stone was in shorter supply than in the south, and the craft of masonry seems to have suffered a decline under succeeding Mwene Mutapas.

Moreover, the Mwene Mutapas' empire itself was short-lived. They did not have the same monopoly of trade that their predecessors at Zimbabwe had enjoyed. And when the Portuguese began to penetrate the area and set up trading posts in the early 17th century, they could deal directly with the Mwene Mutapa's subjects, which greatly undermined his authority.

Sometime in the 16th century, during the reign of the third Mwene Mutapa, both Guruhuswa and Mbire broke away from the empire and became independent states. Because Guruhuswa was a rich gold-producing area, its breakaway was a significant loss to the empire. After this, Mwene Mutapa's power declined and Guruhuswa's power increased. The dominant people in this area were the Rozwi, and their king was called the Mambo. The Rozwi kingdom shared several features with the Mwene Mutapa's empire. They, too, worshiped Mwari, and their Mambo, like the Mwene Mutapa, had priestly functions as well as military and economic ones. In fact, the Rozwi seem to have had some kind of special religious status among the Mashona peoples. The Rozwi also built in stone, and some of the most interesting and decorative of the Rhodesian ruins, such as those at Naletale and Dhlo Dhlo, were built by the Rozwi during the 17th and 18th centuries. Some writers have even suggested that some of the later work at Zimbabwe was done by the Rozwi.

Having conquered Mbire, the Rozwi included Zimbabwe among their domains. Although, according to Garlake, they "never settled or built" there, they "seem to have recognized its spiritual pre-eminence and visited it for special ceremonies as long as they were able." The Mambo, who was specially venerated and kept hidden from the gaze of common people, must have found the great Elliptical Building and the sacred Eastern Enclosure on the hill suitably imposing for his presence.

The Rozwi kingdom came to an end only a few decades before the Europeans finally found Zimbabwe. Hordes of savage Ngoni from Zululand swept through the area during the 1830s. They massacred the Mambo and many of his people, and they sacked Zimbabwe. When Mauch arrived at Zimbabwe in 1871, he found the area inhabited by some Karanga under a chief named Mugabe, who disclaimed any knowledge of the buildings' origin or purpose. However Mauch also found a man who was from a trible related to the Rozwi. His people, he told Mauch, had kept alive the traditions of Zimbabwe, and his own father, a priest, had conducted sacrifices there. Later, Hall found recent deposits of cattle bones in the Elliptical Building, confirmation that sacrifices had taken place. In 1904, during the period of Hall's excavations, the last sacrifice, of some goats, took place at Zimbabwe in the course of a rainmaking ceremony.

Perhaps the strangest aspect of the whole Zimbabwe story is that at the very time the Portuguese were sending back to Europe stories that ancient Ophir had been found, a few hundred miles away from their settlements a living culture was building more "zimbabwes." It would be interesting to know how the Rozwi Mambo or the Mwene Mutapa would have reacted to the news that the invaders were attributing their works to people who lived 2000 years earlier and 3000 miles away. Perhaps with a contemptuous smile.

The Riddle Yet Unsolved

Below: the Elliptical Building seen from the Hill Ruins. Much more investigation still needs to be done if we are ever to fully understand the precedents for the extraordinary stone-building culture that arose here at Zimbabwe. Meanwhile, it stands, a proud memorial to the history of the Mashona and Karanga peoples.

Chapter 7
The Atlantis Mystery

The riddle of Atlantis is among the greatest of the world's unsolved mysteries. Where, for a start, was the exact site of this huge island civilization? Did it really, as early historians reported, vanish from the earth in a day and a night? Small wonder that since the earliest times scholars, archaeologists, historians, and occultists have kept up an almost ceaseless search for its precise whereabouts. Beginning with the Greek philosopher Plato's first description of the lost land that was apparently "the nearest thing to paradise on Earth," this chapter examines in detail the basic evidence for the existence and cataclysmic destruction of Atlantis.

Of all the world's unsolved mysteries, Atlantis is probably the biggest. Said to have been a huge island continent with an extraordinary civilization, situated in the Atlantic Ocean, it is reported to have vanished from the face of the earth in a day and a night. So complete was this devastation that Atlantis sank beneath the sea, taking with it every trace of its existence. Despite this colossal vanishing trick, the lost continent of Atlantis has exerted a mysterious influence over the human race for thousands of years. It is almost as though a primitive memory of the glorious days of Atlantis lingers on in the deepest recesses of the human mind. The passage of time has not diminished interest in the fabled continent, nor have centuries of skepticism by scientists succeeded in banishing Atlantis to obscurity in its watery grave. Thousands of books and articles have been written about the lost continent. It has inspired the authors of novels, short stories, poems, and movies. Its name has been used for ships, restaurants, magazines, and even a region of the planet Mars. Atlantean societies have been formed to theorize and speculate about the great lost land. Atlantis has come to symbolize our dream of a once golden past. It appeals to our nostalgic longing for a better, happier world; it feeds our hunger for knowledge of mankind's true origins; and above all it offers the challenge of a genuinely sensational detective story.

Today the search for evidence of the existence of Atlantis continues with renewed vigor, using 20th-century man's most sophis-

Opposite: Italian Renaissance sculpture of Atlas supporting the earth. The Greeks had long used the Atlas myth to explain how the earth kept its place in the heavens, and Plato incorporated Atlas in his account of the fabulous empire of Atlantis. According to Plato, Atlas was the first king of Atlantis, and the kingdom derived its name from him.

The Idyllic Land

ticated tools in the hope of discovering the continent that is said to have disappeared around 11,600 years ago. Did Atlantis exist, or is it just a myth? Ours may be the generation that finally solves this tantalizing and ancient enigma.

Atlantis is said to have been the nearest thing to paradise that the earth has seen. Fruits and vegetables grew in abundance in its rich soil. Fragrant flowers and herbs bloomed on the wooded slopes of its many beautiful mountains. All kinds of tame and wild animals roamed its meadows and magnificent forests, and drank from its rivers and lakes. Underground streams of wonderfully sweet water were used to irrigate the soil, to provide hot and cold fountains and baths for all the inhabitants—there were even baths for the horses. The earth was rich in precious metals, and the Atlanteans were wealthier than any people before or after them. Their temples and public buildings were lavishly decorated with gold, silver, brass, tin, and ivory, and their principal royal palace was a marvel of size and beauty. Besides being skilled metallurgists, the Atlanteans were accomplished engineers. A huge and complex system of canals and bridges linked their capital city with the sea and the surrounding countryside, and there were magnificent docks and harbors for the fleets of

Below: *The Golden Age*, by the 16th-century German artist Lucas Cranach. Cranach's idyllic land is very like the Atlantis of legend, a utopian country of great beauty and abundant riches, peopled by a wise and virtuous race.

vessels that carried on a flourishing trade with overseas countries.

Whether they lived in the city or the country, the people of Atlantis had everything they could possibly want for their comfort and happiness. They were a gentle, wise, and loving people, unaffected by their great wealth, and prizing virtue above all things. In time, however, their noble nature became debased. No longer satisfied with ruling their own great land of plenty, they set about waging war on others. Their vast armies swept through the Strait of Gibraltar into the Mediterranean region, conquering large areas of North Africa and Europe. The Atlanteans were poised to strike against Athens and Egypt when the Athenian army rose up, drove them back to Gibraltar, and defeated them. Hardly had the Athenians tasted victory when a terrible cataclysm wiped out their entire army in a single day and night, and caused Atlantis to sink forever beneath the waves. Perhaps a few survivors were left to tell what had happened. At all events, the story is said to have been passed down through many generations until, more than 9200 years later, it was made known to the world for the first time.

The man who first committed the legend to paper was the Greek philosopher Plato, who, in about 355 B.C., wrote about Atlantis in two of his famous dialogues, the *Timaeus* and the *Critias*. Although Plato claimed that the story of the lost continent was derived from ancient Egyptian records, no such records have ever come to light, nor has any direct mention of Atlantis been found in any surviving records made before Plato's time. Every book and article on Atlantis that has ever been published has been based on Plato's account; subsequent authors have merely interpreted or added to it.

Plato was a master storyteller who put his philosophical ideas across in the form of apparently real-life events with well-known characters, and his Atlantis story might well have been firmly relegated to the realms of fiction. The very fact that it is still widely regarded as a factual account 2300 years after he wrote it

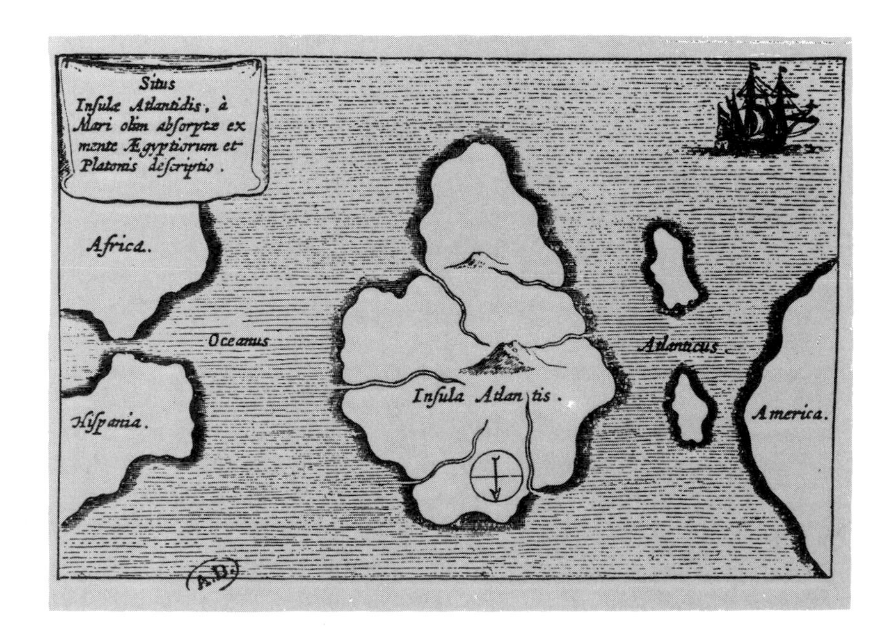

Left: map of Atlantis by the 17th-century German scholar Athanasius Kircher. Kircher based his map on Plato's description of Atlantis as an island west of the Pillars of Hercules—the Strait of Gibraltar—and situated Atlantis in the ocean that has since been named after the legendary land. Unlike modern cartographers, he placed south at the top of the map, which puts America at the right.

Above: Greek philosopher Plato, the first recorder of the story of Atlantis. It appears in two of the dialogues, in which Plato used actual people as mouthpieces for his own philosophical ideas. The story, set down some 2300 years ago, still fascinates and perplexes the world today.

Below: the Athenian statesman Solon. According to Plato, he was the first Greek to learn the story of Atlantis. He was told of the kingdom by priests while visiting Egypt.

shows the extraordinary power of Plato's story. It has inspired scholars to stake their reputation on the former existence of the lost continent, and explorers to go in search of its remains. Their actions were prompted not by the Greek story alone, but also by their own discoveries, which seemed to indicate that there must once have been a great landmass that acted as a bridge between our existing continents.

Why, ask the scholars, are there so many remarkable similarities between the ancient cultures of the Old and New Worlds? Why do we find the same plants and animals on continents thousands of miles apart when there is no known way for them to have been transported there? How did the primitive peoples of many lands construct technological marvels, such as Stonehenge in Britain, the huge statues of Easter Island in the Pacific, and the strange sacred cities of the Andes? Were they helped by a technically sophisticated race that has since disappeared? Above all, why do the legends of people the world over tell the same story of an overwhelming natural disaster and the arrival of godlike beings who brought with them a new culture from afar? Could the catastrophe that sank Atlantis have sent tidal waves throughout the globe, causing terrible havoc and destruction? And were the "gods" the remnants of the Atlantean race—the few survivors who were not on or near the island continent when it was engulfed?

Even without Plato's account, the quest for answers to these mysteries might have led to the belief by some in a "missing link" between the continents—a land-bridge populated by a highly evolved people in the distant past. Nevertheless, it is the Greek philosopher's story that lies at the heart of all arguments for or against the existence of such a lost continent.

Plato intended writing a trilogy in which the Atlantis story plays an important part, but he completed only one of the works, *Timaeus*, and part of the second, *Critias*. Like Plato's other writings, they take the form of dialogues or playlets in which a group of individuals discuss various political and moral issues. Leading the discussion is Plato's old teacher, the Greek philosopher Socrates. His debating companions are Timaeus, an astronomer from Italy, Critias, a poet and historian who was a distant relative of Plato, and Hermocrates, a general from Syracuse. Plato had already used the same cast of real-life characters in his most famous dialogue, *The Republic*, written some years previously, and he planned his trilogy as a sequel to that debate, in which the four men had talked at some length about ideal government.

Plato set the meeting of the four men in Critias' house in June 421 B.C. *Timaeus* begins on the day following the debate recorded in *The Republic*, and the men start by recalling their previous conversation. Then Hermocrates mentions "a story derived from ancient tradition" that Critias knows. Pressed for details, Critias recalls how, a century and a half earlier, the great Athenian statesman Solon had visited Egypt. (Solon was a real person and he did visit Egypt, although his trip took place around 590 B.C., some 20 years earlier than the date given by Plato.) Critias says that while Solon was in Sais, an Egyptian city having close ties with Athens, a group of priests told him the story of

Plato's Account

Atlantis—"a tale that, though strange, is certainly true." Solon made notes of the conversation, and intended recording the story for posterity, but he did not do so. Instead he told it to a relative, Dropides, who passed it on to his son, Critias the elder, who eventually told his grandson, another Critias—the man who features in Plato's dialogues.

In *Timaeus* Critias gives a brief account of what the priests had told Solon. According to ancient Egyptian records there had been a great Athenian empire 9000 years earlier (that is, in about 9600 B.C.). At the same time there had been a mighty empire of Atlantis based on an island or continent west of the Pillars of

Below: *The School of Athens*, by Italian Renaissance artist Raphael, depicts the greatest thinkers of ancient Greece. Beneath the arch are Plato (left) and Aristotle.

"A Day and Night of Destruction"

Below: Greek hoplites, or foot soldiers, pictured on the Chigi vase of the 7th century B.C. Heavily armed infantrymen like these would have taken part in the war between Atlantis and Athens that, Solon was told, had heralded the empire's end. The final battle was over and Atlantis had been defeated when the world was shaken by earthquakes, the floodwater covered the land. The earth swallowed up the Athenian army, and Atlantis disappeared into the ocean depths.

Hercules (the Strait of Gibraltar) that was larger than North Africa and Asia Minor combined. Beyond it lay a chain of islands that stretched across the ocean to another huge continent.

The Atlanteans ruled over their central island and several others, and over parts of the great continent on the other side of the ocean. Then their armies struck eastward into the Mediterranean region, conquering North Africa as far as Egypt and southern Europe up to the Greek borders. "This vast power, gathered into one, endeavored to subdue at one blow our country and yours," said the Egyptian priests, "and the whole of the region within the strait. . . ."Athens, standing alone, defeated the Atlanteans. "But afterward there occurred violent earthquakes and floods; and in a single day and night of destruction all your warlike men in a body sank into the earth, and the island of Atlantis in like manner disappeared in the depths of the sea. For which reason the sea in those parts is impassable and impenetrable, because there is so much shallow mud in the way, caused by the subsidence of the island."

Socrates is delighted with Critias' story, which has "the very great advantage of being a fact and not a fiction." However, the rest of *Timaeus* is taken up with a discourse on science, and the story of Atlantis is continued in Plato's next dialogue, the *Critias*, where Critias gives a much fuller description of the island continent. He goes back to the island's very beginning when the gods

were apportioned parts of the earth, as is usual in ancient histories. Poseidon, Greek god of the sea and also of earthquakes, was given Atlantis, and there he fell in love with a mortal maiden called Cleito. Cleito dwelled on a hill in Atlantis, and to prevent anyone reaching her home, Poseidon encircled the hill with alternate rings of land and water, "two of land and three of water, which he turned as with a lathe." He also laid on abundant supplies of food and water to the hill, "bringing up two springs of water from beneath the earth, one of warm water and the other of cold, and making every variety of food to spring up abundantly from the soil."

Poseidon and Cleito produced 10 children—five pairs of male twins—and Poseidon divided Atlantis and its adjacent islands among these 10 sons to rule as a confederacy of kings. The first-born of the eldest twins, Atlas (after whom Atlantis was named), was made chief king. The kings in turn had numerous children, and their descendants ruled for many generations.

As the population of Atlantis grew and developed, the people accomplished great feats of engineering and architecture. They built palaces and temples, harbors and docks, and reaped the rich harvest of their agricultural and mineral resources. The kings and their descendants built the city of Atlantis around Cleito's hill on the southern coast of the island continent. It was a circular city, about 11 miles in diameter, and Cleito's hill, surrounded by its concentric rings of land and water, formed a citadel about three miles in diameter, situated at the very center of the impressive city.

The kings built bridges to connect the land rings, and tunnels through which ships could pass from one ring of water to the next. The rings of land were surrounded by stone walls plated with precious metals, and another wall ran around the entire city. The outermost ring of water became a great harbor, crowded with shipping.

A huge canal, 300 feet wide and 100 feet deep, linked the great harbor with the sea at the southern end, and joined the city to a vast irrigated plain, sheltered by lofty mountains, which lay beyond the city walls in the north. This rectangular plain, measuring 230 by 340 miles, was divided into 60,000 square lots, assigned to farmers. The mountains beyond housed "many wealthy villages of country folk, and rivers, and lakes, and meadows, supplying food for every animal, wild or tame, and much wood of various sorts, abundant for each and every kind of work." The inhabitants of the mountains and of the rest of the country were "a vast multitude having leaders to whom they were assigned according to their dwellings and villages." These leaders and the farmers on the plain were each required to supply men for the Atlantean army, which included light and heavy infantry, cavalry, and chariots.

Plato and Critias paint a vivid picture of Atlantean engineering and architecture with an attention to detail that bears the hallmark of a very factual account. Critias tells how the stone used for the city's buildings was quarried from beneath the central island (Cleito's hill) and from beneath the outer and inner circles of land. "One kind of stone was white, another black, and a third red, and as they quarried they at the same time hollowed out

Above: men of Crete bringing tribute to the Egyptians, an Egyptian wall-painting of the 15th century B.C. At that time, a great civilization flourished on Crete—a civilization that had trading links with Egypt and other Mediterranean lands. By the time Solon visited Egypt, some 900 years later, the Cretan civilization had fallen. But could it have been Egyptian accounts of Crete that gave rise to the Atlantis myth?

Above: Poseidon, Greek god of the sea and, according to Plato, the founder of Atlantis. Legend tells how, when the Greek gods divided the earth at the beginning of the world, Poseidon was given the island of Atlantis. Poseidon divided Atlantis and its islands among his sons, who ruled as a confederacy of kings. The chief king, however, was the eldest son Atlas, who gave his name to the land he ruled.

docks within, having roofs formed of the native rock. Some of their buildings were simple, but in others they put together different stones, which they intermingled for the sake of ornament, to be a natural source of delight." But it was into their magnificent temples that the Atlanteans poured their greatest artistic and technical skills. In the center of the citadel was a holy temple dedicated to Cleito and Poseidon and this was surrounded by an enclosure of gold. Nearby stood Poseidon's own temple, a superb structure covered in silver, with pinnacles of gold. The roof's interior was covered with ivory, and lavishly decorated with gold, silver, and *orichalc*—probably a fine grade of brass or bronze—which "glowed like fire." Inside the temple was a massive gold statue of Poseidon driving a chariot drawn by six winged horses and surrounded by 100 sea nymphs on dolphins. This was so high that its head touched the temple roof. Gold statues of Atlantis' original 10 kings and their wives stood outside the temple.

Critias tells of the beautiful buildings that were constructed around the warm and cold fountains in the center of the city. Trees were planted between the buildings, and cisterns were designed—some open to the heavens, others roofed over—to be used as baths. "There were the kings' baths, and the baths of private persons, which were kept apart; and there were separate baths for women, and for horses and cattle, and to each of them they gave as much adornment as was suitable. Of the water that ran off they carried some to the grove of Poseidon, where were growing all manner of trees of wonderful height and beauty, owing to the excellence of the soil, while the remainder was conveyed by aqueducts along the bridges to the outer circles; and there were many temples built and dedicated to many gods; also gardens and places of exercise, some for men, and others for horses in both of the two islands formed by the zones [rings of water]; and in the center of the larger of the two there was set apart a racecourse of a stadium [about 607 feet] in width, and in length allowed to extend all around the island, for horses to race in."

At alternate intervals of five and six years the 10 kings of Atlantis met in the temple of Poseidon to consult on matters of government and to administer justice. During this meeting a strange ritual was enacted. After offering up prayers to the gods, the kings were required to hunt bulls, which roamed freely within the temple, and to capture one of them for sacrifice, using only staves and nooses. The captured animal was led to a bronze column in the temple, on which the laws of Atlantis were inscribed, and was slain so that its blood ran over the sacred inscription. After further ceremony, the kings partook of a banquet and when darkness fell they wrapped themselves in beautiful dark-blue robes. Sitting in a circle they gave their judgments, which were recorded at daybreak on tablets of gold.

In the course of time, the people of Atlantis began to lose the love of wisdom and virtue that they had inherited from Poseidon. As their divine nature was diluted and human nature got the upper hand, they became greedy, corrupt, and domineering. Whereupon, says Plato, "Zeus, the god of gods, who rules by law, and is able to see into such things, perceiving that an honorable race was in a most wretched state, and wanting to punish them that they might be chastened and improve, collected all the gods into his most holy abode, which, being placed in the center of the universe, sees all things that partake of generation. And when he had called them together he spoke as follows. . . ."

And there, enigmatically and frustratingly, Plato's story of Atlantis breaks off, never to be completed. Some scholars regard the *Critias* dialogue as a rough draft that Plato abandoned.

Poseidon, the Founder of the Lost Atlantis?

A Reconstruction of Plato's Atlantis

Fable or fact? The truth about Plato's Atlantis remains obscure to this day. The dialogue in which the Greek philosopher described the city was never completed, so it is impossible to know whether Plato based his description on a real country or created an imaginary land to illustrate his philosophical ideas. Whether or not Atlantis ever existed, Plato's account is so detailed that it can be used to reconstruct the city he described.

Poseidon surrounded the hill where his beloved Cleito dwelt by concentric rings of land and water, and the Atlanteans made these an integral part of the city they built around Cleito's hill. Tunnels beneath the land rings enabled ships to sail into the heart of the city, and from the outermost ring of water they could pass through a wide canal to the Atlantic beyond. Bridges linked the city with the land rings.

In the city itself, the Atlanteans constructed a fabulous temple dedicated to Poseidon and a palace "a marvel to behold." Temple, palace, and the surrounding buildings were ornamented with gold and silver, brass, tin, ivory, and *orichalc*—probably bronze. Trees encircled the buildings, and magnificent parks and gardens surrounded the warm and cold fountains Poseidon had made.

Atlantis and the Minotaur Myth

Right: a 19th-century painting of the Minotaur, the bull monster of Greek myth. Can the myth be based on a folk memory of the Atlantis bull ceremony Plato describes?

Others assume he intended to continue the story in the third part of his trilogy, but he never even started that work. He went on, instead, to write his last dialogue, *The Laws*.

Controversy has raged over Plato's story ever since he wrote it, 2300 years ago. Was his account fact, part-fact, or total fiction? Each explanation has its adherents, and each has been hotly defended over the centuries. Plato's story certainly presents a number of problems. Critics of the Atlantis theory claim that these invalidate the story as a factual account. Supporters maintain that they can be accepted as poetic license, exaggeration, or understandable mistakes that have crept in during the telling and retelling of the story over many centuries before Plato reported it.

The greatest stumbling block is the date that the Greek philosopher gives for the destruction of Atlantis. The Egyptian priests are said to have told Solon that Atlantis was destroyed 9000 years before his visit, in about 9600 B.C., which is far earlier than any known evidence of civilization. Supporters of Atlantis point out that modern discoveries are constantly pushing back the boundaries of human prehistory and we may yet discover that civilization is far older than we think. However, Plato makes it clear that in 9600 B.C. Athens was also the home of a mighty civilization that defeated the Atlanteans. Archaeologists claim that their knowledge of Greece in the early days of its development is sufficiently complete to rule out the possibility of highly developed people in that country as early as 9600 B.C. Their evidence suggests that either Plato's story is an invention or he has the date wrong.

Assuming that Plato's facts are right but his date wrong, what evidence do we have to support his account of the origin of the Atlantis story? Bearing in mind that the war was principally between Atlantis and Athens, it seems odd that there were no Greek records of the battle, and that the account should have originated in Egypt. However, Plato has an explanation for this. The Egyptian priests are said to have told Solon that a series of catastrophes had destroyed the Greek records, whereas their own had been preserved. The problem here is that if the Egyptian records existed at the time of Solon's visit, they have since disappeared as completely as Atlantis itself.

Supposing that Solon did hear about Atlantis during his Egyptian trip, is it credible that such a detailed story could have been passed down through the generations as Plato asks us to believe? This is not impossible, because the art of accurate oral transmission was highly developed in the ancient world. Moreover, Solon is said to have taken notes of his conversation with the priests, and Critias claims that these were handed down to his relatives. However, here again we encounter a difficulty. For whereas in one place Critias states that he is still in possession of Solon's notes, in another he declares that he lay awake all night ransacking his memory for details of the Atlantis story that his grandfather had told him. Why didn't he simply refresh his memory from Solon's notes? And why didn't he show the notes to his three companions as incontrovertible proof of the truth of his rather unlikely story?

Above: rhyton or ritual pouring vessel in the shape of a bull's head found during the excavation of the palace of Knossos, Crete. The excavations of British archaeologist Arthur Evans on Crete proved that the bull had held as important a place in the actual life of ancient Crete as that accorded it by Greek legend. His discoveries suggested the possibility of a factual basis for other ancient myths. Had the Minotaur actually existed? Was there a Cretan labyrinth? Could the island of Crete be the Atlantis of legendary fame?

Left: a black-figured Greek vase depicting Theseus, son of the king of Athens, slaying the Minotaur in the labyrinth of Crete. The Greek myths connect the bull with the actual island of Crete as closely as Plato's dialogue connects it with the legendary empire of Atlantis.

Right: the throne room of the palace at Knossos in Crete. At the beginning of this century, Evans discovered in Knossos the remains of a previously unknown civilization contemporary with that of Mycenae in mainland Greece. Evans, who named the civilization Minoan after the legendary Minos of Crete, proved by his discoveries at Knossos that a legend had its basis in historical fact.

Above: Arthur Evans in 1907, a few years after he had made the archaeological discoveries in Crete that won him worldwide fame.

Yet another problem is that Plato dates the meeting of Socrates, Timaeus, Critias, and Hermocrates, during which Atlantis is discussed, as 421 B.C. Plato may have been present during their conversation, but as he was only six years old at the time, he could hardly have taken in much of their discussion, let alone made detailed notes of it. Either his account is based on records made by someone else, or the date is wrong, or this part of his story at least is an invention.

Critics of the Atlantis story believe that it is simply a myth invented to put across the great philosopher's views on war and corruption. Plato used real people in his other dialogues, and put his words into their mouths, too, as a dramatic device to present his ideas. There is no reason, say the detractors, to assume that *Timaeus* and *Critias* are different in this respect. But Plato seems to expect his readers to draw different conclusions. He is at great pains to stress the truth of his account, tracing it back to Solon, a highly respected statesman with a reputation for being "straight-tongued," and having Critias declare that the Atlantis story, "though strange, is certainly true." And why, if his sole intention was to deliver a philosophical treatise, did Plato fill his account with remarkable detail and then stop abruptly at the very point where we would expect the "message" to be delivered? In spite of the errors and contradictions that have found their way into Plato's account, his story of Atlantis can still be viewed as an exciting recollection of previously unrecorded events.

As we saw in the first chapter of the book, history certainly provides us with other examples of supposedly mythical places subsequently being discovered. In 1871 the German archaeologist Heinrich Schliemann excavated in Hissarlik in northwestern Turkey and uncovered Troy just where Homer had placed it over 1000 years previously in his epic poems the *Iliad* and the *Odyssey*. Homer wrote or recited his poems some 500 years before Plato wrote about Atlantis! Schliemann, then, found the historical basis for what European scholars had long dismissed as pure fantasy. Subsequent research has shown that Homer's account of the Trojan War was based on real historical events. As the Irish scholar J. V. Luce observes in his book *The End of Atlantis*: "Classical scholars laughed at Schliemann when he set out with Homer in one hand and a spade in the other. But he dug up Troy and thereby demonstrated the inestimable value of folk memory. Sir Arthur Evans did much the same thing when he found the labyrinthine home of the Minotaur at Knossos." Indeed, Sir Arthur Evans revealed that a highly advanced European civilization had flourished on the island of Crete long before the time of Homer, some 4500 years ago.

This should be justification enough to keep an open mind on Plato's account. The problem is that whereas Troy and Knossos were simply buried, Atlantis could be submerged hundreds or even thousands of feet beneath the waves. And the force of the destruction may have destroyed the remains beyond recognition. However, if Plato's account is based on fact, then we know that the Atlanteans traded with their neighbors. In this case there should be some evidence of their influence and culture in lands that survived the catastrophe. Believers in Atlantis have furnished us with a formidable array of such "proofs." Certainly there are enough puzzling architectural and technical achievements scattered around thc globe to lend support to the idea of a highly advanced, Atlantean-type civilization that was responsible.

Although Plato appears to place Atlantis in the Atlantic Ocean, and early cartographers did likewise, numerous scholars and other Atlantis enthusiasts have since scoured the globe for

Evans and the Secret of Minos

Below: one of a number of reconstructions made by Evans to show how the palace of Knossos must have looked in the heyday of Minoan civilization. The culture Evans discovered was distinguished by the beauty and originality of its art and architecture, and by the comfort and prosperity that its people seem to have enjoyed.

Atlantis and the Modern Occultists

Below: map of Atlantis "at its prime" by British occultist W. Scott-Elliot. The Atlantis myth, unsupported by factual evidence, has been particularly prone to exploitation by those claiming communion with supernatural powers. According to Scott-Elliot, he learned about Atlantis through astral clairvoyance, which had revealed to him the configurations of the earth's landmasses prior to that existing today. The land of Atlantis, he stated, had appeared toward the end of the Mesozoic era and had occupied most of what is now the Atlantic. Populated in turn by various races, each of which was described in detail, Scott-Elliot's Atlantis disappeared about 800,000 years ago.

more likely sites. Surprisingly, these have not always been in the ocean. The lost kingdom of Atlantis has been "found" at various times in the Pacific Ocean, the North Sea, the Sahara Desert, Sweden, southern Spain, Palestine, Cyprus, Crete, the West Indies, and Peru, to name but a few.

Inevitably, with a lack of physical evidence of Atlantis, the occultists have been busy for centuries producing a wealth of information about the lost civilization. They believe that the past is accessible to properly attuned psychics, who can delve into history and see events happening clairvoyantly. Using such methods a number of individuals have produced vivid descriptions of life on Atlantis. Some merely expanded Plato's account. Others gave descriptions so astonishing that it can only be presumed that they were tuning in to some other lost civilization than the one immortalized by Plato. In the 1890s, for example, the English occultist W. Scott-Elliot used astral clairvoyance to reveal that Atlantis occupied most of what is now the Atlantic, more than one million years ago. It was inhabited by warrior tribes, including Rmoahals, black aboriginals who stood 10 to

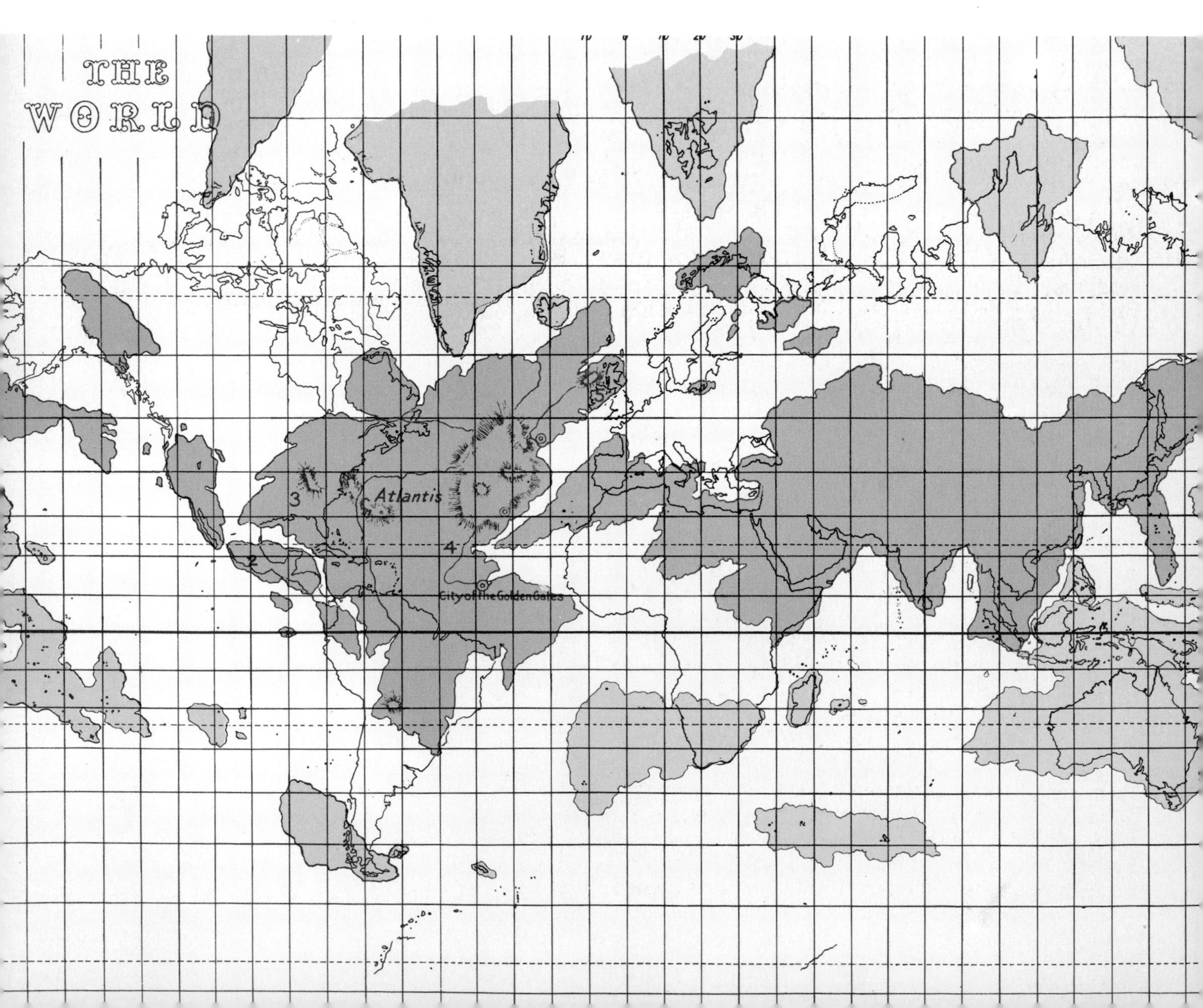

12 feet tall. The ruling race, Scott-Elliot reported, were the Toltecs, who, though only eight feet tall, made slaves of the Rmoahals. Some 200,000 years ago groups of Toltecs emigrated to Egypt and Mexico as well as visiting England. The rulers of Atlantis then took to black magic, and suffered retribution in the form of earthquake and flood, but the emigrants were safe in their new homelands.

Another seer who added to the literature on Atlantis was Edgar Cayce, the famous American clairvoyant prophet and psychic healer who died in 1945. While in a deep trance Cayce gave thousands of "psychic interviews" concerning the supposed previous incarnations of his clients. According to Cayce some of his clients were former Atlanteans, and in describing their lives he added fascinating details of the great civilization. These include references to the Atlanteans' use of what seem to be lasers and masers, described by Cayce in 1942, many years before modern scientists had developed them.

The gist of the many Cayce writings dealing with Atlantis is that the Atlanteans were technically as advanced as we are, and it was the tremendous energies that they developed—possibly nuclear—which brought about their destruction. Many people laugh at Cayce, just as they scoff at Plato's story, but the seer's followers expect to have the last laugh. They believe the earth has begun to undergo major upheavals that will cause large parts of Atlantis to rise again from the sea. In 1940 Cayce predicted that these changes would start around 1968 and 1969, when part of the "western section of Atlantis" would reappear near the Bahamas. Strangely enough, in 1968 a number of underwater formations, including what appeared to be ruined buildings, were sighted off Bimini in the Bahamas. Cayce's followers claim that these "finds" are a fulfillment of the seer's prophecy, and that far more dramatic discoveries will occur over the next 30 years or so. Unfortunately Cayce also predicted that the very upheavals that would uncover the lost continent would also submerge many parts of our existing land, including most of New York City and Japan.

The mystery of Atlantis will not be solved by the study of Plato alone. Clues from a tremendous number of disciplines, and theories from the orthodox to the occult, deserve an objective appraisal. There are those who believe that the quest for the lost continent is merely an expression of mankind's need to believe in a golden age when life was idyllic and men and women were perfect. For them, Atlantis is a dream without foundation. But there are others who view man's ancient legends and mysterious monuments very differently. In their opinion our picture of evolution and civilization is totally inadequate. We choose to ignore the puzzles that do not conform to our cozy picture of development, without realizing that these very enigmas hold the key to a far greater understanding of our past.

The missing link, according to this argument, is Atlantis, and that is why the lost continent still excites such astonishing interest. Find Atlantis, they say, and everything will fall into place. And find Atlantis we may well do, for there is a growing body of people who believe from the clues so far produced that we are now on the very brink of rediscovering the lost civilization.

Above: Edgar Cayce, American clairvoyant and perhaps the most famous and successful psychic healer of all time. While in a state of trance, Cayce conducted psychic interviews with his clients, during which he often mentioned Atlantis. He revealed many fascinating facts about the lost continent and predicted that it would rise again from the sea in 1968. Although no new continent surfaced from beneath the waters in 1968, what appeared to be ruined buildings were observed off the Bahamas.

Chapter 8
The Quest for Atlantis

Where is the site of Atlantis? Ever since the time of Plato, scholars and explorers have searched for—and "found"—Atlantis in every corner of the globe. From the new-found lands of North America in the 17th century to the Brazilian jungles of our own century, from France to Israel, from the Atlantic Ocean to Sweden—the lost land of Atlantis has shimmered like a mirage in every remote corner of the world. This chapter follows the quest, from Africa to Australia, from Siberia to the Caribbean, for this most elusive of all lost lands.

In 1912 the *New York American* published a sensational article. It was written by Dr. Paul Schliemann, grandson of Heinrich Schliemann, the man who discovered Troy. Paul Schliemann announced that he had in his possession coins and an inscribed metal plate belonging to the Atlantean culture. Here at last, it seemed, was proof of the existence of Atlantis.

In his article entitled "How I Discovered Atlantis, the Source of All Civilization," Paul Schliemann explained that the Atlantean artifacts had been left to him by his famous grandfather, who had discovered them during his excavations. Heinrich Schliemann had died before completing his search for evidence of the lost continent. However, he had left his family a sealed envelope containing a number of secret papers about Atlantis, together with an ancient, owl-headed vase. A note on the envelope warned that it should be opened only by a member of the family prepared to swear that he would devote his life to researching the matters dealt with in the papers. Paul Schliemann made that pledge and opened the envelope.

His grandfather's first instruction was to break open the owl-headed vase. Inside he found several square coins of platinum-aluminum-silver alloy and a plate made of a silverlike metal that bore the inscription, in Phoenician: "Issued in the Temple of Transparent Walls." Heinrich Schliemann's notes told of finds made on the site of Troy, including a huge bronze vase containing coins and objects made of metal, bone, and pottery.

Opposite: the gold mask that covered the head and shoulders of the mummified body of Tutankhamun, pharaoh of Egypt in the 14th century B.C. According to American Ignatius Donnelly, the "Father of Scientific Atlantology," ancient Egypt was an Atlantean colony, and its civilization and religion were based on those of Atlantis.

The True Site of Atlantis?

Below: Paul Schliemann's map of the possible location of Atlantis—the dark circles represent the city described by Plato. In 1912 Schliemann, grandson of the discoverer of Troy, published an article setting out what he claimed was conclusive proof of the existence of Atlantis. Most of his evidence, however, turned out to have been lifted without acknowledgment from other writers.

The vase and some of its contents were inscribed with the words: "From King Cronos of Atlantis."

"You can imagine my excitement," wrote the young Schliemann. "Here was the first material evidence of that great continent whose legend has lived for ages. . . ." He went on to state that, by following up these clues with his own investigations, he had finally solved the Atlantis mystery. However, his "research" would appear to have gone no further than a study of the arguments of the pro-Atlantis enthusiasts, because the rest of his article consisted of material clearly culled (without acknowledgment) from their works. Like others before him, Paul Schliemann claimed the cultures of the New and Old Worlds had a common origin in Atlantis. He said he had read the *Troano Codex*, an ancient Mayan text that until then had defied translation. It told of the sinking of an island named Mu, and he had found corroboration of this account in a 4000-year-old Chaldean manuscript from a Buddhist temple in Tibet.

It was at this point that the experts began to have misgivings. Paul Schliemann claimed to have read the *Troano Codex* in the British Museum—but it is preserved in the National Museum of Madrid. And his "translation" was remarkably similar to that made by an eccentric French scholar, which seemed to owe more to a vivid imagination than to a linguistic talent.

Schliemann promised to divulge the full story of his discoveries in a forthcoming book. Like Atlantis, the book never appeared. Nor did the vase, coins, and other precious relics ever see the light of day. Although the Schliemann story was clearly a hoax, this has not stopped the more credulous pro-Atlantists

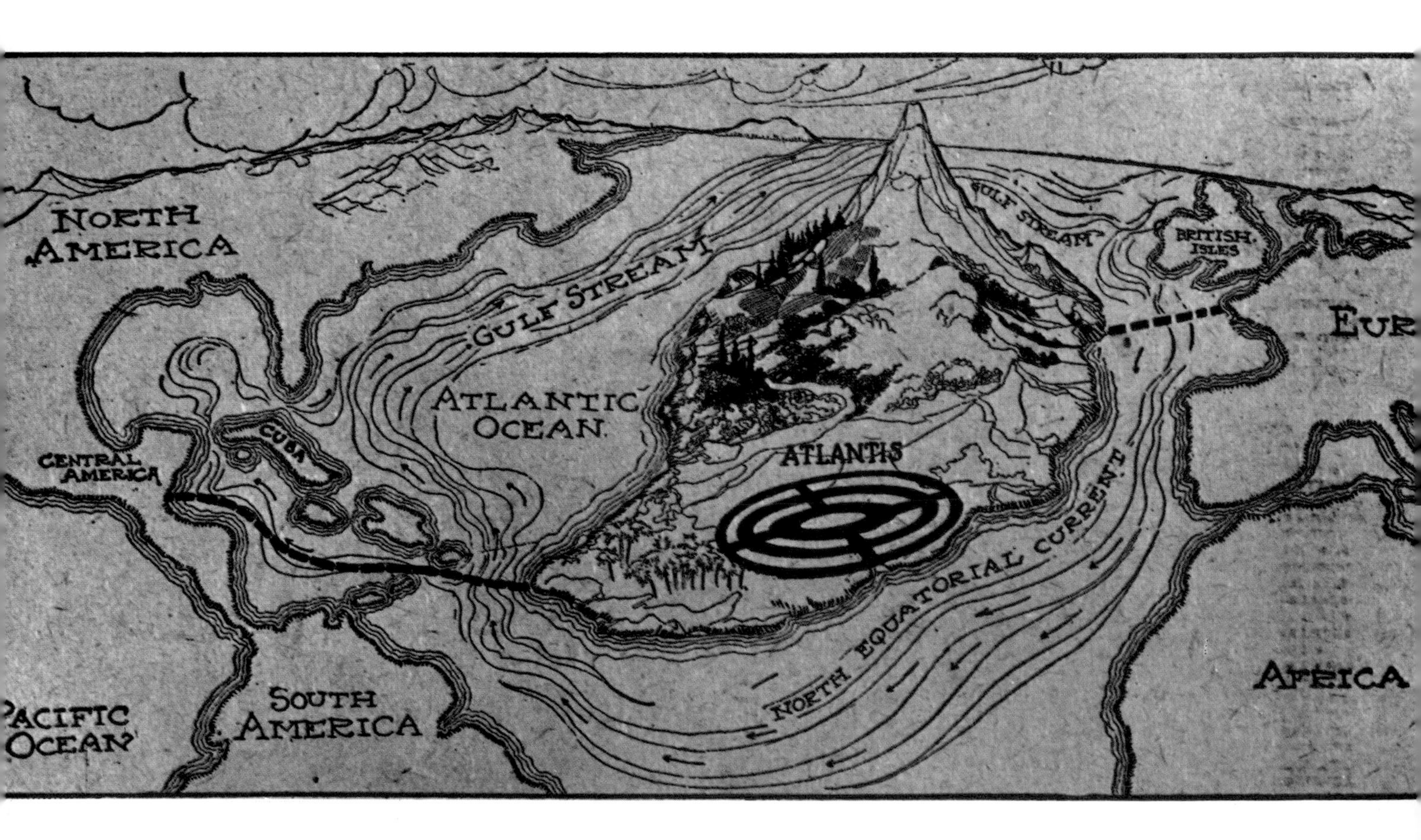

from using it to support their claims, sometimes confusing Paul with his famous grandfather to make matters worse.

This rather sad episode is typical of the numerous false leads that have bedeviled genuine attempts to uncover the truth about Atlantis. Time and again, men of apparent erudition and integrity have claimed the discovery of vital clues. Using ancient manuscripts, folklore, and legends, they have pieced together impressive "evidence" about the sinking of the island continent, the appearance of its inhabitants, what happened to the survivors, and, above all, the true site of Atlantis. Some of these theories, based on inaccurate information, have been rapidly demolished by fellow scholars. Others are so revolutionary in their implications that, if they were proved correct, the entire history of the world would need to be rewritten.

Ever since Plato's time writers, scholars, and explorers have sought—and "found"—Atlantis in almost every corner of the globe. Francis Bacon, the 17th-century English philosopher and statesman, thought that Plato's Atlantis was America. Another 17th-century scholar, the Swede Olof Rudbeck, wrote a lengthy treatise "proving" that Atlantis was Sweden. In the 18th century, French astronomer Jean Bailly—a victim of the French Revolution—traced Atlantis to Spitsbergen in the Arctic Ocean. Francis Wilford, a British officer in India in the 19th century, was convinced that the British Isles were a remnant of the lost continent, and his theory was enthusiastically adopted by the poet William Blake. Other leading theorists and investigators—some of whom have devoted their lives to the subject—have placed Atlantis in North Africa, South Africa, Central America,

Left: Heinrich Schliemann's excavations at Hissarlik. His grandson Paul claimed that he had found some objects of Atlantean origin during his excavations at Hissarlik, and that he had left these to any member of his family prepared to devote his life to the search for the lost continent. It appears, however, that the story was invented by Paul as a publicity gimmick.

Right: English philosopher and statesman Francis Bacon. His unfinished work *New Atlantis* was published in 1627; a year after his death. In it Bacon described a utopian land in the Pacific Ocean whose inhabitants came originally from Plato's Atlantis—situated, according to Bacon, in America. He used this idyllic country to illustrate his educational ideas.

Below: title page of the first edition of Bacon's *Sylva Sylvarum*. It was published in 1627 with *New Atlantis* as an appendix.

Australia, France, the North Sea, Sardinia, Israel and Lebanon, Malta, the Sahara, East Prussia and the Baltic, Siberia, Greenland, Iraq, Iran, Brazil, and the Pacific and Indian Oceans. The peoples of these regions naturally had a vested interest in such theories, because the location of Atlantis in or near their country would give them a reasonable claim to be descended from Atlantean survivors.

It may seem odd that most of the Atlantis theorists mentioned above have chosen *land* areas as the site of a supposedly drowned continent. There are a number of reasons for this, including the obvious one that until recent times extensive underwater exploration has not been possible. Some theorists base their choice on a reinterpretation of Plato's story, believing that he built his account on the memory of some ancient disaster of relatively limited proportions. Others point out that vast areas of our present landmasses were once under water; similarly, areas that are now submerged were once above sea level. According to this argument, Atlantis was submerged, as Plato said, but has since reappeared as one of the countries or areas listed. However, geological evidence does not support this theory. Most geologists agree that, although the earth's surface has undergone many major changes, these have occurred only very gradually over millions of years. As far as they are concerned, large landmasses do not rise and sink rapidly enough to account for the overnight drowning of Atlantis and its reemergence as one of our present-day land areas.

The Atlantis-seekers mentioned so far are, however, in a minority. By far the greater number of scholars who have studied the Atlantis enigma agree with Plato. If the lost continent was anywhere, they believe, it was in the Atlantic Ocean—and they have produced a wealth of material to support their case.

America–or Spitsbergen?

Of all the theorists who have placed Atlantis in the Atlantic, none has argued more persuasively or made a greater impact on the study of Atlantis than the American Ignatius T. T. Donnelly, sometimes called the Father of Scientific Atlantology. Donnelly's enormous physical and intellectual energy brought him success at an early age. Born in Philadelphia in 1831, he studied law and was admitted to the bar at the age of 22. Three years later he and his bride went to Minnesota, where Donnelly and a group of friends had purchased some land near St. Paul and hoped to found a great Middle West metropolis, Nininger City. As part of the campaign to publicize this dream, Donnelly edited and published *The Emigrant Journal*. But Nininger City was never developed, possibly because of the financial depression that occurred in the 1850s.

Above: the 18th-century French astronomer Jean Bailly, a member of the French Academy of Sciences. Besides orthodox scientific works, Bailly wrote a book on ancient astronomy in which he claimed that Spitsbergen was Atlantis, and the source of all Asian civilizations.

Instead, the chubby dynamic Donnelly turned his attention to politics, and was elected Lieutenant-Governor of Minnesota at the age of 28. Four years later he was sent to Congress, where he served for eight years. Donnelly was renowned as a brilliant, forceful, and witty speaker, and rapidly earned the respect of fellow members of the House of Representatives.

Behind the public image, however, Donnelly was experiencing a period of intense loneliness. Soon after his arrival in Washington, his wife had died, and Donnelly turned to study for solace. During his two terms as the member from Minnesota, he spent long hours in the magnificent Library of Congress, soaking up all the information he could.

After his defeat in the election of 1870, Donnelly returned to his home in the ghost town of Nininger City. There, surrounded by his notes and a large personal library, he began writing the books that were to make him famous throughout the world. After years of isolation and poverty during which he persevered with the task in hand to the exclusion of all else, Donnelly produced his masterpiece: *Atlantis, the Antediluvian World.* Published in 1882, this unique study of the lost continent became an overnight sensation. The following year another book, *Ragnarok, the Age of Fire and Gravel*, joined his first as a best seller. This dealt with the cosmic aspects of natural cataclysms such as that which supposedly submerged Atlantis. The extent of Donnelly's influence on the study of Atlantis can be judged by the enormous and continuing success of his books. His first work, for example, has been reprinted 50 times and is still in print today, nearly a century after it was written. Donnelly transformed what had been, until then, a subject of speculation mainly among intellectuals into a popular cult, and one that has survived ever since.

This giant of Atlantology did more than look for confirmation

Donnelly's Theory

of Plato's story. He used it as the basis for a picture of Atlantis that went far beyond anything stated—or that could even have been imagined—by the Greek philosopher. His theories were distilled into 13 "theses":

"1. That there once existed in the Atlantic Ocean, opposite the mouth of the Mediterranean Sea, a large island, which was the remnant of an Atlantic continent, and known to the ancient world as Atlantis.

"2. That the description of this island given by Plato is not, as has been long supposed, fable, but veritable history.

"3. That Atlantis was the region where man first rose from a state of barbarism to civilization.

"4. That it became, in the course of ages, a populous and mighty nation, from whose overflowings the shores of the Gulf of Mexico, the Mississippi River, the Amazon, the Pacific coast of South America, the Mediterranean, the west coast of Europe

Below right: Ignatius Donnelly, author of *Atlantis: the Antediluvian World*, one of the most influential books on the subject ever published. Donnelly, a man of wide-ranging interests and considerable erudition, began his career as a lawyer, subsequently moving to Minnesota where he tried unsuccessfully to found a new city. Turning to politics, at 28 he became Lieutenant-Governor of Minnesota and was later elected to Congress. Donnelly spent much of his free time in Washington reading in the Library of Congress.

Below: cartoon representing Donnelly as Don Quixote, from the *Minneapolis Journal* of February 24, 1891. Although Donnelly was never reelected to Congress he continued to take an active interest in politics throughout his life. He became a member of the Minnesota State Senate, and made two unsuccessful attempts for the vice-presidency of the United States.

and Africa, the Baltic, the Black Sea, and the Caspian were populated by civilized nations.

"5. That it was the true Antediluvian world; the Garden of Eden; the Gardens of the Hesperides; the Elysian Fields; the Gardens of Alcinous; the Mesomphales; the Olympes; the Asgard of the traditions of the ancient nations; representing a universal memory of a great land, where early mankind dwelt for ages in peace and happiness.

"6. That the gods and goddesses of the ancient Greeks, the Phoenicians, the Hindoos, and the Scandinavians were simply the kings, queens, and heroes of Atlantis; and the acts attributed to them in mythology are a confused recollection of real historical events.

"7. That the mythology of Egypt and Peru represented the original religion of Atlantis, which was sun-worship.

"8. That the oldest colony formed by the Atlanteans was prob-

Left: Donnelly's library in Nininger Minnesota, the town he had hoped to build into the greatest city of the midwest. After his defeat in the 1870 election, Donnelly returned to Nininger and began to write his book on Atlantis. First published in 1882, it was still in print, in its 50th edition, in 1949.

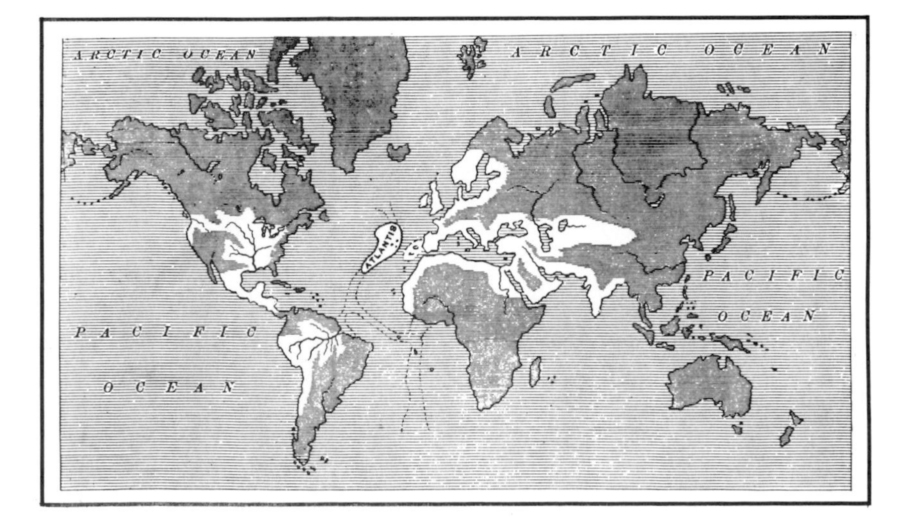

Left: Donnelly's map of Atlantis and its empire, from *Atlantis: the Antediluvian World*. Donnelly believed that all the dark areas were colonized and civilized through contacts with Atlantis.

Arches and Pyramids

ably in Egypt, whose civilization was a reproduction of that of the Atlantic island.

"9. That the implements of the 'Bronze Age' of Europe were derived from Atlantis. The Atlanteans were also the first manufacturers of iron.

"10. That the Phoenician alphabet, parent of all the European alphabets, was derived from an Atlantis alphabet, which was also conveyed from Atlantis to the Mayas of Central America.

"11. That Atlantis was the original seat of the Aryan or Indo-European family of nations, as well as of the Semitic peoples, and possibly also of the Turanian races.

"12. That Atlantis perished in a terrible convulsion of nature, in which the whole island sank into the ocean, with nearly all its inhabitants.

"13. That a few persons escaped in ships and on rafts, and carried to the nations east and west tidings of the appalling catastrophe, which has survived to our own time in the Flood and Deluge legends of the different nations of the old and new worlds."

Donnelly, it seems, had not only "discovered" Atlantis but

Below: the pyramids of Cheops and Khafre in El Giza, Egypt. Donnelly used the fact that peoples in the Old and the New World had built pyramids as a cornerstone in his attempt to prove the existence of Atlantis.

also succeeded in solving nearly all the mysteries of the past at the same time. He maintained that Atlantis was the source of all civilization (Plato made no such claim) and as such had inspired the myths and legends of numerous races—many of which are indeed remarkably similar.

Donnelly argued that the resemblances between many species of American and European animals and plants are due to their having a common origin—Atlantis. Quoting a number of authorities to support his case, he stated that such plants as tobacco, guava, cotton, and bananas were not confined to one hemisphere before Columbus—as was generally thought—but had long been grown in both the New and the Old World. In his view these plants must have crossed the Atlantic by means of an Atlantean land-bridge.

Donnelly also believed that the civilization of ancient Egypt emerged suddenly rather than evolving gradually over thousands of years, thus indicating that it was imported from elsewhere. He quoted the opinion of the 19th-century French writer Ernest Renan to support this view: "Egypt at the beginning appears mature, old, and entirely without mythical and heroic ages, as if the country had never known youth. Its civilization has no infancy, and its art no archaic period." That opinion, together with "evidence" drawn from the religious and cultural beliefs of the ancient Egyptians and from their magnificent achievements, was sufficient to convince Donnelly that Egypt was colonized by survivors of Atlantis who brought with them a ready-made civilization modeled on their former life.

In Donnelly's view, the Mayas of Central America were also of Atlantean origin, partly because they possessed what he believed to be a phonetic alphabet similar to the Old World alphabets, and also because they "claim that their civilization came to them *across the sea in ships from the east*, that is, from the direction of Atlantis."

Another important feature of Donnelly's argument was the incidence of similar culture traits among New and Old World peoples, which he assumed to have a common origin. He cited as evidence the appearance on both sides of the Atlantic of

Above: the Castillo at Chichén Itzá, Mexico. The Castillo was built some 4000 years after the Great Pyramids of Egypt, but it exhibits the same classic pyramid shape. Donnelly did not believe that it was possible for peoples working thousands of miles apart to have arrived independently at the same architectural forms. If "the great inventions were duplicated spontaneously," he wrote, "all savages would have invented the boomerang; all . . . would possess pottery, bows and arrows . . . and canoes. . . ."

Left: Donnelly used these drawings of a section of the treasurehouse of Atreus in Mycenae, Greece (left) and the Arch of Las Monjas in Palenque, Mexico (right) in his book *Atlantis* to illustrate the resemblance between the form of arch used in the oldest Greek building and that employed by certain American civilizations.

The "Bible of Atlantology"

pyramids, pillars, burial mounds, metallurgy, ships, and various other cultural developments. "I cannot believe that the great inventions were duplicated spontaneously . . . in different countries," he argued. "If this were so, all savages would have invented the boomerang; all savages would possess pottery, bow and arrows, slings, tents, and canoes; in short, all races would have risen to civilization, for certainly the comforts of life are as agreeable to one people as another."

Finally, this wide-ranging scholar claimed to have proved the connection between Atlantis and other civilizations through a study of linguistics. New World languages, he declared, are closely related to tongues of the Old World, and he composed parallel tables of words to back his case. For those who had wanted to believe in Atlantis but had felt Plato's account left too many questions unanswered, Donnelly had put flesh on the bones of the legend. Almost every writer on Atlantis who came after him has borrowed from Donnelly's work, which remains the bible of Atlantology. But does it deserve that reputation?

Donnelly's forceful style, his undoubted learning, his enthusiasm, and his air of absolute conviction tend to sweep the reader along with him and mask the false or shaky foundations of some of his arguments. According to L. Sprague de Camp, author of one of the best critical studies of Atlantis, *Lost Continents*, "Most of Donnelly's statements of fact, to tell the truth, either were wrong when he made them, or have been disproved by subsequent discoveries."

Below: Egyptian bas-relief of the head of a young man, dating from about 1370 B.C. His forehead is flattened in a way characteristic of ancient Egyptian portrait heads.

Right: mid-19th century illustration of an American Indian woman and child of the Flat-Head tribe. The woman's forehead is flattened much like that of the Egyptian youth above. Donnelly took the existence of skull deformation in the Old and the New World, with the presence in both of similar architectural forms, as evidence that "the people of both . . . were originally united in blood and race"—the race of Atlantis.

De Camp points out that Donnelly was mistaken in asserting that the Peruvian Indians had a system of writing, or that the cotton plants native to the New and Old Worlds belong to the same species. Donnelly's comparisons between New and Old World alphabets were based on an inaccurate and discredited representation of a so-called "Mayan alphabet," further distorted by Donnelly to create "intermediate forms" between Latin and allegedly Mayan letters. Nor is there a resemblance between the Otomi language of Mexico and Chinese, despite a table of "similarities" that Donnelly published. "I don't know what he used for Chinese," says de Camp, "—certainly not the standard Northern Chinese, the language usually meant by the term."

Errors such as these have gone largely unnoticed, and Donnelly still enjoys a sizable following. Soon after the publication of his first book his correspondence reached gigantic proportions. Even the British Prime Minister William E. Gladstone is said to have written to express his appreciation. Gladstone was so impressed by Donnelly's arguments that he tried to persuade Parliament to vote funds for an expedition to go in search of Atlantis. On the strength of such reactions, Donnelly took to the lecture platform with equal success. Then he turned his back on lecturing to return home and continue writing. Later, he reentered politics, helping to found the Populist Party and twice running for Vice-President of the United States on the Populist ticket. This remarkable, largely self-taught man died in 1901, knowing that he had shaped and laid the foundation stone of modern Atlantology.

Others soon followed, of whom the most outstanding was Lewis Spence, a Scottish mythologist who launched a short-lived magazine called *Atlantis Quarterly* and wrote five books on Atlantis. Spence never achieved the popular appeal of Donnelly, but his theories have won almost as much acclaim among fellow Atlantologists. Even the skeptics have a high regard for Spence. L. Sprague de Camp, for instance, calls Spence "a sane and sober writer," and describes his major work, *The Problem of Atlantis*, as "about the best pro-Atlantis work published to date."

Like Donnelly, Spence takes a serious and scientific approach to his subject. In *The Problem of Atlantis*, which appeared in 1924, he set out to prove four points:

"1. That a great continent formerly occupied the whole or major portion of the North Atlantic region, and a considerable portion of its southern basin. Of early geological origin, it must, in the course of successive ages, have experienced many changes in contour and mass, probably undergoing frequent submergence and emergence.

"2. That in the Miocene (Later Tertiary) times [from 25 to 10 million years ago] it still retained its continental character, but towards the end of that period it began to disintegrate, owing to successive volcanic and other causes.

"3. That this disintegration resulted in the formation of greater and lesser insular masses. Two of these, considerably larger in area than any of the others, were situated (a) at a relatively short distance from the entrance to the Mediterranean; and (b) in the region of the present West Indian Islands. These may re-

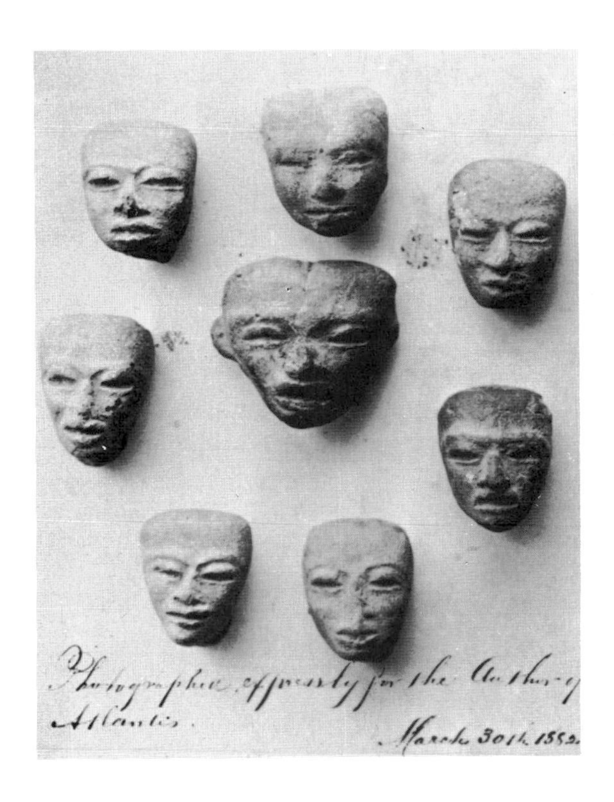

Above: Mexican pottery said by Donnelly to be models of Atlanteans. He believed that some survivors of Atlantis had settled in Mexico.

spectively be called Atlantis and Antillia. Communication between them was possible by an insular chain.
"4. That these two island-continents and this connecting chain of islands persisted until late Pleistocene times, at which epoch (about 25,000 years ago, or the beginning of the post-glacial epoch) Atlantis seems to have experienced further disintegration. Final disaster appears to have overtaken Atlantis about 10,000 B.C. Antillia, on the other hand, seems to have survived until a much more recent period, and still persists fragmentally in the Antillean group, or West Indian Islands."

In order to make these theses acceptable, Spence had to throw out some aspects of Plato's account. Atlantis, he asserted, did not vanish in a day and a night. Its disappearance—the last of many disasters affecting the continent—probably occurred gradually over many years. Nor did he attempt to confirm Donnelly's claim that Atlantis was the source of all civilization.

Above: Scottish Atlantist Lewis Spence. Like Donnelly, Spence approached his subject scientifically, attempting to produce evidence in support of his four theses about Atlantis. Unlike Donnelly's theories, however, Spence's were principally concerned with the geographical existence and disappearance of the lost continent, rather than with the Atlantean civilization and its effects.

Right: artist's impression of a Cro-Magnon man, whose people flourished in Europe about 25,000 years ago. Spence believed that the Cro-Magnons came originally from Atlantis, and he produced an impressive array of evidence to support his claim. As Atlantis disintegrated, Spence asserted, further waves of survivors fled east to Europe. The Cro-Magnon's were followed first by the Caspians, then by the Azilian race.

Although he believed the Atlanteans had a developed culture, he was prepared to accept that they were a Stone Age people, despite Plato's reference to their skillful use of metals.

If Atlantis did exist in the Atlantic Ocean, Spence argued, and disintegrated gradually—finally disappearing at about the time Plato gives (around 10,000 B.C.)—then there should be evidence of its survivors taking refuge in other lands. In the early phases of Atlantis' destruction, man was not a seafarer, and the Atlantean landmass must have been near the coast of other continents to make the journey possible. Spence is able to produce some fascinating evidence for just such an exodus.

The missing link between the Atlanteans and present-day man, according to Spence, consisted of three races of people, the Cro-Magnon, the Caspian, and the Azilian. Quoting a variety of experts Spence demonstrates that none of these races developed in the country where their remains are now to be found. Because most of their settlements were in the coastal areas of south-western France and northern Spain, around the shores of the Bay of Biscay, Spence concluded that they came from a country to the west. None exists there now, and it must have been Atlantis.

The Cro-Magnons were the first to arrive in Europe, at the close of the Ice Age about 25,000 years ago. They appear to have wiped out the Neanderthal people who then inhabited the area, which is hardly surprising because the Cro-Magnons were vastly superior in physique and intellect. The average height of the Cro-Magnon men was 6 feet 1½ inches. They had short arms—a sign of high racial development—and skulls that indicate an exceptionally large brain capacity. Their faces were very broad, with massive chins, high foreheads, and beak noses. The Cro-Magnon people produced amazingly realistic cave paintings—usually of animals, including the bull—and carved equally impressive pictures on their tools and utensils.

Spence and the Lost Continent

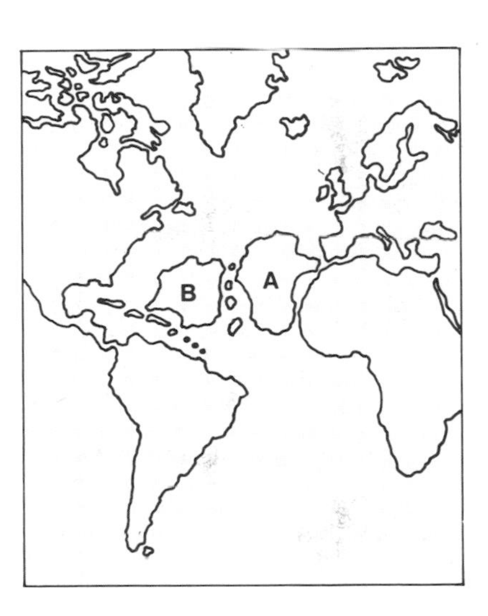

Above: Spence's map of Atlantis (A) and Antillia (B). Spence believed that Atlantis broke up over a considerable period of time rather than disappearing overnight as Plato described. The first stage in the disintegration was its break-up into two smaller landmasses, Atlantis and Antillia. According to Spence, Atlantis later disappeared, but fragments of Antillia still exist—the Antilles or West Indies.

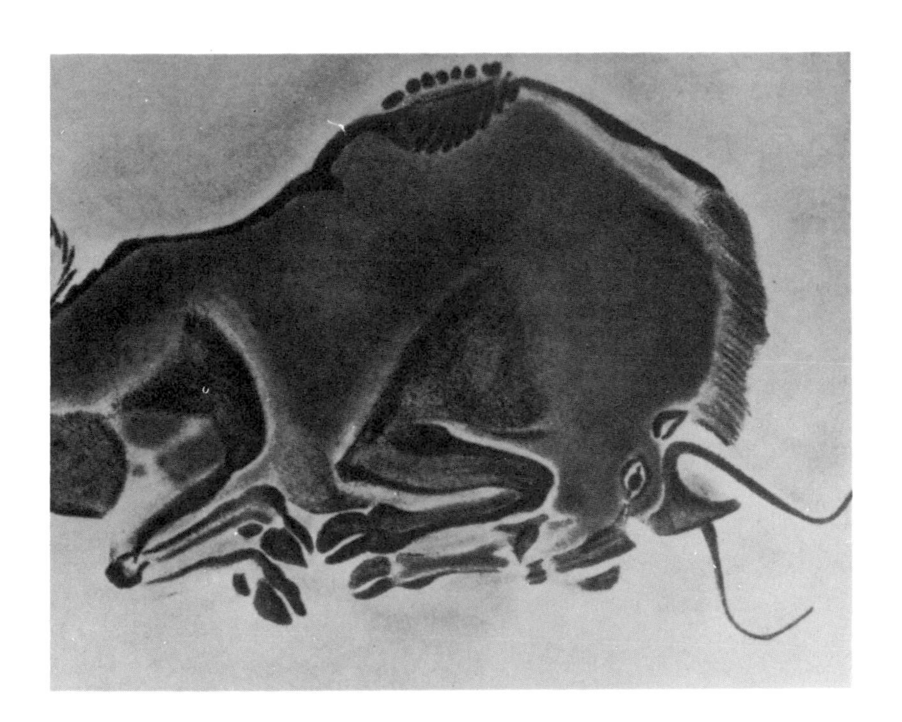

Left: Cro-Magnon painting of a charging bison from the roof of a cave at Altamira, Spain. Spence, identifying the bison with the bull, cites these paintings as evidence of the Cro-Magnons Atlantean origin. The bull, Plato records, had been especially revered by the Atlantean race.

Atlantis and the Sargasso Sea

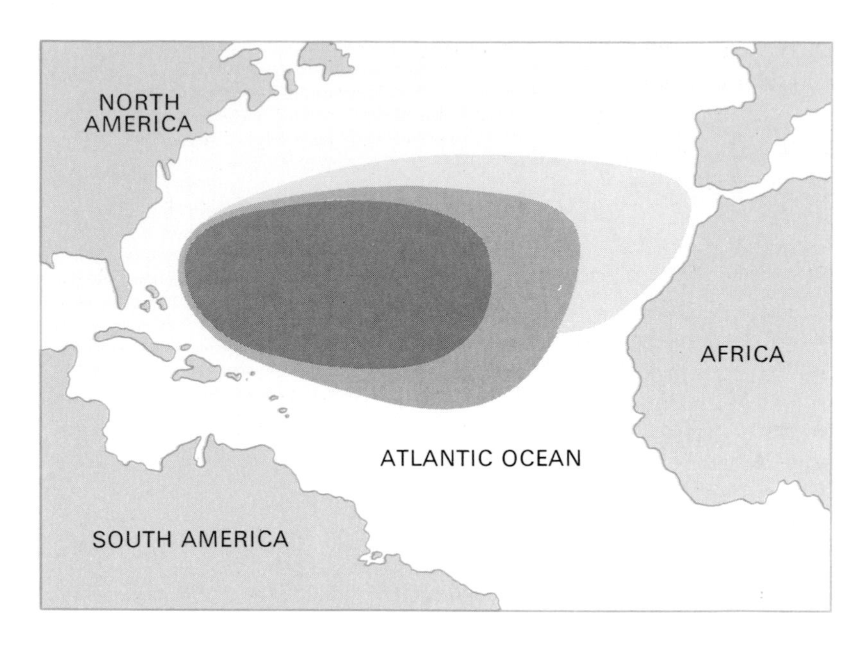

Right: map of the Sargasso Sea, from Spence's book *The History of Atlantis*. The shaded area shows where the seaweed that gave the sea its name and reputation is thickest. The presence of weed in the ocean was once used as a warning of shallow water, which made the Sargasso Sea one of the most popular possibilities as the site of the sunken continent of Atlantis. In his discussion of this theory, Spence quotes Plato's remark that after the disappearance of Atlantis "the sea in these regions has become impassable," which could be taken to refer to the Sargasso Sea.

Above: 19th-century print of sailors collecting seaweed from floating masses in the Sargasso Sea.

This remarkable race flourished for 15,000 years until it was displaced by the Caspian and Azilian invasions. According to Spence, these peoples were also fleeing from Atlantis at later periods in the island's violent history. The Azilians appeared in exactly the same European areas as their predecessors, but archaeologists have found evidence that, unlike the Cro-Magnon people, the Azilians were fishermen, capable of deep-sea fishing. If subsequent cataclysms had destroyed the land-bridge that brought the Cro-Magnons to Europe, said Spence, their successors now had boats in which to flee. Azilian culture appeared in Europe around 10,000 B.C., which ties in approximately with Plato's date for the destruction of Atlantis. Significantly, the Azilians were always buried facing west—toward their homeland, according to Spence.

Spence argued that the Azilians probably founded the civilizations of Egypt and Crete. He believed that Atlantean town planning, as described by Plato, was reflected in the great ancient cities of Carthage and Knossos. In Spence's view, the Mayan culture too derived from Atlantis—as Donnelly had claimed before him. He explained the enormous time gap between the destruction of Atlantis around 10,000 B.C. and the appearance of the Mayan civilization just before the Christian Era by suggesting that some Atlantean refugees had fled westward to Antillia (the second island continent in his theory) and had remained there for thousands of years. It was only when Antillia too was destroyed that they moved on to Central America. Spence believed that the Mayan culture, like that of Egypt, was imported, because it showed no evidence of gradual evolution.

Mankind may have largely forgotten Atlantis over the centuries, argued Spence, but certain animals did not. As an example, he pointed to the curious behavior of the Norwegian lemming. When the lemming population outgrows its local food supply, these small rodents gather in great masses and swim out to sea until they all drown. In Spence's view the lemmings are responding to an instinctive memory of a land that used to exist in the west, where fresh food could be found.

Despite his praise of Spence's book, L. Sprague de Camp is quickly on hand to raise a few healthy objections to some of the author's conclusions. "Even if we confine ourselves to Spence's facts, they turn out less impressive than they seem at first," he writes. "For one thing, Cro-Magnon culture has now been found in the East—in Palestine. Furthermore, despite all these assertions that the cultures of Egypt, Yucatán, and Peru sprang into existence suddenly without a slow transition from primitive culture, modern archaeology has disclosed the gradual evolution of all these cultures from more primitive levels. You can, for instance, trace the growth of Egyptian culture from the neolithic Merimda people, who wore animal skins, lived in mud houses, and farmed in a crude manner, to the highly civilized men of the Fourth Dynasty."

It is easy enough to make mistakes about the development of cultures, says de Camp, simply because relics of more recent times are more numerous and easier to find, and are frequently

Left: miniature illustrating a manuscript of the voyages of St. Brendan, Abbot of Clauinfert, Ireland, in the 6th century A.D. Accompanied by his monks, he set sail into the Atlantic in search of a land where he would find converts to Christianity, and according to the account of his voyage, he was successful in the search. In the minds of Atlantists, such medieval accounts of new lands in the Atlantic Ocean became identified with the Atlantis myth.

Above: Spence used this stone figure found in a grave in Mexico as the frontispiece to his *History of Atlantis*. According to his theory, it represents a soldier wearing Atlantean armor.

Below: reconstruction of the circular harbor at Carthage, the ancient city built by the Phoenicians on the north coast of Africa. Spence remarks on a distinct resemblance between Carthage and the plan of Atlantis as described by Plato. As Carthage was not built until after Plato wrote his dialogue, Spence concludes that it must have been built in the tradition of Atlantis.

bigger and more durable than those built in a culture's earlier stages. In Spence's defense, however, modern Atlantologists point to numerous relics and artifacts that do not appear to fit in with the archaeologists' neat and orderly pattern of development.

As for the lemmings in search of a lost land, de Camp points out that when they become starved by overpopulation they set off willy-nilly in any direction, often swimming rivers in search of food. When they reach the sea they no doubt mistake it for another river and carry on swimming until they drown. Swedish lemmings, he adds, try to swim the Baltic in the opposite direction, which makes nonsense of Spence's theory . . . unless, of course, Atlantis was in the Baltic, as one researcher has suggested.

Lewis Spence, who died in 1955, would probably not have been too perturbed by such criticisms. Although he had worked hard to assemble facts on which to hang his theories, he realized that ultimately they would probably not be sufficient to convince the skeptics. His books do not openly deal with the occult aspects of Atlantology, but Spence was certainly aware that many had endeavored to solve the riddle of the lost continent by nonmaterial methods. Indeed, before writing his first book on Atlantis, Spence had completed an excellent *Encyclopedia of Occultism*, in which he made a first cautious reference to Atlantis.

In time, Spence grew tired of the demand for facts. He began suggesting that the durability of the Atlantis theory might be due to a common "folk-memory" that could actually be inherited rather than preserved through oral or written accounts. There is "a world-intuition regarding the existence of a transatlantic continent," he said, and "we are dealing with a great world-memory, of which Plato's story is merely one of the broken and distorted fragments. . . ." Elsewhere he declared himself in favor of "inspirational methods," which would become "the Archaeology of the Future." In his opinion, "The Tape-Measure School, dull and full of the credulity of incredulity, is doomed," and "the day is passing when mere weight of evidence alone, unsupported by considerations which result from inspiration or insight, can be accepted by the world."

Many Atlantis enthusiasts have been satisfied with inspiration alone, of course, but Spence's views rather clouded his reputation as a scholar. Spence did little to allay his critics when, in 1942, he published a book entitled *Will Europe Follow Atlantis?* This argued that God had destroyed Atlantis because of the wickedness of the Atlanteans and (with the Nazi atrocities in mind) He would do the same to Europe unless it reformed.

For all his idiosyncrasies Spence is probably still the best guide to the Atlantis story. His knowledge of the subject was such that he was consulted by Sir Arthur Conan Doyle during the latter's preparation of his exciting romance *The Lost World*, which concerns an expedition to the Brazilian jungle in search of a mysterious, hidden world. Spence also conducted a correspondence with an English explorer, Colonel Percy H. Fawcett, who was planning a very similar expedition. Fawcett believed that South America might be part of Atlantis, or that the mysterious cities reported to exist in the dense jungles of the Amazon might have been built by Atlanteans who had fled their stricken land.

Fawcett was not alone in linking ancient America with Atlantis Both Donnelly and Spence had used the Mayan culture as evidence in their arguments, and the mysterious early civilizations of the Americas still fascinate and puzzle us today.

"Will Europe Follow Atlantis"

Below: detail of a map of the world made in 1502. The map shows the Antilles, all that remains of the island of Antillia according to Spence.

Chapter 9
The Ancient Legacy

Ever since Hernando Cortes discovered the Aztec civilization in what is now Mexico in 1519, European scholars have puzzled over the origin of such highly developed "lost lands" of the Americas. Aztec or Olmei, Inca or Mayan—all these advanced American civilizations have been attributed to the influence of Old World peoples such as the Egyptians, the Phoenicians, the Irish, the Vikings—or the mysterious Atlanteans. Ancient myths and legends among these American peoples about the coming and promised return of fair-skinned bearded "gods" have strongly encouraged such theories. What is the truth? Is there a vital link between Old and New Worlds? And is that link really Atlantis?

High on a desolate plateau in the Andes stand the ruins of an ancient city, silent, shadowy, and mysterious. This is Tiahuanaco, near La Paz in modern Bolivia. Set at the dizzying altitude of 13,000 feet, amid a wild expanse of barren rock, framed by volcanic mountains, Tiahuanaco is one of the loneliest and most inhospitable places on earth. Yet this city was once the heart of a mighty civilization, built by an unknown people who lived on the shores of Lake Titicaca hundreds—and perhaps many thousands—of years before the arrival of the Incas. Legend has it that Tiahuanaco was built for the worship of Viracocha, the White God, who came to the Indians in the distant past, bringing them all the arts and laws of an advanced civilization. Then Viracocha disappeared across the sea, never fulfilling his promise to return.

Tiahuanaco already lay partly in ruins when the Incas found it in the early 13th century A.D. Three hundred years later the Spanish conquistadors destroyed more of the city in their search for gold. The destruction of Tiahuanaco continued at the end of the 19th century, when most of its remaining treasures were plundered; its fabulous buildings and massive statues were blasted away to provide building materials for the city of La Paz and a roadbed for its railroad. However, enough was recorded by Spanish chroniclers and by travelers from later times for us to be able to gain some impression of the former majesty of this great city and of the powerful and gifted people who built it.

Opposite: idol and altar at Copan, Honduras, drawn by British explorer Frederick Catherwood. In the 1840s Catherwood and American traveler John Stephens discovered relics of pre-Columbian American civilizations. Their discoveries caused a great stir. How, the world asked, could the peoples of America have built such elaborate edifices?

The Riddle of the White God

Tiahuanaco now stands about 15 miles from Lake Titicaca, but the level of the lake has dropped considerably over the centuries and its waters once lapped the very walls of the ancient city. Stairs led from the water up the side of a massive step pyramid, about 150 feet tall, topped by a huge temple. Palaces, temples, and other great buildings stood on the shores of the lake. One Spanish chronicler, Diego d'Alcobaca, reported seeing a paved court 80 feet square, with a covered hall 45 feet long running down one of its sides. The court and hall had been hewn from a single block of stone. "There are still many statues to be seen here today," wrote d'Alcobaca. "They represent men and women, and are so perfect one could believe the figures were alive." Another chronicler held that, "One of the palaces is truly an eighth wonder of the world. Stones 37 feet long by 15 feet wide have been prepared without the aid of lime or mortar, in such a way as to fit together without any joins showing." The Spanish discovered that the colossal stone blocks—some of them weighing as much as 200 tons—used in these buildings were held in place by silver rivets. (It was the removal of these rivets by Spanish mercenaries that caused many of Tiahuanaco's great buildings to collapse in subsequent earthquakes.) The blocks were brought from the volcanic Kiappa region, 40 miles from Tiahuanaco, and, as writer and explorer of South America Pierre Honoré comments in his book *In Quest of the White God*, "As with the pyramids in Egypt, thousands of men must have worked for hundreds of years to erect the enormous buildings of Tiahuanaco, slave labor forced to build on an ever larger, taller, more powerful scale."

The most impressive feature of Tiahuanaco that is still standing is the Gate of the Sun, which may have been the entrance to the city or to its main palace. Cut from a single block of stone, 10 feet high, 6 feet wide, and weighing over 10 tons, it is the largest carved monolith on earth. The gate is crowned by a deeply carved frieze of beautiful and intricate designs, including human figures, animals, birds, and symbols thought by some investigators to denote astronomical observations. Over the center of the gate is a stylized jaguar with human features, holding what may be symbols of thunder and lightning. The frieze was originally inlaid with gold, and the eyes of the figures were made of semiprecious stones. Some of the carvings have been left unfinished, as if something had suddenly interrupted the work of the artists.

According to Spanish chroniclers, the walls and niches of Tiahuanaco's palaces and temples were adorned with statues and ornaments of gold, copper, and bronze, and with stone and clay masks that hung from large-headed gold nails. The holes made by these nails can still be seen today, and some of the nails and other precious objects salvaged from the ruins of Tiahuanaco are on view in La Paz in the Posnansky Museum—named for Arthur Posnansky, a German engineer who tried to save Tiahuanaco from further destruction during the quarrying operations of the 19th century. Pieces in the museum and in private collections include six-foot-high statues covered all over with reliefs, gold figurines weighing between four and six pounds, gold animals and birds, and gold cups, plates, and spoons. These few remaining treasures testify to Tiahuanaco's former

Above: turquoise mosaic mask of Quetzalcoatl, the Aztec god of learning. Aztec legend described Quetzalcoatl as a fair-skinned god who had brought civilization to Mexico from across the sea. Similar White Gods also appear in mythologies of the Incas and the Mayas—the Incas called him Viracocha, the Mayas, Kukulcán. Many believe that these White Gods must be based on a common racial memory of fair-skinned visitors from other lands.

Left: stone figure from the ancient city of Tiahuanaco in what is now Bolivia. The city was discovered by the Incas in the 13th century A.D., later pillaged by the Spanish conquistadors, and largely destroyed in the 19th century to provide building stone. Even from what remains, however, its former splendor is evident. Tradition has it that this magnificent city was built for the worship of the White God Viracocha, and was once inhabited by the Incas. But exactly when it was constructed, and by whom, remains a mystery.

Left: the Gate of the Sun at Tiahuanaco. Once the entrance to a temple or a palace, perhaps, this gateway is surmounted by an intricately carved frieze depicting people, animals, birds, and enigmatic symbols or signs. When the city was at its prime, the frieze was inlaid with gold and semiprecious stones, but—like so many of the other valuable relics of American civilizations—these have long disappeared, plundered by greedy travelers.

Pre-Columbian Achievements

magnificence, and other groups of ruins, including step pyramids, in the highlands and on the coast of present-day Bolivia and Peru indicate the power and extent of the ancient Tiahuanacan civilization.

Tiahuanaco has puzzled archaeologists and historians ever since its discovery. Although our knowledge of the history and development of the civilization of South and Central America has increased enormously in recent years, and the experts have been able to answer some questions about the majestic city, the riddle of its age and of the people who built it is by no means solved.

When archaeologists and explorers of the 19th and early 20th century began rediscovering the magnificent stone citadels of once flourishing civilizations in Central and South America, the effect was electrifying. Most Europeans and North Americans, accustomed to regarding the Middle East as the cradle of civilization, found it hard to believe that the American Indians could possibly have developed such a high degree of cultural and technical achievement without outside help. In the 1840s, when the American traveler John Lloyd Stephens first uncovered the awesome vestiges of Mayan civilization deep in the Honduran jungle, he declared himself convinced that the local inhabitants

Below: Mayan temple at Tuloom in Central America, found by Stephens and Catherwood and drawn by Catherwood. In describing this temple the explorers mentioned that it was so overgrown with creepers and trees that they had found it purely by chance. It was due to the luxuriant growth of the Central and South American jungles that the relics of America's pre-Columbian civilizations remained hidden for so many years.

Left: huge stone head sculpted by the Olmecs, founders of the earliest known American civilization. To a world that had regarded the Middle East as the cradle of civilization, the discovery of a culturally advanced people in the Americas was an amazing one.

Below: 16th-century Peruvian gold statuette of a toucan. The Incas of Peru brought the art of working in gold to seldom equaled heights.

could not have built such structures. Whenever the remains of advanced civilizations were found in the Americas, they were attributed to the influence of Old World peoples such as the Egyptians, the Phoenicians, the Irish, or the Vikings—or to the Atlanteans. Atlantists were quick to seize on the discovery of American pre-Columbian civilizations as further evidence for the existence of a lost Atlantic continent. After all, Plato had mentioned another great continent that lay beyond Atlantis on the other side of the ocean, and had said that Atlantean influence extended to parts of that continent. Direct contact between the Old World and the New prior to the arrival of Columbus in 1492 must have been chancy and sporadic, if it occurred at all, the Atlantists argued, simply because of the vast expanses of ocean that lie between the two. But if the Atlanteans were even half as powerful as Plato had described them, a voyage from their Atlantic home to the Americas would have been easy, especially considering the chain of islands that were said to stretch across the ocean between Atlantis and the outer continent.

Olmecs and Mayas

Did the Atlanteans influence the civilizations of Central and South America? It is a possibility that has to be considered in any attempt to unravel the mysteries of the ancient ruins in this part of the world. If we reject the theory, we are still faced with the questions: Who built these fabulous cities? And how did they acquire the technical skills to do so?

In trying to answer these questions we have to take into account the theory of cultural diffusion. This is based on the belief that separate civilizations would not develop along similar lines without contact with each other. Where we find two or more cultures with the same or similar beliefs, customs, art forms, architecture, or technologies, we can assume, according to the theory, that the people concerned acquired their knowledge from each other, or from a common source. This was the corner-

Above: Olmec pottery statuette. No one knows where the Olmecs came from, but their civilization flourished around the Gulf of Mexico between about 1300 and 400 B.C.

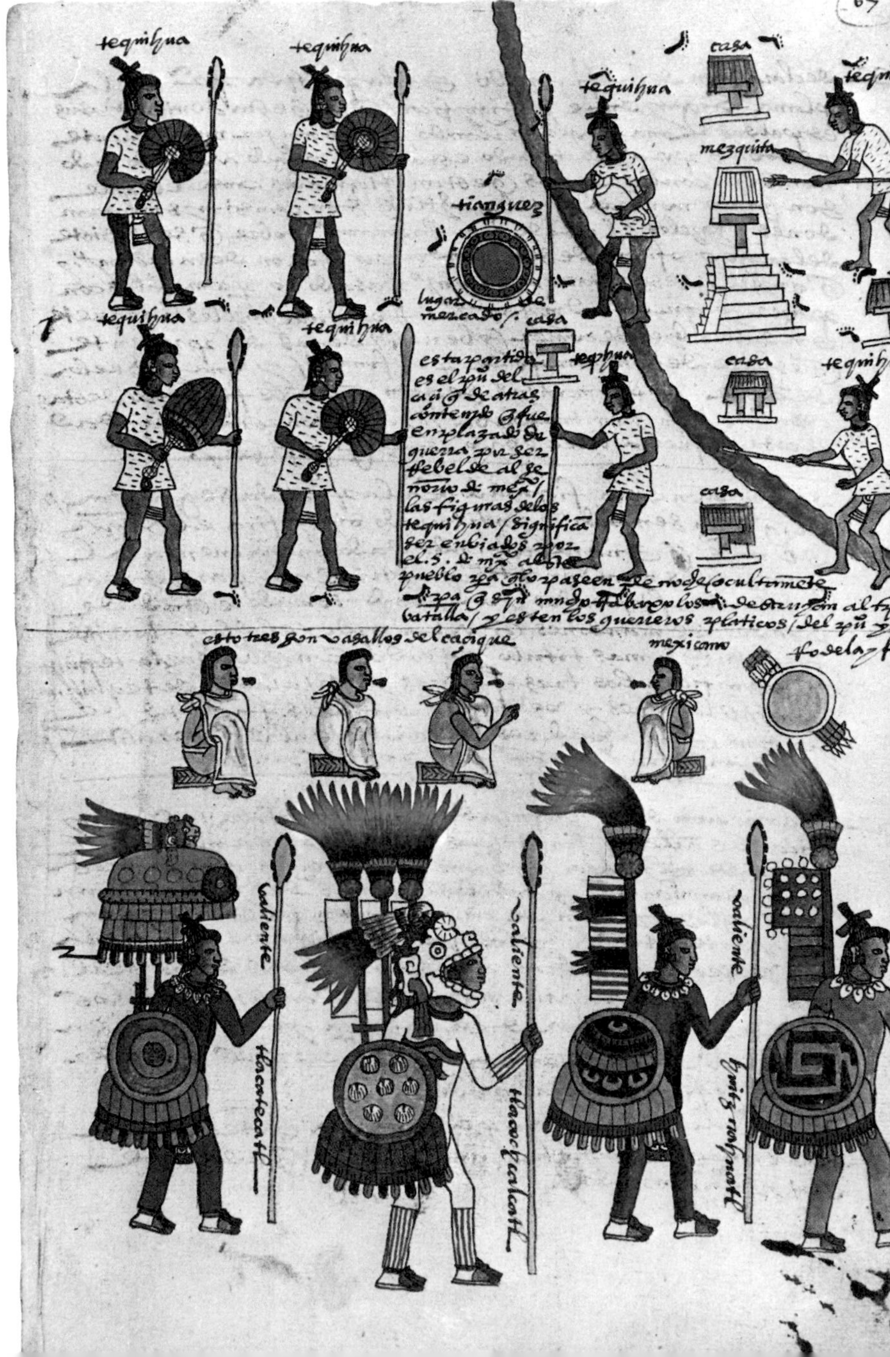

Right: an Aztec scouting expedition and punitive raid, from the *Codex Mendoza*. The Aztecs were a warlike and bloodthirsty people, who spread their rule over a large part of Central America between about A.D. 1350 and their conquest by the Spanish in 1521. The *Codex Mendoza* records the life and history of Mexico under Aztec rule. It was commissioned by the Spanish governor-general after the conquest of Mexico.

Left: Mayan relief of a woman ceremonially mutiliating her tongue. Mayan culture flourished in Central America for about 1000 years.

Above: the Emperor Atahualpa, ruler of the Incas when the Spanish conquistadors arrived in Peru. When his empire fell to the Spanish in 1537, Inca civilization had existed little more than 300 years; yet in that time Inca rule had spread across a vast area.

stone of Ignatius Donnelly's arguments about Atlantis, and although there are many diffusionists who do not believe in Atlantis, almost all latter-day Atlantists believe in diffusion because it fits their case so well. It is because of some remarkable cultural similarities that the civilizations of the Americas share among themselves and with those of the Old World that most believers in Atlantis look upon the now ruined citadels of Central and South America as outposts of the once great Atlantean culture.

Orthodox scholars challenge this view. Today many scholars believe that the pre-Columbian civilizations of the Americas were developed by the American Indians themselves, independent of any chance contact they may have had with the outside world. The only trouble from the scholars' point of view is that they have so far been unable to trace with any certainty the starting point of civilization in the Americas. No sooner do they uncover the origins of one civilization in this part of the world than another equally advanced civilization appears right behind it. This, of course, comes as no surprise to Atlantologists, who are convinced that a fully developed civilization was imported into the Americas in the first place.

Before examining this claim in detail, we need to take a look at what archaeologists know of the people in whose lands the mysterious citadels of the Americas have appeared. They are principally the Olmecs, the Mayas, the Incas, and the Aztecs. The Olmec civilization is the oldest so far known in the Americas, and was founded along the Gulf of Mexico in what are now the

Was Atlantis the Mid-Atlantic Link?

states of Veracruz and Tabasco. No one knows where the Olmecs came from, but their civilization is thought to have flourished from about 1300 B.C. to 400 B.C., and their colossal monuments and sculptures show them to have been gifted artists and engineers. They also possessed a written language, apparently resembling that of the Mayas, whose origins are equally mysterious. The Mayan culture arose in Guatemala some time between 400 and 100 B.C. and flourished there for 1000 years, during which the Mayas built over 100 city-states with magnificent temples, palaces, pyramids, and plazas. The Mayas called themselves "lords of the earth," and their influence quickly spread toward the north, west, and southwest, covering a large part of Central America. Then, between A.D. 700 and 1000, for reasons that are still unknown, they abandoned their homeland and its thriving cities and moved to the arid and inhospitable Yucatán. Their attempts to rebuild their empire were thwarted by invasions and internal strife, and the Mayan civilization gradually declined. By the time the Spaniards arrived in 1511 it possessed only a shadow of its former greatness.

The Aztecs of Mexico were relative latecomers on the American scene. Their civilization flourished from about 1350 until the Spanish conquest of 1521. They inherited much of their culture from their predecessors, but their own art and architecture was so splendid that the leader of the Spanish conquistadors declared their capital Tenochtitlán (now the site of Mexico City): "The most beautiful city in the world." While the Aztecs were building Tenochtitlán, the Incas of South America were establishing their considerable empire that stretched from the Columbia-Ecuador border to central Chile, taking in parts of present-day Peru, northern Argentina, Bolivia, Chile, and Ecuador. The Incas, who founded their capital of Cusco around A.D. 1200 and whose empire crumbled before the Spaniards in 1537, traced their ancestry back in legend to the builders of Tiahuanaco, which they regarded as the cradle of their civilization.

The history books, then, paint a picture of a whole series of rapidly developing American civilizations, far less ancient than those of the Old World, and archaeological examination of the ruins generally confirms this simplified view of the various peoples of the Americas. But some scholars disagree. Tiahuanaco, for example, has been the center of debate for decades because the experts cannot agree about when the city was built. At one time it was widely believed to date from around 1000 B.C. Today,

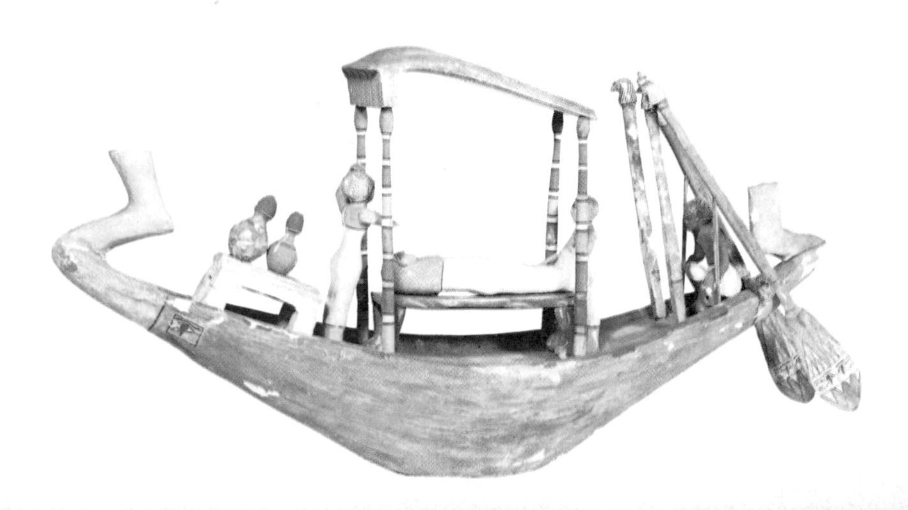

Right: model of a papyrus boat, found in an ancient Egyptian tomb.

Left: reed boats on the waters of Lake Titicaca in Bolivia. These vessels are similar to those of ancient Egypt in shape, materials, and construction. According to the theory of cultural diffusion, such similarity would be impossible unless the civilizations had had contact, or had acquired their knowledge from a common source. Atlantists believe this source to be the lost continent of Atlantis.

Below: Norwegian anthropologist Thor Heyerdahl's reed boat *Ra II*. In 1969 Heyerdahl attempted an Atlantic crossing in *Ra II* to prove that the ancient Egyptians could have brought civilization to the Americas. The expedition got within 600 miles of Central America, which confirmed the possibility of such a journey being concluded successfully.

the generally accepted view is that its impressive buildings were erected several centuries after the beginning of our era—estimates vary from about A.D. 100 to 800. Some scholars believe several cities were built on the same site. Arthur Posnansky, who made valiant efforts to preserve the ruins of Tiahuanaco, came to the conclusion that the last city was built 16,000 years ago. Other researchers claim that Tiahuanaco is a quarter of a million years old.

It has been suggested that Tiahuanaco was originally built at sea level and that the land on which it now stands and Lake Titicaca were thrust upward a distance of about two miles during a convulsion of the earth many thousands of years ago. This theory is based on the discovery of a "water mark" line on the surrounding mountains, which stretches for over 300 miles and consists of the calcified remains of marine plants, indicating that these slopes were once part of the seashore. Significantly Lake Titicaca has a very high salinity and oceanic fauna, as do other lakes in the area. This theory would certainly account for the presence of what appears to be a ruined seaport close to Tiahuanaco and might also explain why the city was abruptly abandoned by its builders and how it first fell into ruin.

According to some German and local archaeologists, Tiahuanaco was abandoned around 9000 or 10,000 B.C.—which conveniently coincides with the date given by Plato for the destruction of Atlantis. Atlantologists conclude that the catastrophe that caused Atlantis to sink into the ocean also pushed a large area of the west coast of South America some two miles above sea level. If this theory were proved correct and Tiahuanaco was built before the catastrophe, it would be over 11,000 years old.

Another curious feature of the area has not escaped the cultural diffusionists and the Atlantologists. The boats that sail on the salty waters of Lake Titicaca are identical with the papyrus boats of ancient Egypt. Their shape, the material used, and the method of construction are the same. Coincidence? Evidence of direct contact between ancient Egypt and the New World? Or one more clue that a long-lost civilization once influenced great areas of the globe?

South America is probably one of the last places on earth to be keeping its secrets from us. Many lost cities have been found in the dense, almost impenetrable jungle since the turn of the century, and no one can guess how many more, filled with treasures and works of art, are hidden beneath the thick and tangled canopy of tropical vegetation. It is an area that cannot easily be mapped from the air, and explorers enter this "Green Hell" at their peril.

Among the adventurers who have dared to risk death in their search for ancient ruins, the name of Colonel Percy H. Fawcett is particularly remembered because of the mystery surrounding the fate of his final expedition to South America. Fawcett was convinced that the ruins of Atlantis or some of its daughter cities lay beneath the jungles of Brazil, and in the 1920s, after 20 years in the British Army as a military surveyor, geographer, and engineer, he turned to exploration. He went on several expeditions to Brazil, during which he traveled extensively through

Below: Percy Harrison Fawcett, leader of one of the most famous expeditions ever to set out in search of a lost land. While traveling in South America, Fawcett came into possession of a map showing the location of a lost city that he called "X." In 1925 Fawcett set out in search of X with his son Jack and a friend, but no member of their party was ever seen again.

uncharted country populated by hostile tribes. Fawcett was an acknowledged expert on the area and how to survive its hazards.

During these explorations a map came into his possession. It was said to have been 150 years old and to have been drawn by a man who had found a lost city deep in the Mato Grosso region of southwest Brazil. The city was said to be surrounded by a wall and to stand in acres of cultivated land. In 1925, accompanied by his 20-year-old son Jack and a young friend named Raleigh Rimmel, Fawcett set off in search of this city, which he was sure would prove to have links with Atlantis. Before his departure, he declared: "Whether we succeed in penetrating the jungle and come out alive, or whether we leave our bones there, of this I am certain: the key to the mystery of ancient South America, and perhaps of the whole of prehistory, can be found if we are able to locate these old cities . . . and open them up to science. Their existence I do not for a moment doubt—how could I? I myself have seen a portion of one, and that is the reason why I observed it was imperative for me to go again. The remains seemed to be those of an outpost of one of the largest cities, which I am convinced is to be found together with others, if a properly organized search is carried out. Unfortunately I cannot induce scientific men to accept even the supposition that there are traces of an old civilization in Brazil. But I have traveled through regions unknown to other explorers and the wild Indians have told me time and again of the buildings, the characteristics of their old inhabitants, and the strange things to be found there."

The Search for the Lost Land

Below: Jack Fawcett and Raleigh Rimmel at Dead Horse Camp during the expedition in search of X. The last message ever to be received from the party came from Dead Horse Camp—in it, Fawcett wrote that he had heard of another ruined city beside a large lake. The world waited in suspense to hear whether or not Fawcett had found the city, but there was never any further news of their party.

Did Fawcett Communicate?

With those words, Fawcett and his two companions left for their last great adventure. Their final message came from Dead Horse Camp in the Xingú Basin, where they reported hearing of yet another ruined city on the edge of a large lake. Then they disappeared into the jungle, never to be seen again. The chances are that they were captured and killed by hostile Indians or that they all died from fever. But as the world waited for news of the Fawcett expedition, other theories were advanced. Some believed that the party had found the lost city but, for reasons best known to themselves, had decided not to return to England. Others suggested that the Indians had taken the explorers to the lost city but had either killed them or held them prisoner afterward so that no one else would come looking for the secret. Mediums tried to contact Fawcett in the next world, but their psychic explorations shed little light on the true outcome of his expedition.

Nevertheless, one alleged spirit communication does stand head and shoulders above the others. This purports to be a long communication from Fawcett, dictated over a number of years through the hand of a woman who was to become one of the world's most famous automatic writing mediums.

Geraldine Cummins, a young Irish writer, was already a well-known medium when her friend, E. Beatrice Gibbes, asked her to try communicating with the lost explorer. Miss Cummins would go into a light trance during which her hand would be allegedly controlled by spirit people who would write messages. It was 10

Above: these bones were found in a shallow grave in the jungle in 1951, 26 years after Fawcett's disappearance. Exhibited in Rio de Janeiro as Fawcett's, they were later proved not to be his.
Right: the jungle grave in which the unidentified bones were found in 1951. This photograph was taken by Brian Fawcett.

years after Fawcett had disappeared when the two women first attempted to establish contact with him. They apparently succeeded, but Fawcett told them he was not dead. He was in a semi-conscious state, still in the South American jungle, but his spirit was able to communicate. Four communications were made in 1936, after which they were abandoned for 12 years. When Fawcett again communicated, in 1948, he said he had died.

It would be easy to dismiss these messages as utter nonsense if it were not for the fact that Geraldine Cummins was a very talented psychic widely respected in psychical research. She submitted to numerous tests during her long lifetime, and was apparently able to receive communications of incredible detail and accuracy from people about whom she knew nothing. Researchers are still debating whether in the best of these cases Geraldine Cummins was really in touch with the dead person, or whether she was using clairvoyance to discover information that she could not know normally. There is no doubt, however, that she did possess remarkable paranormal powers. So, even if she was not in touch with Fawcett, the possibility exists that she did have supernormal access to facts about the fate and findings of his expedition.

The communicator claiming to be Fawcett wrote that he had seen pyramids in the jungle. He had apparently been given drugs that enabled him, when in the vicinity of a certain pyramid, to travel back in time. The forest would become transparent and another landscape would appear before his eyes, superimposed on the jungle. He could then see the pyramids as they had been in the distant past and the people who lived at that time. He described the pyramids as Egyptian in appearance.

"You must accept my assurance that the last relics of an ancient civilization, Egyptian in character, are to be found in central South America," he wrote. "With my living eyes I have seen these ruins. . . . I believe that, if the climate were not so oppressive and we could bring gangs of men here, excavating under skilled direction, a whole ancient civilization would be revealed—the secret of the Lost Continent would be divulged; a flood of light thrown on a period that is prehistoric, and our origins more clearly realized."

The communicator said that sun worship was the basic principle of this civilization, and he added: "The Atlanteans knew more or less the nature of electricity, which is dependent on the sun yet is allied to other air forces. Of course, there is more than one kind of electricity. The kind that is known to men was discovered by these Atlanteans, but they used their kind of electricity in a different way from us. They realized that it might be used, not merely to give light—queer globular lights—but that it might also be employed in connection with the shifting of weights. The building of the pyramids is solved when you know that huge blocks of stone can be manipulated through what I might call blast-electricity. . . . You will think me mad . . . but I, who have seen this ancient world, walked through its streets, halted before the porticoes of its temples, descended into the great subterranean world wherein electricity and air are combined and fused, can assure you that the men who came before modern history was recorded knew more about matter and light, about

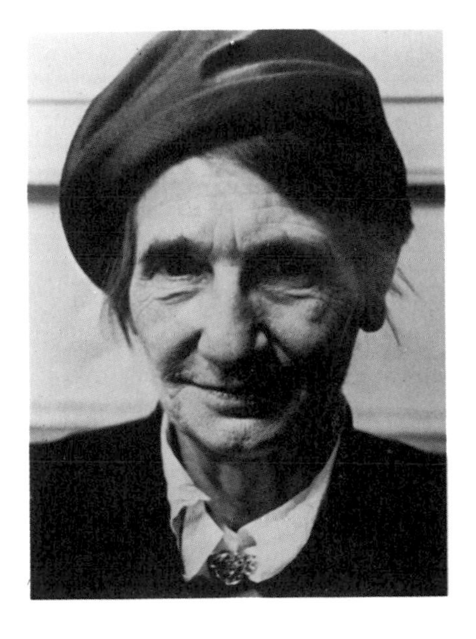

Above: medium Geraldine Cummins apparently communicated with Fawcett's spirit often in the mid-1930s. Messages she received described a strange civilization Fawcett told her he had found in the jungle, which he seems to have believed to be Atlantis. In 1948 Fawcett finally told Cummins that he was dead.

Right: the Temple of the Inscriptions in Palenque, Mexico, on its 65-foot-high stepped pyramid.

Left: the Funerary Crypt in the Temple of the Inscriptions. Beneath the relief-carved stone slab lay a large sarcophagus containing a man's skeleton and a quantity of treasure. Until the discovery of this crypt in 1952, it was believed that although the pyramid as an architectural form was common to the Old and the New World, the functions of Old and New World pyramids differed. The former were principally tombs, the latter used mainly as temples. When the crypt in the Temple of the Inscriptions was uncovered, a similarity of purpose was also revealed.

the ether and its properties, than the scientists of the 20th century can ever know or imagine."

The scripts went on to claim that it was not natural forces but massive explosions in these subterranean electricity reservoirs that destroyed Atlantis. Do these writings give us a fantastic glimpse of Atlantis, or are they simply the outpourings of a highly imaginative brain? It is not a question we can answer with certainty. There is undoubtedly a widespread belief that ancient peoples were able to move great weights by unknown means, though scholars have come back with quite mundane solutions to such problems. The ancient Egyptian pyramids have often been cited in this connection despite the experts' assurances that thousands of labourers *were* capable of moving and assembling the huge blocks used in their construction.

In the Americas, too, we find immense buildings made of huge blocks of stone, often greater than those of the Egyptian pyramids. Time and again we learn that the stones were cut with such precision that the joins between them were scarcely detectable, and required no mortar. Yet the people who designed and built these architectural masterpieces possessed neither iron nor steel. Nor was bronze in general use, for either tools or weapons. Many temples, and even cities, were built high in the mountains, where the problems of terrain and altitude made their construction even more difficult.

Of all these cyclopean structures, the one that raises the biggest question mark over the Americas is undoubtedly the pyramid. Understandably, the sight of these impressive monuments calls to mind the Egyptians. Is it possible that two quite separate civilizations, living at different times, evolved the same structure and the technique to build it?

L. Sprague de Camp can be relied on to throw cold water on any Atlantis or other diffusionist theory not backed by scientific evidence. "Mayan architecture, like that of Egypt three or four thousand years earlier, began by developing stone structures in imitation of the existing wooden houses . . ." he writes in *Lost Continents*. "Their structures included astronomical observatories, ball-courts in which they played a kind of cross between basket-ball and soccer, dance-platforms, vapor-baths, shrines, reviewing-stands, stadiums, city walls, causeways, and pyramids, comparable in bulk, though not in height, with those of Egypt. However, the pyramids of the Mayas and Aztecs have nothing to do with those of Egypt, which were built several thousands of years earlier and moreover evolved from tombs, while the New World pyramids evolved from temple platforms."

But for once, de Camp cannot have the last word. Despite his assertion that Egyptian and American pyramids differ in that the former evolved from tombs and the latter from temples, some New World pyramids were used for burial in a similar way to those in Egypt. And that, say the Atlantologists, is stretching coincidence too far.

Palenque, Link With the Pyramids

It was in 1952, when Professor Alberto Ruz Lhullier was investigating the Mayan ruins near Palenque in southeast Mexico, that the burial aspect of American pyramids was confirmed. Among the ruins in Palenque is an impressive step pyramid known as the Temple of the Inscriptions. Inside this pyramid, Lhullier found a passage blocked with rubble. When this was removed and the professor had reached what he took to be the base of the pyramid, he discovered a heavy stone door. Behind it lay a chamber, 12 feet by 7 feet, whose floor consisted of a slab decorated with reliefs. Using an elaborate system of ropes and pulleys, Lhullier and his team finally managed to lift the 12-cwt slab. Beneath it they found a large, red stone sarcophagus containing the skeleton of a man, and a quantity of jade treasure, including a death mask placed over the man's skull. The walls of the tomb were covered with stucco relief figures of men in archaic costume—possibly ancestors of the Mayans who built the city near Palenque.

Above: this jade mosaic funerary mask covered the face of the man whose skeleton was found in the Funerary Crypt of the Temple of the Inscriptions in Palenque. The eyes were made of shell and obsidian, and the whole was fastened to a wooden backing that had rotted away before the tomb was found.

Commenting on this remarkable find, Michael Coe, Professor of Anthropology at Yale University, writes in his book *The Maya*: "It is immediately evident that this great man, certainly a late seventh- or early eighth-century ruler of Palenque, had the Funerary Crypt built to contain his own remains; further, that he might have had the entire temple pyramid above it raised in his own lifetime. Thus it seems that the Temple of the Inscriptions was a funerary monument with exactly the same primary function as the Egyptian pyramids. And this, of course, leads one to look upon most Maya temple pyramids as sepulchral monuments, dedicated to the worship of deceased kings."

A similar find was made as early as 1896 by Edward H. Thompson, the U.S. Consul in Yucatán and one of the early explorers of the great Mayan city of Chichén Itzá. Among the ruins of Chichén Itzá Thompson discovered a small pyramid containing the bones of seven human skeletons, and a cave housing a tomb.

The Egyptian connection does not end there. One of the most brilliant sites of American civilization, built by a people who apparently had close ties with the Mayas, is a city known by its Aztec name of Teotihuacán. It is an extraordinary place near Mexico City, consisting of a vast complex of ruins that were already overgrown when the Spaniards reached America. It is dominated by pyramids, one dedicated to the sun and another to the moon. The base of the sun pyramid measures 740 feet by 725 feet—exactly the same as the base of the Cheops pyramid in Egypt. The height of the Mexican structure is 215 feet, half that

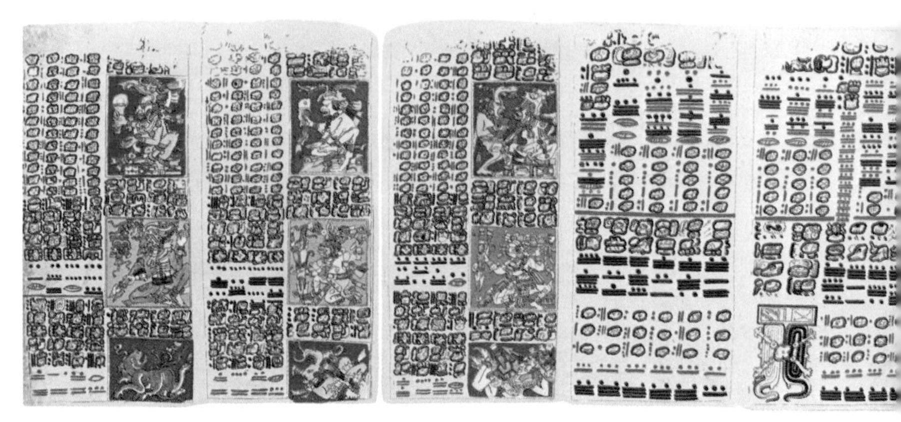

Above: the "Calendar Stone" from the Aztec capital Tenochtitlán, carved with symbols of the days, months, and suns. The Aztecs based their calendar on that of the Mayas.

Above right: a page from the *Dresden Codex*, one of only three Mayan books that have survived to the present day. Although Mayan writing is still largely undeciphered —principally because so few examples exist—it is known that this page contains astronomical calculations on the planet Venus. In the opinion of some experts, Mayan astronomy was far in advance of that of the Greeks and Romans; the accuracy and range of Mayan knowledge still astounds scholars.

of the Egyptian one. Again we have to ask if this is just a strange coincidence or does it have tremendous significance?

Teotihuacán was a city of 100,000 people. Its streets and houses were laid out to a precise grid plan, and the homes of the wealthy were decorated with paintings and frescoes. The city's major buildings were constructed sometime between A.D. 100 and 300, and Teotihuacán was sacked and burned in A.D. 856 by the Toltecs—contemporaries of the Mayas who later overran much of the Mayan empire in Yucatán.

In the Mayan city of Tikal in Guatemala the pyramids are of a height and steepness that astonished the early explorers. One rises to 230 feet, making it the highest known building in the Americas before the construction of New York's first skyscrapers. And in nearby Uaxactún, the oldest Mayan city yet excavated, archaeologists discovered a feature unique in the world: a pyramid within a pyramid.

The Mayas erected *stelae*—carved stone columns—bearing inscriptions that recorded important events. At Tikal a series of stelae was raised to mark the passage of each 20 years between A.D. 629 and 790. On each was the date, the age of the moon, and symbols of the gods ruling at the time. Stelae are not unique to the Mayas. They are an Asian device that the Egyptians, Greeks, and Romans also used.

One of the greatest puzzles about the past is how so many ancient peoples, without our modern technical aids, were able to transport massive building stones over great distances, fashion them precisely, and erect them with such ability that they have stood for thousands of years. The island of Malta in the Mediterranean, for example, is rich in megalithic remains. The primitive men who erected Malta's giant monuments also dug large underground tunnel networks and subterranean chambers. We do not know who these people were or why they carried out this work. Stonehenge is perhaps the most famous example of Stone Age skill that is beyond our comprehension. This ancient circle of stones in southern England, built about 1800 B.C., attracts a quarter of a million visitors a year. "We today can name no man or tribe who had all these qualifications [to erect the stones] at any time in the period of British prehistory," says the official guide to Stonehenge. A recent theory suggests that a party of Egyptians was responsible for its construction because a basic measurement used by its builders was also used by the Egyptians.

More Proof From the Pyramids?

It is widely believed that the builders of Stonehenge, whoever they were, possessed a considerable knowledge of astronomy. We find a similar knowledge among the peoples of Central America.

In the opinion of French historian Raymond Cartier, "In many fields of knowledge the Mayas outclassed the Greeks and Romans. They were expert astronomers and mathematicians, and thus brought to perfection the science of chronology. They built domed observatories with a more exact orientation than those of 17th-century Paris, e.g. the Caracol erected on three terraces in Chichén Itzá. They had a precise calendar based on a 'sacred year' of 260 days, a solar year of 365 days, and a Venusian year of 584 days. The exact length of the solar year has been fixed, after long calculation, at 365·2422 days; the Mayas estimated it at 365·2420 days, i.e. correct to three places of decimals."

The Mayas showed astonishing mathematical skill. While the Romans were still using a cumbersome method of counting, the Mayas invented a system of numbering that has all the features of modern arithmetic. Yet they used only three symbols: a bar for the number five, dots for each unit up to four, and a stylized shell for zero. Above all, the Mayas developed a form of picture-writing, based on a similar system to that used in Egyptian hieroglyphs. Because Diego de Landa, a Spanish monk who became Bishop of Yucatán, burned all the Mayan literature he could lay his hands on, only three Mayan books remain for study, and Mayan writing is still largely undeciphered.

While acknowledging the remarkable achievements of the early American civilizations and their striking similarities to Old World cultures, it is only fair that we also consider the feat-

Below: the Pyramid of the Sun at Teotihuacán near Mexico City. In the early centuries of the Christian era, Teotihuacán was a magnificent metropolis covering an area of more than eight square miles, and ruling an empire including most of what is now Mexico. When European explorers first investigated the city, they discovered that the base of the pyramid is exactly the same size as that of the Pyramid of Cheops in Egypt—740 by 725 feet—and that it is exactly half as tall. Could this simply be an amazing coincidence, or is it further proof that there were links between the Old and New Worlds thousands of years ago?

The Return of the White God

ures they did *not* share with Old World civilizations. They had no plow, very few metal tools, no Old World diseases, no Old World domestic animals, and no wheels—except on toys. Indeed it is one of the great mysteries of the American cultures that they never extended the use of wheels from toys to full-size vehicles. Atlantologists and other diffusionists make much of the supposed resemblances between Mayan and ancient Egyptian writing, but although the two scripts are based on similar principles, the signs and language are completely different. Those who argue that the early American civilizations developed under the influence of a greater people, such as the Atlanteans or the Egyptians, must explain all these anomalies.

Probably the most important objection to the theory that Atlantean refugees founded the cultures of the Americas is the enormous time lag between the date given by Plato for the destruction of Atlantis and the emergence of the civilizations of the Olmecs and Mayas, let alone those of the Aztecs and Incas. Either we must believe, like Lewis Spence and others, that the Atlanteans escaped to another continent and only moved on to the Americas at a much later stage, or we must accept that these cultures were the echo of others equally great that date back many thousands of years—as some investigators of Tiahuanaco maintain. Atlantologists point out that the peoples of the Americas seem to have been content to reproduce the same patterns of art and architecture over and over again, as if they were copying models provided by others, and that they do not seem to have progressed from an advanced starting point. However, orthodox scholars contest the view that the civilizations of the Americas sprang up suddenly, and are convinced that these cultures evolved, albeit rapidly, from more primitive beginnings. Certainly the claim by some Atlantologists that the Mayas derived their peaceful nature from the Atlanteans does not stand up to close examination. The Mayas may not have been as bloodthirsty as the later Aztecs, but they were undoubtedly warlike and they indulged in human sacrifice.

On the other hand we cannot ignore the persistent legends of the ancient American peoples that tell of visits from fair-skinned "gods" with beards who came from across the sea in the mists of prehistory, bringing the Indians the arts of civilization. This tradition was common to the Mayas, Aztecs, Incas, and other culturally advanced peoples of pre-Columbian America, though each culture called the White God by a different name. To the Mayas he was Kukulcán; the Toltecs and Aztecs knew him as Quetzalcoatl; and the Incas called him Viracocha.

The discovery of artifacts depicting men with beards and narrow, beaked noses, who look quite un-Indian, appears to some investigators to back up the legends and to provide further evidence that another people influenced American culture. The famous Norwegian anthropologist and diffusionist Thor Heyerdahl is reportedly convinced that "a people, or more exactly a group of men, with fair skin, aquiline noses, and bushy beards exercised a decisive influence on the development of the American civilizations and in particular on those that flourished in the Andes, in ancient Peru."

The legends of the White God were the undoing of these great

Below: Aztec greenstone mask of Quetzalcoatl. Aztec effigies of the White God range from those whose features look typically Indian such as this, to representations of those who appear to be a completely different race. Were they drawn from the artist's imagination or were they based on fact? Were the Americas once visited by travelers from the east?

civilizations, for they welcomed the fair-skinned Spanish conquistadors as gods, and their kingdoms crumbled.

Dr. Michael Coe, a leading expert on Olmec civilization, believes that the earliest site of the Olmecs is in San Lorenzo, Mexico. Radiocarbon dating of samples from San Lorenzo indicates that the monuments at this site were constructed no later than 900 or 800 B.C., and perhaps considerably earlier. "We have, therefore, found the oldest civilized communities thus far known in Mesoamerica," says Dr. Coe. "Nonetheless, by pushing back the earliest Olmec civilization to such an early date—to a time when there was little else but simple village cultures in the rest of Mexico and Central America—the lack of antecedents is an embarrassing problem. We now have no idea where the Olmec came from or who built the mounds and carved the sculptures of San Lorenzo. Whoever they were, these pioneers must have been unusually gifted in engineering as well as art. . . ."

So, despite attempts to make the civilizations of ancient America appear normal, if remarkable, it seems that there is a mystery that remains unsolved. Perhaps the South American jungles will provide more ruins and more clues. Or perhaps Atlantis will be found, and give us the answers. Unless, of course, the answer lies not in the Atlantic but in the Pacific, in the shape of yet another lost continent.

Below: envoys from Aztec emperor Montezuma presenting gifts to the Spanish conquistador Hernando Cortés. Aztec mythology told how the White God Quetzalcoatl had left Mexico, promising one day to return. When the fair-skinned Spaniards reached the Aztec Empire, they were at first mistaken for the returning god, and welcomed by the Aztecs.

Chapter 10
A Lost World in the Pacific

When Dutch explorers stumbled upon strange giant monuments on a tiny island in the South Pacific, they were understandably bewildered. The islanders could tell them nothing about them. Who carved them and set them up? Why were they erected? What happened to the lost civilization that created these mysterious monoliths? Easter Island remains one of the greatest enigmas in the world. The added complication of a picture-writing nobody has satisfactorily decoded has made Easter Island the focus of all kinds of amazing theories. This chapter tries to put these theories in some kind of perspective.

In the evening twilight of Easter Sunday 1722, a Dutch fleet chanced upon a tiny island in the South Pacific—and launched a controversy that has lasted ever since. Admiral Jaakob Roggeveen and his men reached the island too late in the day to explore. They dropped anchor and waited until dawn next day before moving closer to the shore to look for signs of life. At first light they saw a series of small fires on the shore. Then, as the sun climbed slowly above the horizon, an astonishing sight met their eyes. All along the shore, people of different skin colors were apparently worshiping in front of colossal statues.

Roggeveen named the island Paasch Eyland, or Easter Island, because of the day on which his fleet had first sighted it. He and his men spent only a few hours there, but they did take a closer look at the enormous statues. These proved to be huge elongated heads, all very similar and of varying heights. Roggeveen was able to break a piece from one of the statues with his bare fingers and the Dutch explorers concluded it was made from clay and soil mixed with pebbles. In fact, the statues were made from solid rock that had deteriorated with age and erosion. This was discovered by a Spanish expedition under Felipe Gonzalez, which reached the island in 1770. The Spaniards hit the statues with pickaxes, causing sparks to fly.

If the Easter Island statues had been molded, as the Dutch explorers believed, there would have been no mystery. But with the realization that the statues had been hewn from rock a

Opposite: monumental stone heads brood over the slopes of the extinct volcano Rano Raraku on Easter Island in the Pacific. Similar monoliths line the island's coast and appear to have marked its roads. The people who inhabited Easter Island when European explorers first arrived there could tell their visitors nothing about the construction of the statues. Who sculpted them, and why they were erected, remains one of the greatest mysteries in the world.

problem arose. How did the inhabitants of this tiny island develop the skill to sculpt the statues and, more important, how did they transport the huge heads and erect them on an island devoid of trees and ropes large enough for the purpose? Later European explorers discovered that, although the Easter Islanders held the statues in awe, they seemed to know nothing about their construction. And as time went by, a new enigma emerged. The Easter Islanders possessed a number of engraved wooden boards, known as *rongorongo* boards or "singing tablets," that appeared to be inscribed with a form of picture-writing. Yet none of the islanders could read the boards with any exactness, and they remain undeciphered. Where did this writing come from? Was it invented by the statue-builders? Is it really writing at all? These and other questions about the perplexing Easter Island civilization have exercised the minds of scholars for 200 years.

Easter Island is dominated by three extinct volcanoes, Rano Raraku, Rano Kao, and Rano Aroi. It is only 13 miles long and 7 miles across at its widest points, and it rises out of the South Pacific in splendid isolation. Its nearest inhabited neighbor is Pitcairn Island—refuge of the *Bounty* mutineers—1200 miles to the west. In the opposite direction, 2300 miles of open ocean lie between Easter Island and the coast of northern Chile.

Below: French explorer Jean de la Pérouse's expedition visits Easter Island in the 1780s. At that time the statues were still surmounted by red stone topknots that have since fallen off. The statues baffled all the early explorers, who could not understand how a people with few mechanical skills had been able to sculpt and erect these huge heads.

Civilization of the Distant Past

Yet a people settled on this barren stretch of land, with its boulder-strewn landscape and porous soil. There are no fresh-water rivers or streams and the strong, salt-laden winds prevent the growth of tall plants or trees. There was no animal life to hunt, and life for the early settlers must have been arduous in the extreme. But they multiplied, and apparently developed (or had brought with them) a form of writing. They built roads, temples, and a solar observatory, and carved some 600 massive stone heads with elongated ears. Many of these statues were set up along the coast of the island. Some were erected on the slopes of Rano Raraku, and others appear to have marked the island's roads. The largest of the coastal statues is 33 feet high and weighs 80 tons. It was once surmounted by a 12-ton cylindrical topknot, carved from red stone and measuring six feet high by eight feet wide.

It is hardly surprising, then, that Easter Island has figured prominently in numerous theories about the earth's early civilizations and their origins, particularly as the island's inhabitants at the time of its discovery—who bore no resemblance to the stone colossi—seemed as mystified by the statues as the visitors. Nearly 200 stone heads, including one 66 feet high, are still in the quarry, suddenly abandoned during production, adding one more intriguing element to the enigma.

In the absence of any immediate acceptable solution to the Easter Island problem, scholars and visionaries have been free to give their imagination full rein in an attempt to find the answer. Many have speculated that the island is either part of a sunken Pacific continent, or an outpost of such a lost land. Inevitably, because the Americas sit between the Atlantic and Pacific oceans, much of the "evidence" for a lost Atlantic continent that influenced the cultures of ancient America has been offered in support of a vanished Pacific civilization, also supposed to have carried its arts and skills to the American Indians.

In 1864 a French scholar, the Abbé Charles-Étienne Brasseur

Left: part of a cast of an Easter Island rongorongo board, inscribed with what appears to be picture writing. Early explorers found that the Easter Islanders could not read the boards. Like the stone heads, they seem to be relics of a civilization of the distant past.

Below: Mayan alphabet, set down by Diego de Landa, 16th-century Spanish Bishop of Yucatán. The Abbé Charles-Etienne Brasseur, a French scholar, used de Landa's alphabet to translate the Mayan *Troano Codex*. His translation told of a land called Mu that had sunk beneath the sea. Other theorists compared de Landa's alphabet with Cretan Linear A script to prove a connection between Mu and Crete.

MAYAGLYPHS DELANDA'S ALPHABET			CRETAN SCRIPT LINEAR A		
Ca					
U					
E					
H					
T					=ta
C					
X „sch"					
U					
Z					
A					
A					
PP		p glottal		=Po	B =PA
O					
N					
B					

de Bourbourg, came across an abridged copy of a treatise on the Mayan civilization in the library of the Historical Academy of Madrid. This treatise, entitled *Account of the Affairs of Yucatán*, had been written by Diego de Landa, the Spanish Bishop of Yucatán, who destroyed all but three books of the Mayans' extensive literature and substituted Christian teachings. After this appalling act of vandalism de Landa became interested in the Mayan culture and tried to learn Mayan writing—a complicated system combining ideographic signs and phonetic elements to produce word-glyphs. As a result he compiled a "Mayan alphabet" and included it in his treatise.

The discovery of this alphabet excited Brasseur. He already had a considerable interest in the civilizations of the New World, and he believed he could use de Landa's alphabet to decipher the three surviving Mayan books. Armed with the alphabet and aided by a lively imagination, he immediately set about translating one of the books, the *Troano Codex*—half of the two-part *Tro-Cortesianus Codex* preserved in Madrid. Soon he revealed that the book told of a volcanic catastrophe and of a land that sank beneath the waves. But there were two symbols in the Mayan manuscript that Brasseur was unable to account for. They bore a very faint resemblance to de Landa's "M" and "U," so he put them together and produced Mu—the name he gave to the submerged land.

Naturally, Brasseur's discovery of the de Landa alphabet caused excitement among historians and scholars, but this quickly turned to disappointment when attempts to translate other Mayan writing with this "key" produced incoherent nonsense. To this day only about one third of the Mayan glyphs are understood, but enough is now known about the language to assert that the *Troano Codex* deals with astrology and not with the destruction of Mu. The other two books—the *Dresden Codex* and the *Codex Perezianus*, preserved in Dresden and Paris respectively—appear to concern astronomy and religious ritual. Although de Landa's alphabet has been shown to be based on erroneous principles, and Brasseur's translation has been discredited, the story of Mu has survived and grown, as others have sought to prove the existence of a lost continent, using the same tools. Whereas Brasseur believed Mu to be the name once used for Atlantis, others have adopted it for a South Pacific continent.

Brasseur's contemporary and fellow countryman Augustus Le Plongeon, a physician and archaeologist of some repute, was the first man to excavate Mayan ruins in Yucatán, where he and his American wife Alice lived for many years. Le Plongeon, a resplendent figure with a waist-length beard, attempted his own translation of the *Troano Codex*, drawing a good deal of his inspiration from the work of Brasseur and from a liberal interpretation of pictures found on the walls of ruins in the Mayan city of Chichén-Itzá. Le Plongeon's "translation" retraced the story of the sunken continent of Mu with an extravagance that made Brasseur's account pale in comparison. At the heart of his account is the rivalry of two Muvian princes, Coh and Aac, for the hand of their sister Moo, the Queen of Mu. Prince Coh won, but was killed by his jealous brother who immediately took over the country from Queen Moo

At the height of this drama, the continent began to sink. Moo fled to Egypt, where she built the Sphinx as a memorial to Prince Coh, and, under the name of Isis, founded the Egyptian civilization. Other Muvians escaped from their sinking homeland to Yucatán, where they recorded their history and erected temples to their leaders. Le Plongeon claimed that Egyptian hieroglyphs and Mayan writings were alike—a belief not shared by the specialists in these languages—and even maintained that Jesus spoke Mayan on the Cross.

In the 1880s Augustus and Alice Le Plongeon settled down in Brooklyn to write several books on their experiences and discoveries. The best-known of these was Le Plongeon's *Queen Moo and the Egyptian Sphinx*—published in 1896 and still in print—which included the author's claim to have found the charred entrails of Prince Coh, preserved in a stone urn, during his excavations of Mayan ruins.

Le Plongeon's "translation" of the *Troano Codex* was far more readable—if no more reliable—than Brasseur's. Here is the part of Le Plongeon's version that deals with the destruction of Mu: "In the year 6 Kan, on the 11th Muluc in the month Zac, there occurred terrible earthquakes, which continued without interruption until the 13th Chuen. The country of the hills of mud, the land of Mu was sacrificed; being twice upheaved it suddenly disappeared during the night, the basin being continually shaken by the volcanic forces. Being confined, these caused the land to sink and to rise several times in various

The Enigmatic Mayan Alphabet

Below: section from the Mayan *Troano Codex*, which is preserved in Madrid. It is now known that the *Troano Codex* is concerned with astrology, but in Brasseur's version it appears to suggest the existence of a lost civilization. His translation includes elements of the Atlantis legend such as volcanic catastrophe and the disappearance of the civilization under the sea.

The Mu Mystery

places. At last the surface gave way and ten countries were torn asunder and scattered. Unable to stand the force of the convulsion, they sank with their 64,000,000 inhabitants 8060 years before the writing of this book."

According to the Frenchman, he found records in Yucatán stating that "the Hieratic head [high priest] of the land of Mu prophesied its destruction, and that some, heeding the prophecy, left and went to the colonies where they were saved."

Like Brasseur, Le Plongeon believed that Mu and Atlantis were one and the same land. Basing his argument on his interpretations of Mayan wall paintings and inscriptions, he placed the sunken continent in the region of the Gulf of Mexico and the Caribbean Sea, to the east of Central America.

At about the same time, another Frenchman, Louis Jacolliot, was also writing about a lost continent. He had a new name for it, Rutas, and a new source, a collection of Sanskrit myths collected during a stay in India. According to Jacolliot, these myths told of a land named Rutas that sank in the Indian Ocean. But he interpreted them as referring to a Pacific landmass that formerly covered the region now occupied by the Polynesian islands. Plato's Atlantis story, he argued, was merely an echo of this tremendous event, and the sinking of Rutas caused India and other lands to rise from the sea.

From the 1880s onward, support for the existence of a lost Pacific continent began to appear with surprising frequency, and from sources that were even more surprising. A New York dentist, Dr. John Ballou Newbrough, claimed angelic inspiration for his account of a vanished land called Pan. Newbrough, a spiritualist medium, published the story of Pan in *Oahspe*, a book allegedly produced by automatic writing (hand writing said to occur without the individual's conscious control). The book was subtitled *A Kosmon Bible in the Words of Jehovah and his Angel Ambassadors*. It was first published in 1882, and has since been largely ridiculed for its misinformation and unfulfilled prophecies.

According to *Oahspe*, man appeared on earth 72,000 years ago as a result of the union between the angels and a species of seal-like animals. Newbrough's book contains a map of the earth in antediluvian times showing the triangular continent of Pan in the North Pacific. Pan sank beneath the waves 24,000

Right: Augustus Le Plongeon, the French archaeologist who was the first to excavate the Mayan ruins in Yucatán. Le Plongeon made his own translation of the *Troano Codex*, based on Brasseur's version and on Mayan pictures he had discovered at Chichén Itzá. His translation is a colorful account of the history of the lost Mu, in which he suggests that Muvians were the ancestors of both the Mayas and the ancient Egyptians.

Far right: Le Plongeon's wife Alice, who accompanied and assisted him in the Yucatán.

Left: Le Plongeon excavating in Mexico. The picture is reproduced in Le Plongeon's account of his theories, *Queen Moo and the Egyptian Sphinx*, in which the statue shown is identified as Prince Coh. According to Le Plongeon, Coh and Aac were princes of the lost continent of Mu, and rivals for the hand of their sister Queen Moo. In fact, this statue appears to be in the characteristic pose of the so-called "chacmool" sculptures imported to Mayan lands by the Toltecs.

years ago. However, it is scheduled to rise again in the very near future. *Oahspe* tells us that Pan will begin to resurface in 1980, and when its cities and the records of its civilization are finally exposed we will have no difficulty in deciphering its books or learning about its culture, because *Oahspe* very thoughtfully supplies us with a Panic dictionary and a Panic alphabet.

Not all proponents of a lost Pacific continent needed the help of angels to formulate their ideas. A New Zealander, Professor J. MacMillan Brown, drew upon his knowledge of geology, archaeology, and anthropology to explain the mystery of Easter Island. He argued that there had once been either a continent or a densely populated archipelago in the South Pacific, inhabited by white men, and that Easter Island had served as a collective burial ground for the people of neighboring islands. The professor pointed to similarities between the monuments and customs of the Polynesian people and those of the Peruvian civilizations, believing that South American culture had reached that continent from the west. Although Professor Brown has been described as "a man with a mind both simple and excessively imaginative," parts of his theory find support today in a new interpretation of Polynesian culture by modern experts.

Below: Mayan painting discovered by Le Plongeon. He interpreted it as the preparation for cremation of the body of Prince Coh who, after winning the hand of Queen Moo, had been murdered by Aac. Le Plongeon describes how Coh's body has been opened to extract his heart, while the members of his family make preparations for the ceremony. The mourners are almost naked, Le Plongeon writes, because after contact with the dead they will have to undergo a ritual purification.

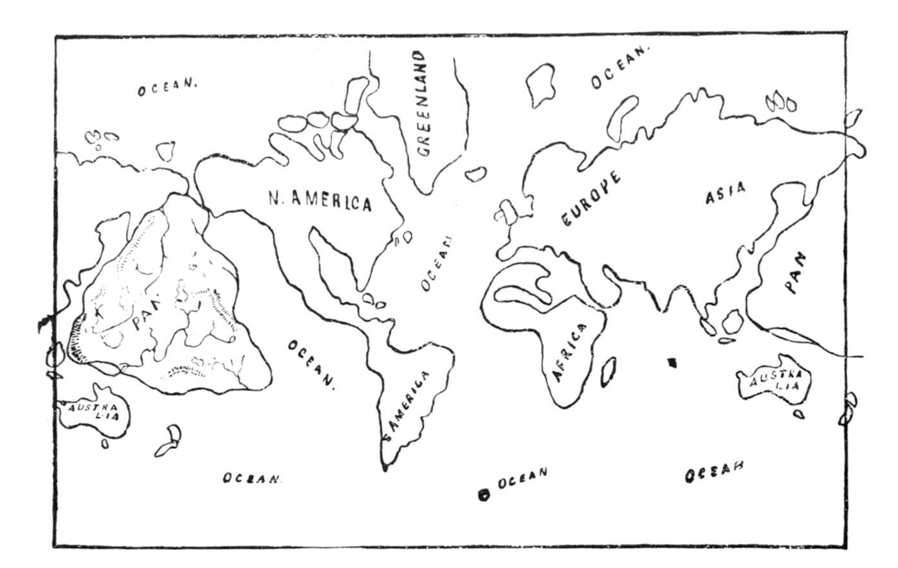

Right: John Ballou Newbrough's map of the submerged continent Pan, which he believed occupied much of the North Pacific.

The professor published his theory in the form of a book, *Riddle of the Pacific*, which appeared in 1906. Shortly afterward, between 1908 and 1926, the German explorer Leo Frobenius made discoveries in Yorubaland—part of Nigeria—that led him to believe he had discovered Atlantis. He identified the Nigerian god Olokon with Poseidon, and argued that the Yoruba culture contained many elements, such as the short bow and tattooing, that he said were non-African. He went on to state his belief that civilization had begun on a lost Pacific continent. It had spread from there to Asia, then to the west, giving rise to the Egyptian and Atlanto-Nigerian civilizations.

All these protagonists had merely set the stage for the appearance of the most outrageous supporter of a vanished Pacific continent. James Churchward, a small, thin Anglo-American, was already in his 70s when he first revealed the results of a lifetime's research on the subject. His first book, *The Lost Continent of Mu*, published in 1926, made fascinating reading, though acceptance of its contents demands a high degree of gullibility on the part of the reader. Nevertheless, Churchward's name is now almost synonymous with Mu's, and his book is still in print.

Churchward based his theory on two sets of tablets, one of which no one has had the privilege of studying except a priest in whose temple the tablets were allegedly preserved. In his first book Churchward claims to have seen these "Naacal tablets" in an Indian temple; elsewhere he says he studied them in Tibet. The other set of tablets is a collection of some 2500 stone objects found in Mexico by an American engineer named William Niven. These objects, which look like flattened figurines, were made in great numbers by the Aztecs and other Mexican peoples. No one else seemed to think there was anything on them worth deciphering, but Churchward claimed to be able to "read" their bumps and curlicues. They are symbols that originated in Mu, he said, and they convey deep and mysterious meanings. He dated the Niven tablets as at least 12,000 years old, and claimed that they and the Naacal tablets contain extracts from the Sacred Inspired Writings of Mu.

Churchward's first book begins with these compelling

Below: inhabitants of Pan, from *Oahspe*, Newbrough's personal version of the Bible in which he recorded his theories about Pan.

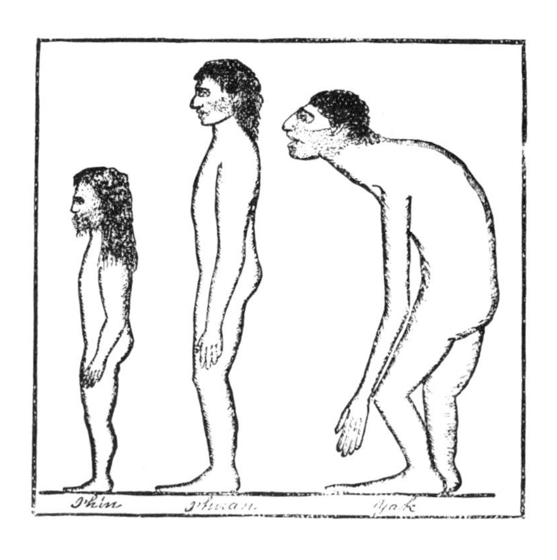

words: "The Garden of Eden was not in Asia but on a now sunken continent in the Pacific Ocean. The Biblical story of creation—the epic of the seven days and the seven nights—came first not from the peoples of the Nile or of the Euphrates Valley but from this now submerged continent, Mu—the Motherland of Man.

"These assertions can be proved by the complex records I discovered upon long-forgotten sacred tablets in India, together with records from other countries. They tell of this strange country of 64,000,000 inhabitants, who, 50,000 years ago, had developed a civilization superior in many respects to our own. They described, among other things, the creation of man in the mysterious land of Mu."

Churchward explains that he saw the sacred Naacal tablets during a stay in India (or Tibet, depending on which of his books we are reading). While he was studying the bas-reliefs in a certain temple, he became friendly with the temple's high priest. He discovered that the man was interested in archaeology and ancient records, "and had a greater knowledge of those subjects than any other living man." The high priest began teaching Churchward how to read the peculiar inscriptions on the temple walls, and Churchward spent the next two years studying this strange language, which "my priestly friend believed to be the original tongue of mankind." Churchward learned that only two

The Lost Lands of Pan and Mu

Below: painting by James Churchward from his book on Mu, which he described as a continent in the central Pacific Ocean. He captioned this illustration as "A Volcanic Cataclysm such as completed the destruction of the Maya edifices in Yucatán after the earthquakes had shaken them to their foundations. The Yucatán Maya, the builders, were virtually wiped out. 9500 B.C." In fact, the Mayas established themselves in Yucatán only after A.D. 700, more than 1600 years after Churchward's date for their fall.

The Submerged Continent of Mu

Below: one of the Naacal tablets that Churchward claimed to have discovered in an Indian temple, and from which he learned the history of Mu. This tablet, Churchward explains, tells of the creation of the first man, of his division into man and woman, and of how their progeny peopled the world.

other priests in India knew this language.

Interpreting the temple writings proved difficult, because many apparently simple inscriptions had hidden meaning, "which had been designed especially for the Holy Brothers—the Naacals—a priestly brotherhood sent from the motherland [Mu] to the colonies to teach the sacred writings, religion, and the sciences." One day, in the course of a conversation with Churchward, the priest revealed that there were a number of ancient tablets in the temple's secret archives, which were believed to have originated either in Burma or in the vanished land of Mu itself. He had never seen the tablets, only the containers in which they were kept. Although he was in a position to examine the tablets, the high priest had not done so because they were sacred records not to be touched.

Churchward argued that the tablets might not be packed away properly and could be deteriorating, a view that the priest eventually shared, and so the containers were opened. According to Churchward the tablets, written in the same dead language that he had been studying, described in detail the earth's creation, the appearance of man, and the land on which he evolved—Mu.

Having learned that more tablets were preserved in other Indian temples, Churchward set off on an unsuccessful quest for them. He then turned to a study of the writings of old civilizations, which confirmed his belief that the Chaldeans, Babylonians, Persians, Egyptians, Greeks, and Hindus had been preceded by the civilization of Mu.

"Continuing my researches, I discovered that this lost continent had extended from somewhere north of Hawaii to the south as far as the Fijis and Easter Island, and was undoubtedly the original habitat of man. I learned that in this beautiful country there had lived a people that colonized the earth, and that the land had been obliterated by terrific earthquakes and submersion 12,000 years ago, and had vanished in a vortex of fire and water."

According to Churchward, Mu was a beautiful, tropical country with vast plains covered with rich grazing grasses and

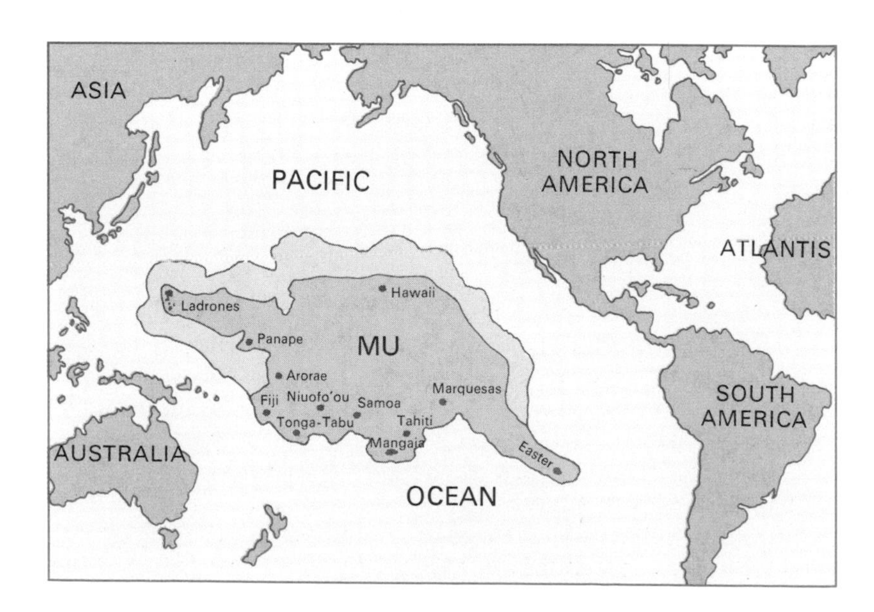

Right: Churchward's map of Mu, covering most of Polynesia in the Pacific Ocean. According to his theory, Mu sank beneath the sea some 13,000 years ago, leaving only the Polynesian islands visible above the waves. The survivors of the cataclysm, crowded onto these small islands, reverted to savagery and became cannibals.

tilled fields. There were no mountains, "for mountains had not yet been forced up from the bowels of the earth," but there were low, rolling hills, shaded by tropical vegetation. Many "broad, slow-running streams and rivers, which wound their sinuous ways in fantastic curves and bends around the wooded hills and through the fertile plains," watered the land and produced luxuriant flowers and shrubs.

Churchward peoples his graphic picture of the vanished continent with gaudy-winged butterflies, humming birds, lively crickets, mighty mastodons and elephants, and a population of 64,000,000 noble human beings enjoying "a gay and happy life."

The inhabitants of Mu consisted of ten tribes all under one government, ruled by an emperor, the Ra Mu. "The dominant race in the land of Mu was a white race, exceedingly handsome people, with clear white or olive skins, large, soft, dark eyes, and straight black hair. Besides this white race, there were other races, people with yellow, brown, or black skins. They, however, did not dominate."

The Muvians built broad, smooth roads running in all directions like a spider's web, and the stones from which the roads were constructed were matched so perfectly that not a blade of grass could grow between them. They were great navigators, and they made all the other countries on the planet their colonies. It was an idyllic life, and on cool evenings pleasure ships, filled with gorgeously dressed, jewel-bedecked men and women, rejoiced at their good fortune. "While this great land was thus at its zenith," Churchward's account continues, "center of the earth's civilization, learning, trade and commerce, with great stone temples being erected, and huge statues and monoliths set up, she received a rude shock; a fearful visitation overtook her."

Earthquakes and volcanic eruptions shook the southern parts of the continent, destroying many cities. Tidal waves flooded the land, and the lava piled up into high cones that are still to be seen today in the form of the Pacific islands. Eventually the Muvians were able to rebuild these cities, and life returned to normal. Then, many generations later, a similar but far greater catastrophe struck Mu, and "the whole continent heaved and rolled like the ocean's waves." Churchward is not one to miss the drama of such an event. "With thunderous roarings the doomed land sank," he writes. "Down, down, down she went, into the mouth of hell—'a tank of fire.'" Then 50 million square miles of water poured over the continent, drowning the vast majority of its noble inhabitants.

The only visible remains of the great continent were its lava cones, which formed chains of small islands, covered to capacity with the survivors of the cataclysm. With no clothing, no tools, no shelter, and no food, these formerly peace-loving people had to become cannibals in order to survive. The colonies that Mu had founded continued for a while, but without the help of the motherland they eventually flickered out. Churchward asserts that Atlantis was one of these colonies, and suffered a similar fate to Mu 1000 years later.

Churchward claimed that his findings solved the mysteries surrounding the first inhabitants of the South Sea islands and the

Above: Princess Arawali of Arorai Island in the Gilbert group. This photograph was reproduced in Churchward's book to prove the descent of the Pacific islanders from the inhabitants of Mu. The fan Arawali carries, Churchward asserts, is ornamented with the royal escutcheon of Mu.

Churchward and the Sinking of Mu

Below: North American Indian picture, interpreted by Churchward as an illustration of the destruction of the continent of Mu. The picture is surmounted by the plumed serpent, which—according to Churchward—is God of Creation. Beneath the serpent, the Thunder Bird, symbolizing the creative forces, holds in its talons the Killer Whale, the ocean waters. But the whale is dead, indicating that the waters have completed the catastrophic destruction of Mu.

origins of the ancient American civilizations. "On some of the South Sea Islands, notably Easter, Mangaia, Tongatabu, Panape, and the Ladrone or Marianas Islands," he writes, "there stand today vestiges of old stone temples and other lithic [stone] remains that take us back to the time of Mu. At Uxmal, in Yucatán, a ruined temple bears inscriptions commemorative of the 'Lands of the West, whence we came;' and the striking Mexican pyramid southwest of Mexico City, according to its inscriptions, was raised as a monument to the destruction of these same 'Lands of the West'."

Even those readers prepared to believe that Churchward was privileged to see the ancient Naacal tablets may wonder how he was able to decipher them—and the Niven tablets that also supplied part of his story—so quickly. However, Churchward has an explanation for this. Like many occultists, he believed that it is possible for a suitably gifted person to decipher the secret language of symbols (said to have been used by all the ancients to record their wisdom) simply by staring at the symbols until their meaning emerges from the student's inner consciousness. It was this technique, in which he was aided by the teachings of the Indian (or Tibetan) high priest, that enabled Churchward to recover the forgotten history of Mu.

In considering the possibility that there was once a huge continent in the Pacific, we need to take a fresh look at the islands now occupying that area. The place deserving the closest scrutiny is undoubtedly Easter Island with its huge sculptures and associated mysteries. Why did the people of such a tiny island build so many very similar stone heads? Why, instead of carving them one at a time, were they producing as many as 200 simultaneously in their quarry when they suddenly abandoned their work?

Some have suggested that the island was part of Mu, and the place at which the stone monuments were carved before being transported to other parts of the continent. Others believe Easter Island to have been a burial ground, a sacred area of Mu

Right: drawing by Churchward of "the probable condition underlying Mu before her submersion." The earth beneath the continent, Churchward stated, was honeycombed with chambers filled with explosive volcanic gases. Pressure caused cracks and fissures in the rocks, and the gases escaped upward leaving the chambers empty behind them. With no "bolstering gases" to support their roofs, they collapsed and Mu sank beneath the sea.

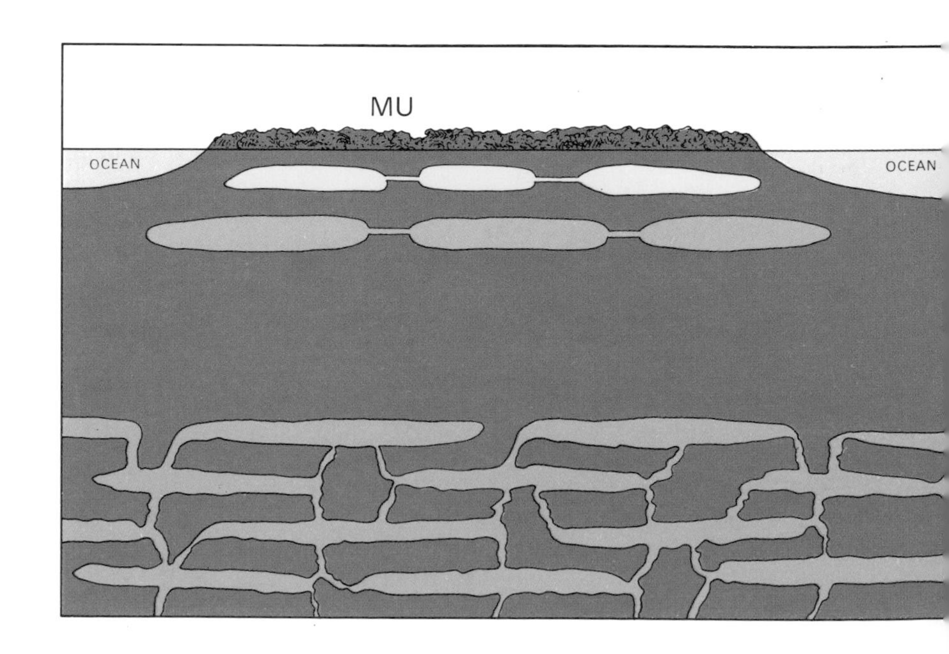

Above: Churchward's painting of the submersion of Mu. He wrote that "*the whole continent* heaved and rolled like the ocean's waves. The land trembled and shook like the leaves of a tree in a storm. Temples and palaces came crashing to the ground. . . ." That night, the continent broke up and was engulfed first by fire, then by the waves.

that became an island when the rest of the continent sank.

The man who has done most in our time to popularize Easter Island and to solve its riddles is Thor Heyerdahl, the Norwegian anthropologist who, in 1947, led the famous Scandinavian *Kon-Tiki* expedition from South America to Polynesia. He subsequently organized expeditions to the Galápagos Islands in 1952 and to Easter Island in 1955. Heyerdahl is convinced that all the Polynesian islands were originally settled by people from South America. When he first published his theory, in 1941, most scientists disregarded the possibility of South American influence on Polynesia because of the vast expanse of ocean that lies between South America and the nearest South Pacific islands. It seemed unlikely, to say the least, that the South American Indians with their frail reed and balsa wood craft could have crossed thousands of miles of ocean to carry their culture to Polynesia. Most authorities believed that the Polynesians had come from the other direction, from Asia. Heyerdahl agreed that Asian immigrants *had* reached the Polynesian islands, but he was convinced that they were preceded by colonizers from South America.

To help prove his case, Heyerdahl and his team built the balsa wood raft *Kon-Tiki* based on the traditional materials and techniques used in the construction of South American boats. In 1947, he and five companions set out aboard the raft from Callao, Peru. They spent 101 days at sea, allowing the South Equatorial Current and the prevailing trade winds to carry them 4300 nautical miles to the little Polynesian atoll of Raroia

Heyerdahl and the Mystery of Easter Island

in the Tuamotu Archipelago.

The voyage made Heyerdahl famous, but many scientists remained skeptical. To show a thing can be done is not the same as proving it was done, said the critics. And even if people from South America had reached Polynesia, this did not prove that there was regular contact across the ocean or that the sailors from Peru founded the culture of the Polynesian islands, as Heyerdahl suggested. Orthodox scientists were even more outraged when Heyerdahl suggested that the civilizers from Peru might have been the fair-skinned, bearded men enshrined in Indian legend, who had previously influenced the development of the American civilizations.

However, Heyerdahl is a careful scientist, and he has carried out a great deal of research among the American Indians and the Polynesians in order to provide evidence for his theories. His expedition to Easter Island in 1955 was the first to undertake a thorough archaeological study, including modern techniques such as radiocarbon dating, and he combined his examination

Above: long-eared Easter Islander in the 1770s. The Peruvian Indians also elongated their ears like this.

Right: one of the giant Easter Island statues, its red topknot restored by archaeologists, gazes over the Pacific landscape as it first did hundreds of years ago. Some believe that these statues are all that remains of an ancient Pacific civilization, and that Easter Island was part of a landmass that has sunk beneath the waves.

of the island's past with a practical approach to such problems as how the Easter Island statues were transported.

Why is it that Easter Island, the most remote and inaccessible of all the countless Polynesian islands, should be the very one among them to possess the most abundant and spectacular archaeological remains? And why, alone in Polynesia, should it have a system of writing? asked Heyerdahl. He believed that the key to these questions lay in the island's situation. Of all the inhabited Polynesian islands, Easter Island is the nearest to South America—and the farthest from Asia. It is likely to have been the first island colonized by settlers from South America, whereas migrants from Asia would have reached it last.

Heyerdahl's excavations, backed up by radiocarbon dating tests, showed that a considerable population lived on Easter Island around A.D. 380—about 1000 years earlier than anyone had hitherto suspected. Heyerdahl believes that these people came from Peru, bringing with them their stoneworking techniques. They built temples, roads, and a solar observatory that resemble the magnificent constructions found in ancient Peru. Their temples were astronomically oriented, altarlike elevations, evidently built by specialized stonemasons.

This cultural period was succeeded by another around A.D. 1100, when a new wave of immigrants overran the island. These people showed similar—but not identical—stone-carving skills to their predecessors, and Heyerdahl believes that they too came from Peru. It was during this period that the giant statues were carved and placed on terraced stone platforms that contained burial vaults. The huge heads, depicting long-eared men, recall the practice among the Inca and other Peruvian Indians of elongating the ears by inserting ornamental plugs into the lobes.

According to Heyerdahl, the statue-builders controlled the island for nearly 600 years, but around 1680 the production of statues stopped abruptly, and from then on the giant heads were gradually toppled or destroyed. In Heyerdahl's view, this occurred as the result of another invasion of the island, this time by Polynesians arriving from the direction of Asia. Archaeological evidence suggests that from about 1680 onward the island underwent a period of decadence and warfare, and Easter Island legends tell of a lengthy conflict between "the short ears" (whom Heyerdahl identifies with the Polynesian invaders) and "the long ears" (the statue-builders). The "short ears" eventually won, wiping out the "long ears" and destroying their civilization. The Polynesians were left in control of the island, unable to carve the statues or read the rongorongo boards left by their predecessors. Apart from the remaining statues, the only picture we now have of the earlier settlers is the wood carving, produced by the hundred for commercial purposes by today's Easter Islanders. It shows an emaciated person with goatee beard, aquiline nose, and long ear lobes. The islanders claim that these were the people their ancestors found and exterminated.

Apart from the early date ascribed to Easter Island civilization, one of the most remarkable discoveries made by Heyerdahl was that when the first settlers arrived on Easter Island there were trees in abundance. The settlers had to cut them down in order to clear the way for the transportation of stones from

Above: Thor Heyerdahl (left) with historian Bjørn Landström. Heyerdahl has done more than anyone to solve the mystery of Easter Island.

Below: the balsa-wood raft *Kon-Tiki* nears the end of its 4300-mile drift across the Pacific from Peru to the Tuamotu Islands. The voyage was undertaken by Heyerdahl and five companions to try to prove Heyerdahl's theory that Polynesia was first colonized from the Americas, not from Asia. He believes that civilization reached Easter Island from the same source.

Disproving the Theory of the "Lost Continent"

Right: modern inhabitants of Easter Island insert long poles under a fallen statue prior to raising it. They work under the direction of Heyerdahl, who was trying to show that their ancestors could have moved the huge statues.

Right: the poles are used as levers to allow stones to be piled under the head of the statue.

Opposite top: the heap of stones under the statue gradually grows until the great head is almost vertical. At this stage, ropes are used to prevent it toppling over. It took 12 men 18 days to raise the statue using only these primitive tools.
Opposite bottom: Heyerdahl and an islander in front of the newly raised head. Heyerdahl's work showed how the sculptures could have been erected, and his theories might explain their existence without the need for a "lost continent." If Peruvians had settled on Easter Island, as his sea voyage in *Kon-Tiki* had indicated was possible, they could have been responsible for the giant stone figures.

the quarry. The trees were still there when the statue-builders arrived. Thus the means of moving and erecting the giant statues is no longer a mystery. Indeed Heyerdahl arranged for some of the present-day inhabitants to erect a fallen statue by levering it up with long poles and ropes and gradually blocking piles of small rocks underneath it. It took 12 men 18 days to raise the 25-ton statue—but they did it.

Heyerdahl still has his detractors. Critics point out that, despite the apparent similarities between the stoneworking techniques of Easter Island and Peru, there are fundamental differences between the two. The Easter Islanders built rubble walls that they faced with thin slabs of stone, whereas the Peruvians built with solid blocks of stone. What is more, the Peruvians could not have brought writing to Easter Island, because they themselves had no written language. Indeed, many scholars believe that the inscriptions on the rongorongo boards are not, strictly speaking, a system of writing at all, but rather a device to jog the memory of the storytellers or hymn-singers who used the symbols as reminders of the key elements of their story when reciting lengthy ritual chants. Above all, the critics attack Heyerdahl's use of legend to support his theories, because the legends themselves are often contradictory. They also point out that the Easter Islanders and the Peruvian Indians were not alone in elongating their ear lobes. This practice is also found in Polynesian islands much closer to Asia.

Nevertheless, Heyerdahl's tireless endeavors in support of his claims and his undoubted contribution to our knowledge of

Easter Island have led to a reevaluation of the idea of cultural contact between South America and Polynesia, and a number of scientists now accept at least part of his theory concerning the history of Easter Island.

Heyerdahl has shown that it is possible to explain the mysteries of Easter Island without recourse to a lost continent. But even if his claims are correct, they need not mean that such a continent never existed in the Pacific. If the continent sank 12,000 years ago, as Churchward maintained, it could well have taken all evidence of its existence with it. Easter Island may be one of its peaks, even if the cultures whose remains now litter its surface appear to have no connection with Mu.

The Pacific region seems so rich in unsolved mysteries and enigmatic finds that almost any theorist, however outlandish, will probably find some "evidence" for his ideas in this part of the globe. Until a more thorough archaeological examination of the area has been carried out, it would be unwise to jump to any firm conclusions. After all, in many ways the huge Pacific Ocean —the world's largest at 68,000,000 square miles—with its volcanic history and strings of islands, might seem to be a more promising site for a vanished continent than the much smaller Atlantic (31,830,000 square miles).

Lemur Catta Linn.

Chapter 11
Lemuria-the Missing Link?

Ever since the mid-19th century, men have puzzled over the lemur. This small mammal, halfway between a monkey and a squirrel, is found mainly in Madagascar, but also in Africa, India, and the Malay Archipelago. How, argued the biologists, could the identical animal have settled in such widely scattered territories? The answer was simple. They proposed Lemuria, a lost continent spanning the Indian Ocean, as the only feasible solution. Where they right? And assuming they were, what would such a lost land mean in terms of the origins of mankind itself? This chapter explores the arguments—and the evidence.

The descendants of a long-lost race from a vanished continent are alive and well and living on the slopes of Mount Shasta in northern California. So claimed an article in the *Los Angeles Times Star* of May 22, 1932. The writer of the article, reporter Edward Lanser, said he had first learned about these people while traveling at night on the *Shasta Limited*, the train taking him to Portland, Oregon. From the train's observation car Lanser had seen strange red and green lights illuminating Mount Shasta. The conductor of the train told him that these were the work of "Lemurians holding ceremonials." Understandably intrigued, and sensing a scoop for his newspaper, Lanser made an expedition into the Mount Shasta wilderness in search of these mysterious beings, said to be the last descendants of the earth's first inhabitants.

Lanser drove to the town of Weed where he heard tell of a "mystic village" on Mount Shasta and talked to other investigators who had seen the Lemurians' ceremonial lights, during the daytime as well as at night. But no one had ever been able to enter the "sacred precincts" of the Mount Shasta colony—or if they had, they had not returned to tell the tale. One man, however, had managed to become an expert on this strange Lemurian settlement: "the eminent scientist Professor Edgar Lucin Larkin." According to Lanser, Professor Larkin, "with determined sagacity, penetrated the Shasta wilderness as far as he could—or dared—and then, cleverly, continued his investiga-

Opposite: the ring-tailed lemur, from a German work on natural history published in 1775. The lemur, a small mammal related to the human, is found mainly in Madagascar, but also lives in other countries bordering the Indian Ocean. In the 19th century, those who accepted Charles Darwin's theory of the evolution of species found it difficult to explain how the lemur had reached the other countries, separated from Madagascar by wide expanses of sea. It was suggested that all the habitats of the lemur might once have been connected by a continent that had vanished. Because this theory arose as an explanation for the lemur's distribution, the lost continent was named Lemuria.

Lanser and the Lemurians of Mount Shasta

tions from a promontory with a powerful long-distance telescope."

Peering through his telescope the professor had seen a great temple in the midst of the Lemurian village. It was a splendid piece of architecture, carved from marble and onyx, which rivaled the beauty of the magnificent Mayan temples in Yucatán. Although the investigators seemed frightened to trespass on the Lemurians' sacred terrain, the evidence was that they were a peace-loving, friendly community, apparently leading the same kind of life as their ancestors had done before their homeland sank beneath the sea.

Lanser reported that the people of Weed had occasionally met Lemurians and were able to give a good description of them. They were "tall, barefoot, noble-looking men, with close-cropped hair, dressed in spotless white robes." The town's storekeepers had good reason to like them. The Lemurians purchased huge quantities of sulfur, salt, and lard, paying with large gold nuggets—worth far more than the merchandise—that they apparently mined from Mount Shasta.

How had this ancient people been able to remain undetected for so long? Lanser provided the answer in his remarkable account. The Lemurians, he said, possessed "the secret power of the Tibetan masters," which enabled them to blend with their surroundings and vanish at will, and they encircled their village with an "invisible protective boundary" to keep intruders out. According to Lanser, the Lemurians' scientific knowledge was

Right: Mount Shasta in California. In 1932, Mount Shasta was named as the home of a colony of Lemurians in a feature article in the *Los Angeles Star*. According to the writer of the article, the Mount Shasta Lemurians had emigrated to the United States from their homeland in the Indian Ocean. They lived a secluded life on the mountain, but sometimes ventured into a local town to buy supplies. Strangely enough, no one walking on the mountain had ever seen the colony. Not surprisingly, the article was soon proved to be a fraud.

far greater than ours. And although they had lived in America—which they called Gustama—for several hundred thousand years, they had not forgotten their homeland. Their strangely lit ceremonials on the slopes of Mount Shasta were held in honor of the long-lost Lemuria.

Those readers of the *Los Angeles Times Star* who took Lanser's story without a pinch of salt were to be disappointed. Lanser's report contains the only allegedly eye-witness account of the Mount Shasta Lemurians ever published, and no subsequent investigators have found the mystic village or its strange inhabitants. Either these mysterious people never existed or they have since blended irretrievably into their surroundings. Professor Larkin, who studied the Lemurians through his telescope, turns out to be no "eminent scientist," as Lanser claimed, but an elderly occultist who ran the Mount Lowe Observatory in California. Unlike its neighbor, the Mount Wilson Observatory, which is a great scientific institution, the Mount Lowe Observatory was a tourist attraction operated by the Pacific Electric Railway, and Larkin's job was to show visitors the stars through a small telescope. Larkin died in 1924—eight years before the publication of Lanser's article.

Mount Shasta had already been a subject of mystical speculation long before Lanser wrote his Lemurian story. In 1894 a writer named Frederick Spencer Oliver published an occult novel entitled *A Dweller on Two Planets*, under the name "Phylos the Tibetan." In this book the narrator meets his Master, a

Identifying the "Missing Link"

Chinese named Quong, on Mount Shasta, where sages have established a community to preserve the wisdom of the ancients. Having inducted him into their order, the sages take the narrator to visit Venus in his spiritual body and also teach him to remember his previous incarnations. These include a life on Atlantis, where he rose from miner's son to prince of the realm. He then got involved with two women at once, which proved to be his undoing.

Although we can dismiss the Lanser story as a fascinating piece of fiction based on another piece of fiction, we cannot discard the Lemurians in the same way. Their country of origin, Lemuria, was first suggested in the mid-1800s by scientists trying to account for striking resemblances between the rocks and fossils of Central India and South Africa and for the spread of certain fauna and flora between these continents. One animal that puzzled them particularly was the lemur, a small mammal related to both men and monkeys. The lemur, which looks like a cross between a monkey and a squirrel, lives mainly on the island of Madagascar, but is also found in Africa, India, and the Malay archipelago.

The debate over the lemur emerged in the wake of Charles Darwin's great thesis on evolution, *On The Origin of Species*, published in 1859. At this time there were two schools of thought: either God had created the various species and put them on earth in the form that we know them, or they had evolved over millions of years. If the former were the case, then God could put His creations wherever He liked—limiting similar species to a particular area of the globe, or placing them on continents thousands of miles apart. But if similar species had evolved in one place from a common ancestor, as Darwin and his supporters thought, the geographical spread of those species had to be in accordance with the limitations of the global picture. In the evolutionists' scheme of things, the lowly lemur presented a problem, because some means had to be found by which it could have crossed the ocean to its present areas of distribution.

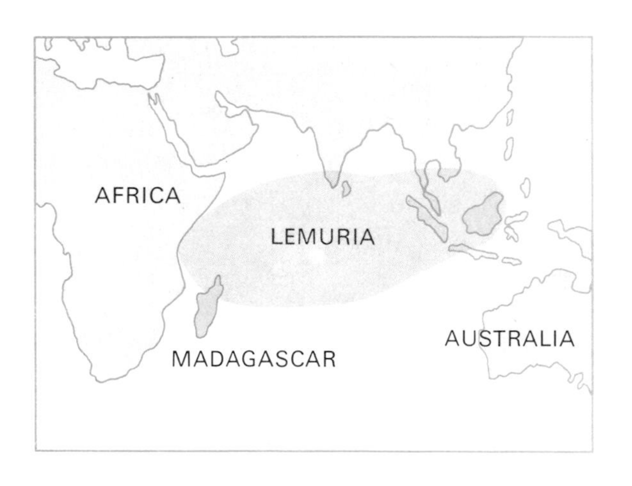

Above: Ernst Haeckel's map of the probable site of Lemuria in the Indian Ocean, joining Madagascar, Africa, India, and the Malay Peninsula—the homelands of the lemur. Haeckel, a naturalist and a keen advocate of Darwin's theories, believed an Indian Ocean continent was necessary to explain how the lemur had arrived in its present habitats.

Biologists were quick to come up with the obvious solution to the dilemma. The areas now inhabited by the lemur must once have been connected in one vast continent, which still existed at the time when mammals were evolving. The English zoologist Philip L. Sclater suggested that the continent be called "Lemuria" in honor of the lemur.

Many eminent people were ready to accept the possibility of such a continent. Alfred Russel Wallace, who independently developed the theory of evolution simultaneously with Darwin, wrote: "This is undoubtedly a legitimate and highly probable supposition, and it is an example of the way in which a study of the geographical distribution of animals may enable us to reconstruct the geography of a bygone age. . . . It [Lemuria] represents what was probably a primary zoological region in some past geological epoch; but what that epoch was and what were the limits of the region in question, we are quite unable to say. If we are to suppose that it comprised the whole area now inhabited by Lemuroid animals, we must make it extend from West Africa to Burmah, South China and Celebes, an area which it possibly did once occupy."

Left: Ernst Haeckel on an expedition to Ceylon in 1882. Darwin's theory of evolution proposed that humans were descended from the apes, but in the mid-19th century no fossils connected ape and man had yet been found. Haeckel believed that the intermediate evolutionary stages had taken place on Lemuria, and that the fossil evidence had disappeared with the continent.

Above: British naturalist Alfred Russel Wallace. Wallace, a respected scientist who independently reached a theory of evolution similar to Darwin's, gave scientific backing to Haeckel's idea. He supported the Lemuria theory as a feasible explanation of the geographical distribution of animals and plants in the lands around the Indian Ocean.

Among the most ardent supporters of Lemuria was the German naturalist Ernst Heinrich Haeckel. In a burst of enthusiasm he suggested that if Lemuria had existed it could solve a hotly disputed matter of far greater significance than the spread of the lemurs—namely, the origin of man.

"Of the five now existing continents," Haeckel wrote in the 1870s, "neither Australia nor America nor Europe can have been this primeval home (of man), or the so-called 'Paradise' the 'cradle of the human race.' Besides Southern Asia, the only other of the now existing continents which might be viewed in this light is Africa. But there are a number of circumstances (especially chronological facts) which suggest that the primeval home of man was a continent now sunk below the surface of the Indian Ocean, which extended along the South of Asia, as it is at present (and probably in direct connection with it), towards the east, as far as Further India and the Sunda Islands; towards the west as far as Madagascar and the southeastern shores of Africa. We have already mentioned that many facts in animal and vegetable geography render the former existence of such a South Indian continent very probable. . . . By assuming this Lemuria to have been man's primeval home, we greatly facilitate the explanation of the geographical distribution of the human species by migration."

At the height of the great debate on evolution no fossil remains of man, or of forms intermediate between apes and man, had been identified. (Although fragments of Neanderthal man had already been found, they were only later identified.) Some scientists therefore concluded that the land on which man evolved had disappeared, taking the evidence with it, and Lemuria seemed a good candidate for the site of man's emergence. Our subsequent knowledge of man's family tree and his gradual evolution has done away with the need for a Lemuria-type place of origin, just as other theories have been found to account for the distribution of the lemur, but this information came too late to stop Lemuria taking its place alongside Atlantis and Mu as a great lost continent. No sooner had scientists made the cautious suggestion that Lemuria might have existed than the occultists brought it to life with vivid accounts, derived from supernormal sources, of its inhabitants and their civilization. As a result, Lemuria is now an apparently imperishable feature of the thinking of most leading occult groups.

Below: H. P. Blavatsky, founder of the Theosophical Society and an ardent supporter of the Lemuria theory. The existence of Lemuria was seized on by occultists and adapted to their own mystical ideas. Madame Blavatsky believed that the inhabitants of Lemuria were the third of the seven "root races" into which she divided mankind.

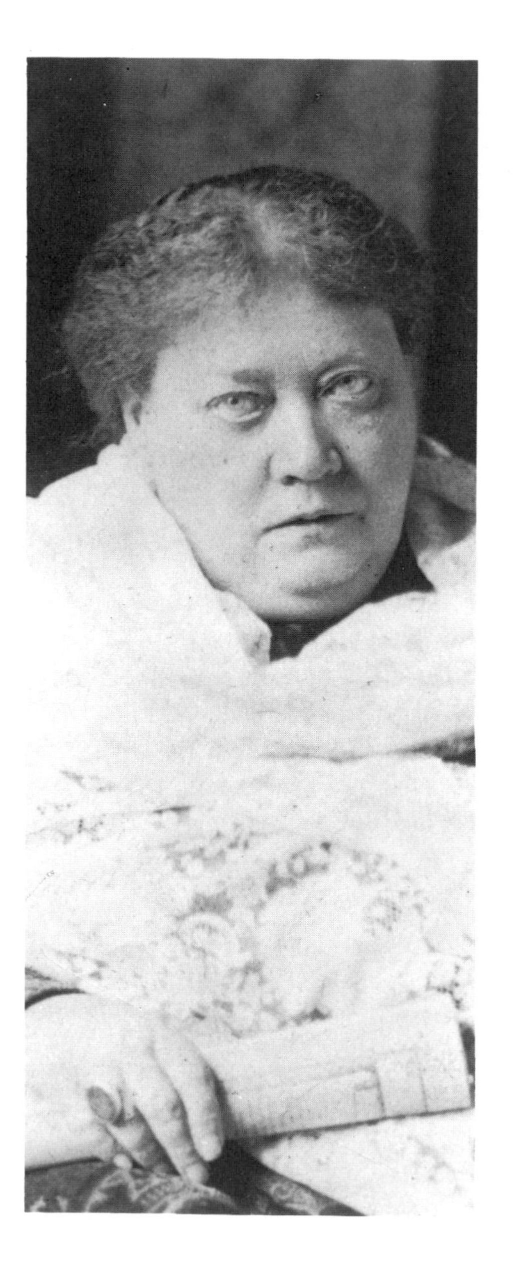

Madame Helena Petrovna Blavatsky, the greatest of modern occultists and founder of the occult group known as the Theosophical Society, started the ball rolling. In 1888 she published a vast work, *The Secret Doctrine*, which set out her philosophy and gave its readers an insight into the ancient wisdom imparted to her by the Brotherhood of Mahatmas, ethereal beings who were said to run the world from their Tibetan headquarters. Madame Blavatsky maintained that her book was based on an ancient work called the *Book of Dzyan*, which the Mahatmas had shown her during the astral visits they paid her. The *Book of Dzyan*, she says, was written on palm-leaf pages, and had been composed in Atlantis in the now forgotten Senzar language. Besides describing Atlantis it dealt with the lost continent of Lemuria.

It is not easy for the reader to understand the full meaning of Madame Blavatsky's writings, or those of the mysterious *Book of Dzyan* from which she quotes at length. She writes: "After great throes she cast off her old Three and put on her new Seven Skins, and stood in her first one. . . . The Wheel whirled for thirty crores more. It constructed Rûpas; soft Stones that hardened, hard Plants that softened. Visible from invisible, Insects and small Lives. . . ."

Describing the emergence of life on earth, Madame Blavatsky declares that we are the "Fifth Root Race" to inhabit the earth, and that our planet is destined to have seven such races, each composed of seven subraces. The First Root Race, invisible beings made of fire-mist, lived on an Imperishable Sacred Land. The Second, who were just visible, inhabited the former Arctic continent of Hyperborea. The Third Root Race was the Lemurians, gigantic, brainless, apelike creatures. The Fourth Root

Race was the fully human Atlanteans, who were destroyed through black magic. We are the Fifth, and the Sixth will evolve from us and return to live on Lemuria. After the Seventh Root Race, life will leave our planet and start afresh on Mercury.

According to Madame Blavatsky, some of the Lemurians had four arms, and some had an eye in the back of their heads, which gave them "psychic vision." They had no spoken language, using telepathy instead as their method of communication. They lived in caves and holes in the ground, and although they had no proper brain they could use their willpower literally to move mountains. Their homeland, Lemuria, occupied practically the whole of the Southern Hemisphere, "from the foot of the Himalayas to within a few degrees of the Antarctic Circle." Although their continent was swept away before the Eocene epoch—which occurred from 60 million to 40 million years ago—their descendants survived to become the Australian Aborigines, Papuans, and Hottentots.

After Madame Blavatsky's death in 1891 her successor, Annie Besant, wrote at length on the subject of Lemuria and its people, as did another leading British Theosophist, W. Scott-Elliot. He put the flesh on the bones of Madame Blavatsky's Lemuria with an astonishing account based on occult revelations he had received from the "Theosophical Masters." He was helped further by having had "the privilege . . . to be allowed to obtain copies—more or less complete" of a set of maps showing the world at critical stages of its history. They form the basis of six world maps reproduced in Scott-Elliot's book *The Story of Atlantis and The Lost Lemuria*, published in 1896 and still kept in print by the Theosophical Society.

The Seven "Root Races" of Man

Scott-Elliot enlarged on Madame Blavatsky's description of Lemuria. He said that this huge continent took shape when the great northern continent of Hyperborea—his and Madame Blavatsky's designated home of the Second Root Race—broke up. The Manus, the unseen supervisors of the universe, then chose Lemuria for the evolution of the Third Root Race. Their first attempt at producing human life resulted in jellylike creatures, but in time the Lemurians' bodies hardened and they were able to stand up.

From Scott-Elliot's description, the Lemurians were far from beautiful. They were between 12 and 15 feet tall. Their faces were flat, apart from a protruding muzzle, and they had no foreheads. Their skin was brown, and their eyes were set so wide apart that they could see sideways as well as forward. As for the Lemurians' third eye in the back of the head, that now forms the pineal gland in our brains. The capacity to see out of the backs of their heads was particularly useful to the Lemurians, because their heels stuck out so far at the back that they could walk backward as well as forward.

The Lemurians started out as egg-laying hermaphrodites, but by the time their fifth subrace evolved they were reproducing as we do. However, during their sexual progress they foolishly interbred with beasts, producing the apes that still populate our planet. This upset the Lhas, supernatural beings whose duty it was, at this stage of the cosmic plan, to incarnate on earth in human bodies to help the evolving Lemurians. So the Lhas

refused to carry out their appointed task. Beings from Venus saved the day by offering to take the place of the Lhas. The Venusians—called "Lords of the Flame"—had already developed a highly advanced civilization on their own planet, and they taught the Lemurians how to achieve individual immortality and reincarnation. By the time of the seventh subrace, the Lemurians had mastered the basic arts of civilization and had begun to look human. The Lapps and the Australian Aborigines are among their descendants on earth today.

During the period of the sixth and seventh subraces Lemuria began to break up as various parts of the continent sank. But a peninsula of Lemuria that extended into the North Atlantic grew into Atlantis. Then the Fourth Root Race, the Atlantean, appeared on what was left of Lemuria. Some of its first subrace, the Rmoahals, moved to Atlantis. Others stayed behind and interbred with the Lemurians to produce a race of half-breeds, who looked like blue-skinned American Indians. The Rmoahals were black-skinned, and stood between 10 and 12 feet tall. The Rmoahals who settled in southern Atlantis waged continual war on the remaining Lemurians, but as time went on some Rmoahals moved to the north of Atlantis, where their skins became lighter and their stature shorter. Their descendants were the Cro-Magnons of Europe.

Next to arrive on the scene, according to Scott-Elliot, were the Tlavatlis. This second Atlantean subrace originated on an island off Atlantis that is now the site of Mexico. Gradually the human race was feeling its way toward self-government, and the appearance of the third subrace, the Toltecs, ushered in the golden age of Atlantis. The Toltecs enjoyed a superb culture for 100,000 years until they resorted to sorcery and phallic worship. There was a rebellion, and the followers of the "black arts" overthrew the emperor and replaced him with their own king. The Toltecs then degenerated, and were soon at war with the Turanians, the fourth subrace, who had meanwhile emerged on Atlantis. The Turanians were a brutal and ruthless people, and practiced complete sexual promiscuity in order to boost their population for warfare. Their direct descendants were the Aztecs.

During these wars—some 800,000 years ago—a great catastrophe caused most of Atlantis to disappear, reducing it to a relatively small island. At the same time, a number of islands began to grow in size on their way to becoming the continents we know today. Many of the surviving Turanians left for Asia where they evolved into the more civilized seventh subrace, the Mongolians. In the meantime, the fifth and sixth subraces, the Semites and the Akkadians, came into being on Atlantis. The Semites inhabited the northern region of Atlantis, which is now Scotland and Ireland, and were a quarrelsome people who constantly provoked fights with their neighbors, the peaceful Akkadians.

Another disaster 200,000 years ago split what was left of Atlantis into two islands—Ruta, ruled by surviving Toltec sorcerers, and Daitya, occupied by Semite sorcerers. The next phase in the destruction occurred 80,000 years ago when a further catastrophe submerged Daitya and made Ruta an even smaller island. It was the final sinking of Ruta—also called

The Amazing Inhabitants of Lost Lemuria

Opposite: a Lemurian, as described by occultist W. Scott-Elliot in his account of the continent, *The Lost Lemuria*. Like Madame Blavatsky, Scott-Elliott divided mankind into root races, and this "average, commonplace" Lemurian belonged, so he wrote, to the fifth subrace of the third root race. He was a gigantic, ungainly being, between 12 and 15 feet tall, with long arms and legs permanently bent at elbow and knee, and huge hands and feet. His heels projected backward because, in the early stages of their evolution, Lemurians could walk backward as efficiently as forward—to aid them further, they had a third eye in the back of their head. This creature's two primary eyes were set far apart, so that he could see sideways as well as forward, and lurked beneath a roll of flesh that took the place of a forehead. His whole face was curiously flattened, his skin dark, and his general aspect hideous—as was that of the huge reptile he led by a rope of twisted creeper. Lemurians, Scott-Elliot asserted, domesticated these sinister monsters and used them as companions in the hunt.

The Mapping of the Lost Continent

Poseidonis—in 9564 B.C. that inspired Plato's story. Before the disaster that destroyed Daitya, a selected band of Semites moved into Central Asia where they evolved into the Aryans, the Fifth Root Race, who include the modern Hindus and Europeans.

There was far more to Scott-Elliot's story than this complex account of racial evolution. He was able to list the great achievements of the Atlanteans, such as the domestication of leopard-like animals and the creation of the banana. Atlantean alchemists made huge quantities of precious metals. Atlantean scientists invented gas-bombs and aircraft propelled by jets of *vril*-force, a mentally directed, invisible force first dreamed up by a Victorian novelist. These aircraft, owned only by the rich, flew at 100 mph and had a ceiling of 1000 feet. They were even capable of vertical takeoff, and Scott-Elliot's description of this aeronautical feat is not too different from the "jump jet" technique used today.

Another detail-packed interpretation of the lost continents of Atlantis and Lemuria came from the pen of Rudolf Steiner, a tall, dark-eyed Austrian who broke away from the Theosophists in 1907 to form his own Anthroposophical Society. Steiner's *Cosmic Memory: Atlantis and Lemuria*, published in 1923, is still in print through Rudolf Steiner Publications, the publishing

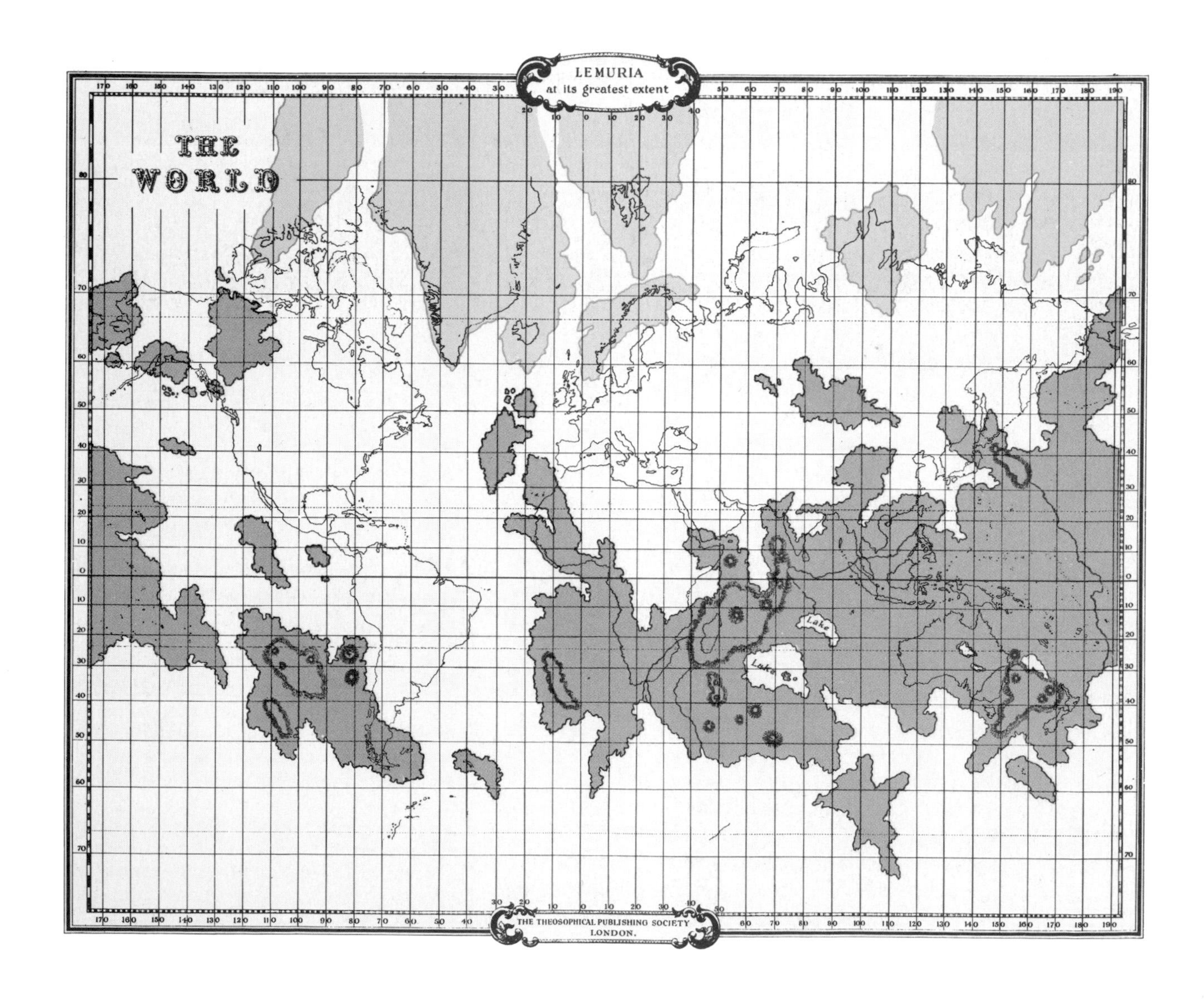

Below: Scott-Elliot's map of the continent of Lemuria "at its greatest extent." The map was based, he wrote, on a "broken terra-cotta model and a very badly preserved and crumpled map," amplified by occult memories of the period in earth's history the map represents. Scott-Elliot was reluctant to assign a precise date to his representations of Lemuria, but did state that the continent probably looked like this from the Permian into the Jurassic—that is from approximately 280 million to 180 million years ago.

enterprise that also prints other Atlantis classics such as the works of Donnelly and Le Plongeon. Steiner claimed to have derived his view of the lost continents from consultation of what he called the "Akasha Chronicle"—a spiritual record of the past available only to the initiated. Nevertheless, many of his ideas are obviously drawn from the work of Madame Blavatsky.

Steiner's Lemurians were feeble-minded, but they had enormous willpower by which they could lift heavy weights. Young Lemurians were taught to bear pain as an aid to developing this willpower. The Lemurians were endowed with souls, and they slowly developed the rudiments of speech. During their period as egg-laying hermaphrodites, the Lemurians made do with a single eye, but their vision improved along with their discovery of sex. According to Steiner, while their souls dominated their bodies, the Lemurians remained bisexual, but when the earth entered "a certain stage of its densification," the increasing density of matter forced a division of the sexes. The Lemurians were unenthusiastic about this change, and for a long time they regarded sexual intercourse as a sacred duty rather than a pleasure. The Lemurian women remained far more spiritual than their menfolk.

Below: Scott-Elliot's second map of Lemuria, representing the continent at a later period in its history. The earth's landmasses were so arranged, according to Scott-Elliot, through the Cretaceous period and into the Eocene—from some 136 million to some 60 million years ago. At that time, "great catastrophes" had begun the dismemberment of Lemuria, but its final destruction was still far off. The occultist never professed that these maps were perfectly accurate, but he thought they were probably correct in important details.

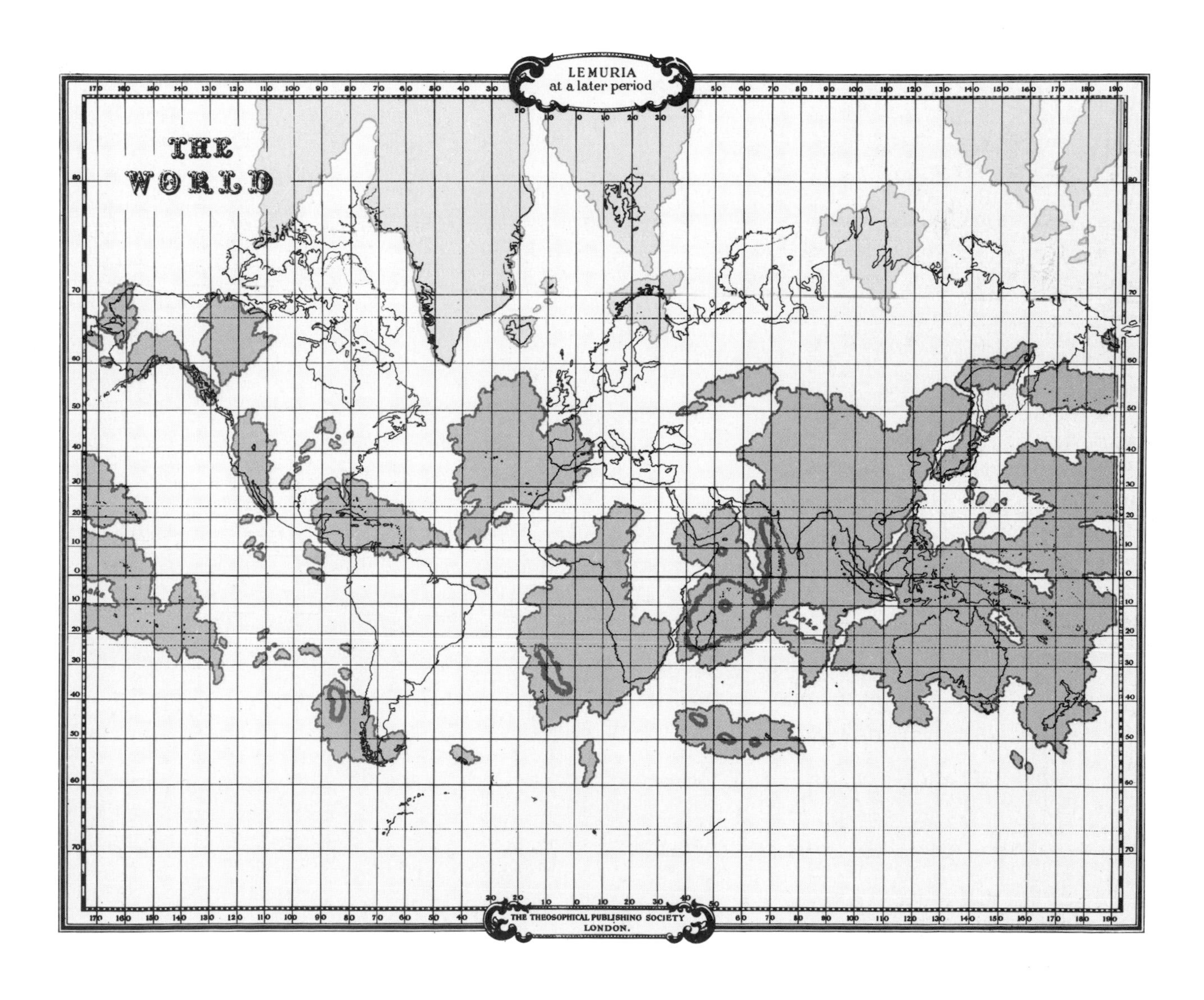

Right: Austrian occultist Rudolf Steiner, Theosophist, member of Ordo Templi Orientis, and later founder of his own quasi-Rosicrucian movement, Anthroposophy. In 1923 Steiner published an account of Lemuria that he asserted came from mystical sources, but it was obviously heavily influenced by the work of Madame Blavatsky. Steiner credited the Lemurians with being in some respects remarkably advanced. By controlling the life force, he said, they flew heavier-than-air machines.

Steiner's Atlanteans, like the Lemurians, were unable to reason but they did possess good memories. They were educated in a way that enabled them to hold a vast store of images in their minds, and each problem was solved by remembering a precedent. When confronted with a novel situation, however, this system left them floundering. The Atlanteans had learned to control the "life force," which they were able to use to power their aircraft.

They had also discovered the magical power of certain words, which they used to heal the sick or to tame wild animals. They wove the branches of living trees to form their houses and cities. Toward the end of their racial history, when the Semites emerged, the Atlanteans had begun to lose their mastery of the life force and were allowing individualism to take over. However, the Semites developed reasoning and a conscience to take themselves a step further along the evolutionary scale, and their descendants, the Aryans, refined these qualities further still.

So what began as mere speculation in the minds of biologists looking for a land-bridge in the Indian Ocean has developed into a complex occult world picture centered on both Atlantis and Lemuria, which—depending on whose account is regarded as the most authoritative—might once have been joined together in a single massive continent that covered practically the entire Southern Hemisphere and stretched all the way into the North Atlantic.

It would be easy to dismiss Blavatsky, Scott-Elliot, and Steiner as cranks or fools, and their accounts as highly romanticized fiction with mass appeal. But would that be entirely fair? Do we know enough about man's spiritual and mental abilities to rule out the possibility of being able to step back in time? The field of parapsychology is a thriving if frustrating one, but there are certainly enough paranormal phenomena now under study for us to keep an open mind on the possibility of astral clairvoyance. Indeed some occultists have claimed that Plato himself might have used this method in compiling his Atlantis story.

It is intriguing to note that many early maps of the world showed a continental landmass in the Southern Hemisphere, long before anyone had ever mentioned Lemuria. The landmass, placed in the South Pacific, was named *Terra Australis Incognita*, "the great unknown southern continent," and no one was more surprised than the European explorers of the 16th and 17th centuries to discover little but sea in the vast Pacific Ocean. It has been argued that the belief in *Terra Australis Incognita* originated in the human desire for symmetry, which caused the Greeks to suppose that equal amounts of land were distributed, in symmetrical fashion, around the globe. Although this idea was modified by the voyages of Columbus and others, most people continued to think it reasonable that the same amount of land should be found below the equator as above it. The discovery of Australia in the 17th century failed to solve the problem, being too small and too barren a land to fulfill people's expectations about the great southern continent, and even when the great British explorer Captain James Cook had shown beyond doubt that no such continent existed in the South Pacific, some people clung to the idea that it must once have been there. Believers in this lost continent argue that our very desire for symmetry may be a manifestation of a deep, latent *knowing*—a collective subconscious memory of the land on which our ancestors evolved.

The problem with the occultists is that their stories go back so far in time. Scientists assure us that if such enormous changes in the earth's surface as the occultists describe did occur, they would have taken place long before man appeared on the planet. By the time our species was emerging the earth's crust was relatively peaceful, and has remained so ever since.

Probably most people today would prefer to fall in with an orthodox view of the earth backed by scientific evidence. But before we dismiss the occultists and their beliefs there is one important question that requires an answer: Why do the ancient myths and legends of practically every people tell of a tremendous catastrophe that once shook the earth? Perhaps the scientists are mistaken after all.

Did Lemurians Really Control the "Life Force"?

Atlantean Airships

The vast continent of Lemuria perished, according to W. Scott-Elliot, through volcanic action. But a northern peninsula in the Atlantic Ocean survived Lemuria's fiery destruction, and there the fourth root race of man evolved. This was the Atlantean race, and civilization first emerged in its home, the legendary Atlantis.

The civilization of Scott-Elliot's Atlantis sounds like a modern SF dream. Its scientific knowledge was in any case far in advance of that of the late 19th century, when Scott-Elliot wrote. He even credited the Atlanteans with the invention of airships, powered in their early days by life force or *vril*, but in later times by a "force not yet discovered by science." This mysterious fuel enabled the Atlantean upper classes—for whose sole use the airships were originally reserved—to travel at up to 100 miles an hour.

Atlantean airships were built first from wood, later from a metallic alloy, but in either case they appeared "seamless and perfectly smooth, and they shone in the dark as if coated with luminous paint." They were boat-shaped, with a ramming nose, and decked over to protect their passengers at speed. At first they carried only a few passengers; later, fighting airships holding 50 or 100 men were built.

Chapter 12
Legends of Fire and Flood

Tales of terrible devastation caused by volcanic eruption, fire, or flood are strangely common to the myths and legends of peoples throughout the world. Are they, as some historians and archaeologists suggest, based upon folk memories of a single worldwide holocaust? Or, as seems equally probable, is each legend founded on a smaller, more localized event? And if some almighty catastrophe did occur, what effect did it have upon the present distribution of the world's continents? Once again, Atlantis, Mu, and Lemuria are vital elements in the arguments of the experts. But what is the real answer?

The earth was at peace. A mild climate enveloped the planet and man had responded well to the beneficence of nature. He had learned to cultivate and harvest his crops. He had domesticated animals to help make his life easier. Various civilizations were beginning to blossom. Then a terrible and all-encompassing catastrophe shook the earth.

The sky lit up with a strange celestial display. Those who saw in this a portent of disaster fled for shelter. Those who watched and waited perished as the sky grew dark and a fearful rain fell upon the earth. In places the rain was red like blood. In others it was like gravel or hailstones. And it brought down fire from the sky, too. Nothing escaped this global holocaust. Men and animals were engulfed. Forests were crushed. Even those who reached the caves were not safe. Darkness gripped the earth and tremendous quakes convulsed the planet. Mountains were thrown up to the heavens and continents were sucked beneath the seas as the stricken earth rolled and tilted. Hurricane winds lashed the planet's wretched surface and tidal waves swept across vast stretches of land. Fearful explosions shook the world as molten lava spewed out from the broken crust. A terrible heat hung over the planet and in places even the sea boiled.

Some, miraculously, lived through this horrific turmoil. After many long days of darkness the mantle of gloom was lifted from the earth and the survivors slowly began rebuilding their lives. A catastrophe of such proportions would account for the

Opposite: a 19th-century artist's representation of the biblical story of the destruction of Sodom and Gomorrah. Such tales of a terrible devastation caused by volcanic eruption, fire, or flood are common to the mythologies of peoples throughout the world. Are they based on folk memories of an appalling holocaust by which the entire earth was once shaken? Or is each legend founded on a smaller, more localized event?

Terrifying Events of Ancient Myth

Right: Akkadian cylinder seal of the 3rd century B.C., depicting Zu, the bird-man, led for judgment before Ea, god of the deep. This reproduction is larger than the actual seal. One of the first flood myths belonged to the earliest civilizations of the Tigris-Euphrates valley. It told how Ea warned the earth of a disastrous inundation that was soon to come.

sinking of a huge continent such as Atlantis—but did such an event ever take place?

If it did, we might expect to find evidence of it in the myths, legends, and folklore of the people who survived. It is a remarkable fact that almost all races have a tradition, handed down through countless generations, of a catastrophe that nearly ended the world. Not only are these legends similar in essence, they are also frequently similar in detail, to such an extent that it is tempting to assume they all share a common origin: a terrifying event of global proportions.

The Babylonian *Epic of Gilgamesh*, which is around 4000 years old and records traditions of an even earlier age, tells of a dark cloud that rushed at the earth, leaving the land shriveled by the heat of the flames: "Desolation . . . stretched to heaven; all that was bright was turned into darkness. . . . Nor could a brother distinguish his brother. . . . Six days . . . the hurricane, deluge, and tempest continued sweeping the land . . . and all human life back to its clay was returned."

From ancient Hindu legend comes an account of the appearance in the sky of "a being shaped like a boar, white and exceedingly small; this being, in the space of an hour, grew to the size of an elephant of the largest size, and remained in the air." After some time the "boar" suddenly uttered "a sound like the loudest thunder, and the echo reverberated and shook all the quarters of the universe." This object then became a "dreadful spectacle," and "descended from the region of the air, and plunged head-foremost into the water. The whole body of water was convulsed by the motion, and began to rise in waves, while the guardian spirit of the sea, being terrified, began to tremble for his domain and cry for mercy."

Hesiod, a Greek poet of the 8th century B.C., writes of a legend involving the earth and the heavens. The story centers around a fiery, serpentlike creature, an aerial monster mightier than men and gods alike, that wreaks terrible havoc upon the earth: "Harshly then he thundered, and heavily and terribly the earth reechoed around; and the broad heaven above, and the sea and streams of ocean, and the abyss of earth. But beneath his immortal feet vast Olympus trembled, as the king uprose and earth groaned beneath. And the heat from both caught the dark-

Opposite: flames spurt and colossal clouds of vapor, smoke, and ash billow from the sea as a submarine volcano surfaces to form an island. This photograph of Surtsey's birth in 1963 off southwest Iceland shows the way in which many oceanic islands began.

Above: *The Seventh Plague of Egypt*, a 19th-century painting of one of the terrible vengeances that, according to the Bible, God wreaked upon the enemies of the Jews. The Bible tells how Moses "stretched forth his rod toward heaven: and the Lord sent thunder and hail, and fire ran along the ground. . . ." In the view of cosmologist Immanuel Velikovsky, this archetypal catastrophe was part of a series of natural disasters caused by a comet nearly colliding with the earth.

colored sea, both of the thunder and the lightning, and fire from the monster, the heat arising from the thunderstorm, winds, and burning lightning. And all earth, and heaven, and sea were boiling. . . ."

From Iceland we have further evidence of a global catastrophe in the *Poetic Edda*, a collection of ancient Scandinavian legendary poems of unknown antiquity:

"Mountains dash together,
Heroes go the way to Hel,
and heaven is rent in twain. . . .
The sun grows dark,
The earth sinks into the sea,
The bright stars from heaven vanish;

Fire rages,
Heat blazes,
And high flames play
'Gainst heaven itself."

The legends of the Cashinaua, the aborigines of western Brazil, tell of the time when "The lightnings flashed and the thunders roared terribly and all were afraid. Then the heaven burst and the fragments fell down and killed everything and everybody. Heaven and earth changed places. Nothing that had life was left upon the earth."

In North America, the Choctaw Indians of Oklahoma have a tradition about the time when "The earth was plunged in darkness for a long time." A bright light eventually appeared in the north, "but it was mountain-high waves, rapidly coming nearer."

The Samoan aborigines of the South Pacific have a legend that says: "Then arose smell . . . the smell became smoke, which again became clouds. . . . The sea too arose, and in a stupendous catastrophe of nature the land sank into the sea. . . . The new earth (the Samoan islands) arose out of the womb of the last earth."

The Bible, too, contains numerous passages that refer to terrible conflagrations. Psalms 18:7-15 is one example: "Then the earth shook and trembled; the foundations also of the hills moved and were shaken. . . . The Lord also thundered in the heavens, and the Highest gave his voice; hail stones and coals of fire. . . . Then the channels of waters were seen, and the foundations of the world were discovered. . . ."

These are but a few of the vast number of legends dealing with great cosmic events and cataclysmic destruction on the face of the earth. The ancient records of Egypt, India, and China, the mythology of Greece and Rome, the legends of the Mayas and the Aztecs, the biblical accounts, and those of Norway, Finland, Persia, and Babylon, all tell the same story. So, too, do the people of widely separated countries, such as the Celts of Britain and the Maoris of New Zealand.

Archetypal Catastrophes

What on earth, or in heaven, could have caused such seemingly worldwide catastrophe? The accounts quoted above are taken from two masterly works on the subject, both of which offer the same explanation. One is Ignatius Donnelly's *Ragnarok: The Age of Fire and Gravel*, published in 1883, whose title is drawn from the legend of *Ragnarok* (wrongly translated as "the darkness of the gods" and "the rain of dust") contained in the Scandinavian *Poetic Edda*. The other is *Worlds in Collision*, which appeared in 1950, and is the most famous of several books by Immanuel Velikovsky, a Russo-Israeli physician whose theories have made him as controversial a character as Donnelly before him. Both men suggest that a comet which came into close proximity with the earth caused the terrible events remembered by the ancient peoples of the world. They agree on many points of evidence, such as the myths and legends, and the sinking of Atlantis features in both works. But they take different stands in their search for scientific proof of their theories.

Above: the Fenris wolf devours the god Odin, a scene from the Norse legend *Ragnarok*. Donnelly mistranslated Ragnarok as "rain of dust" and used the word as the title of his book on the comet theory.

Donnelly devotes a large part of his book to a discussion of the drift, or *till*—a vast deposit of sand, gravel, and clay that lies above the stratified rocks of the earth's surface. The origin

Velikovsky's Venus Theory

of the till puzzled many geologists, and Donnelly's explanation was that it had rained down from the heavens as the earth passed through a comet's tail. He argued that the comet's tail would have been moving at close to the speed of light when the earth passed through it, so only half the planet would have been covered by the till, and he sought to produce evidence to confirm his theory.

Velikovsky, though agreeing that a close earth-comet encounter lay behind the ancient catastrophe legends, has no use for the till theory—which was a foundation stone of Donnelly's treatise—and he observes: "Donnelly . . . tried in his book *Ragnarok* to explain the presence of till and gravel on the rock substratum in America and Europe by hypothesizing an encounter with a comet, which rained till on the terrestrial hemisphere facing it at that moment. . . . His assumption that there is till only in one half of the earth is arbitrary and wrong."

Right: the beautifully colored comet Humason, which appeared in the night skies in 1961. If Velikovsky's theory of cosmic evolution is correct, the planet Venus once looked like this as it sped toward the earth, bringing disaster in its train.

Below: Immanuel Velikovsky. In 1950 Velikovsky published his controversial theory of planetary encounters in *Worlds in Collision*, which set people speculating on the evolution of the universe.

Neither Donnelly nor Velikovsky was the first to argue that a comet had caused havoc on this planet. The English scientist William Whiston, who succeeded Sir Isaac Newton at Cambridge, wrote a book in 1696, *New Theory of the Earth*, which attempted to prove that a comet caused the biblical Flood. There was also a belief, at the time of Aristotle, in the 4th century B.C., that a comet had joined the solar system as a planet.

But Velikovsky has pieced together a far more startling picture of cosmic activity. It began, he believes, when a planetary collision caused Jupiter to eject a comet, which went into an eccentric orbit. This brought it close to the earth in about 1500 B.C., causing global catastrophes. The comet returned 52 years later and did further damage to the earth. Its approaches even caused the planet to stop and then rotate in the opposite direction, changing the position of the poles and altering the earth's orbit. The hydrocarbon gases of the comet's tail showered down on the earth in a rain of gravel and fire that formed the petroleum deposits we now use to power our automobiles and airplanes.

The comet, having left much of its tail behind, then had a close encounter with Mars, causing that planet to leave its orbit and, in turn, to come dangerously close to the earth in the 8th and 7th centuries B.C. Meanwhile the comet joined the solar system as a planet—the one we now call Venus.

When this theory was first published, in 1950, it caused a sensation. Since then Velikovsky has become something of a cult figure, particularly among young people, though the scientific community has largely dismissed his ideas as nonsense.

L. Sprague de Camp probably expresses the opinion of most orthodox scientists and scholars in his succinct and damning

Below: the planet Venus. Velikovsky believes that Venus began its life between 4000 and 5000 years ago as a vast comet, which caused havoc in the universe before taking its own planetary place. It was a near collision between the comet Venus and the earth that caused the catastrophic natural disasters recorded in legends throughout the world.

Hanns Hörbiger and the Lost Continents

appraisal of Velikovsky's "mad" theory. He writes in *Lost Continents*: "Despite the impressive build-up . . . Velikovsky neither establishes a case nor accounts for the success of the Copernicus-Newton-Einstein picture of the cosmos which he undertook to supersede. Some of his mythological references are wrong (for instance he uses the Brasseur 'translation' of the *Troano Codex*); the rest merely demonstrate once again that the corpus of recorded myth is so vast that you can find mythological allusions to back up any cosmological speculation you please. The Babylonians left clear records of observations of Venus 5000 years ago, behaving just as it does now. . . . Moreover, the theory is ridiculous from the point of view of physics and mechanics. Comets are not planets and do not evolve into planets; instead they are loose aggregations of meteors with total masses less than a millionth that of the earth. Such a mass—about that of an ordinary mountain—could perhaps devastate several counties or a small state if struck, but could not appreciably affect the earth's orbit, rotation, inclination, or other components of movement. . . . And the gas of which the comet's tail is composed is so attenuated that if the tail of a good-sized comet were compressed to the density of iron, I could put the whole thing in my briefcase!"

So that disposes of Velikovsky—or does it? Seven years after his book was published, man made his first tentative steps into space. Since then earthlings have landed on the moon, and space vehicles have probed our nearest planetary neighbors. So far, these explorations appear to have confirmed some of Velikovsky's predictions about our planetary system. He had stated that, because Venus is a newcomer to the system, it is still giving off heat. This was thought to be nonsense at the time, and the consensus of astronomical opinion was that the surface temperature of Venus was around 65°F. Radio astronomy and the arrival of space vehicles in the vicinity of the planet have proved

Below: Hanns Hörbiger's picture of the earth before the continents of Atlantis and Lemuria were submerged. His map shows the routes by which migrants from the lost continents brought civilization to the rest of the world. Hörbiger accounted for the disappearance of these huge landmasses by a theory of "cosmic gravity," a force attracting all the bodies in a stellar system toward a central sun, and smaller bodies to larger ones. It was this force that had pulled the moon into the earth's orbit, setting up such stresses on earth that Atlantis and Lemuria had sunk into the sea.

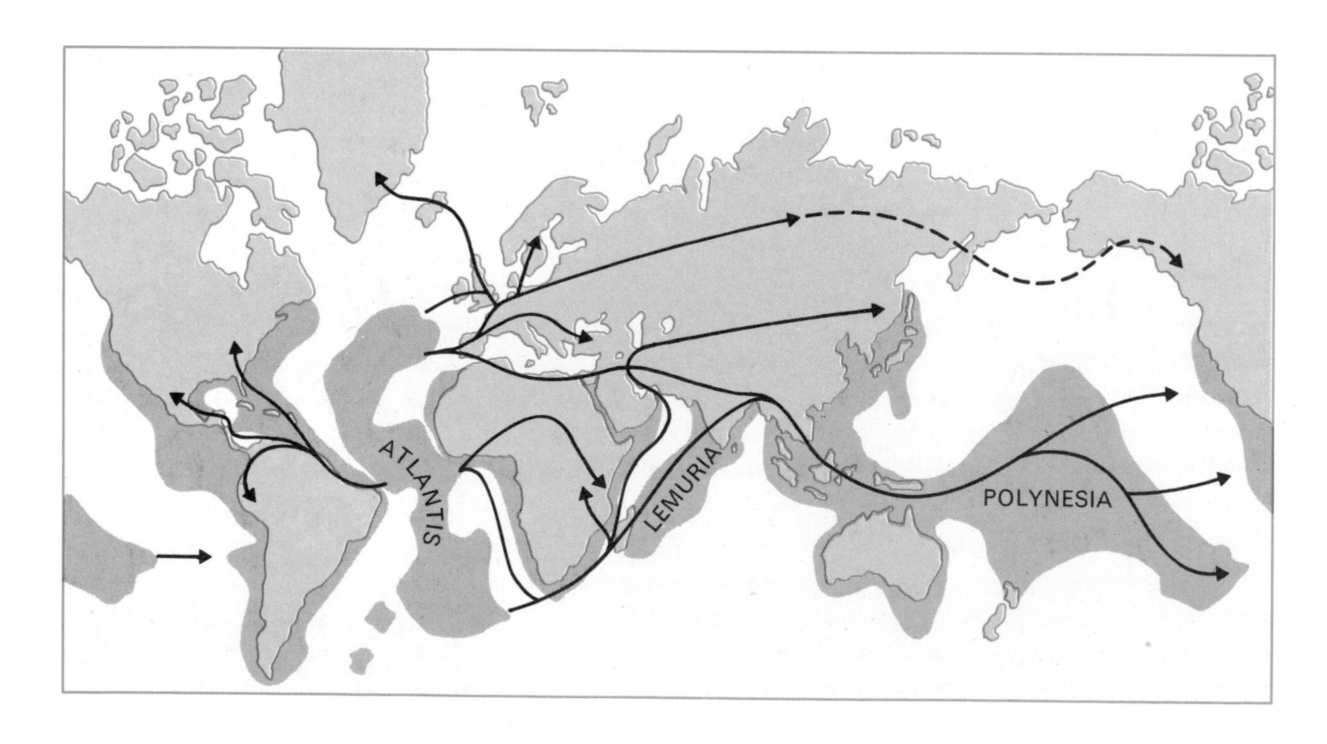

Left: reconstruction of the Gate of the Sun at Tiahuanaco, Bolivia. In common with other Atlantists, Hörbiger believed that it was the Atlanteans who had brought civilization to the New and Old Worlds, and who were responsible for the construction of the vast edifices of olden times.

Velikovsky right. Mariner II, when it passed Venus in December 1962, detected a temperature of over 800°F, and subsequent investigations have revealed a temperature of approximately 990°F.

The results of the Mariner probe—the first to provide reliable information about the planet—showed that, just as Velikovsky had maintained, Venus is enclosed in an envelope of hydrocarbon gases and dust. It was also revealed that Venus rotated retrogradely, a sign that either it had been disturbed or it had evolved in a different way from other planets. A Russian probe that soft-landed on the planet in October 1975 was able to relay information for 53 minutes before the extremely high pressure of the atmosphere caused it to stop transmitting. But it was enough for the Russian scientists to declare that Venus is a young planet, and still "alive."

Interviewed about these findings by a British newspaper, Velikovsky commented that they confirmed his theory. His book contained many other predictions about Mars, Jupiter, the earth, and the moon. "And about 30 of them have since been proved right," he claimed. If subsequent probes confirm other details of his theory, it would not be the first time that science has had to change its thinking about the history of the earth and its partners in the solar system.

Velikovsky weaves the destruction of Atlantis into his theory by suggesting that the continent sank as a result of the first approach of the Venus comet, though in order to make this idea fit his scheme he has to alter Plato's dating of the Atlantis catastrophe. There is one zero too many in Plato's date, says Velikovsky. Atlantis sank not 9000 years before Solon's trip to Egypt, but 900 years before Solon—in about 1500 B.C.

The idea that a comet destroyed Atlantis was not a new one. It had previously been put forward in 1785 by the Italian scholar

Below: portrait head from Tiahuanaco. Hörbiger argued that the "pure Nordic features" of this man are evidence of the common descent of the American Indians and the Aryan Germans from the original civilized Atlantean race.

Gian Rinaldo Carli—although he dated the catastrophe at 4000 B.C.—and was taken up again in the 1920s by a German writer called Karl George Zschaetzch, whose main aim was to prove the racial superiority of the Aryans by providing them with a pedigree that went all the way back to Atlantis.

Another theory to account for the Atlantis catastrophe came from Hanns Hörbiger, an Austrian inventor and engineer. Hörbiger maintained that the universe is filled with "cosmic building stuff," consisting of hot metallic stars and "cosmic ice." The collision between a hot star and a block of cosmic ice generates a tremendous explosion, throwing pieces of star material and ice particles into space. These bodies spiral inward toward the sun, causing another explosion, which covers the nearest planets with a thick coating of ice. Hörbiger believed the Milky Way to consist of ice particles, and maintained that Venus and Mercury were sheathed in ice, as was the moon. According to Hörbiger's theory, the earth had possessed several moons before the present one. Each of these moons caused violent earthquakes and floods on the earth at the time of its capture by our planet, and finally shattered, showering its fragments onto the earth's surface. These events gave rise to the catastrophe myths, and it was the capture of our present moon that caused both Atlantis and Lemuria to sink. Hörbiger predicted that the eventual breakup and fall of our present moon would probably wipe out life on earth.

Hörbiger's theory, published in 1913, attracted millions of followers, and made him as much of a cult figure as Velikovsky is today. But whereas space exploration and our increased knowledge of the universe have disproved most of Hörbiger's assertions, many of Velikovsky's ideas are still living up to the expectations of his followers, who foresee them becoming the accepted scientific thinking of a future era. Unless and until that day comes, however, we need to examine the catastrophe legends and the theories of lost continents in the light of current scientific belief. The picture then becomes far less promising.

Orthodox scientists dismiss the idea of a global catastrophe of the kind described by Velikovsky and others. How, then, do they explain the legends? The answer is that, universal though the disaster legends may seem, they are descriptions of separate events that occurred at different times and were fairly localized. They concern tremendous earthquakes, great volcanic eruptions, massive flooding of river valleys, and inundation of areas below sea level. These events, spanning many centuries and not linked in any way, gave rise to the legends, which were doubtless exaggerated as they were handed down from one generation to the next.

Take Noah's flood, for example. According to the Bible, this great deluge drowned every living thing on earth—apart from the few survivors in the ark. It is now considered likely that this story was based on a real flood that submerged something like 40,000 square miles of the Euphrates Valley some time between 5400 and 4200 B.C. China and the lowlands of Bengal have seen similar great floods, and these, too, could have given rise to deluge legends. Many geologists believe that the Mediterranean was once a fertile valley below sea level, which was flooded long

Was there One Flood or Many?

Opposite: *The Deluge*, a 19th-century depiction of the great flood with which, according to the Bible, God punished the world. So vast was the cataclysm that, apart from those warned by God, every living thing perished. Today orthodox scholars believe that the flood described in the Bible was based on an inundation that swamped the Euphrates Valley some 7000 years ago. To those ancient peoples it must have seemed as though the entire world had been drowned.

Below: Noah's ark rides the floodwaters, watched over by God. Noah, warned by God of the approaching flood, saved his family and one male and female of every animal species in his ark.

Above: Japanese artist Hokusai's print of a tidal wave, another of the natural disasters that can devastate the earth. A tidal wave breaking on the shore causes immense damage and many deaths. It can be set off by an earthquake or volcanic eruption, and the combination of earth tremor, fire, and flood appears in many myths about the end of the world.

ago by the Atlantic in one terrible rush. The flooding of the former Zuider Zee (now Ijssel Lake) in the Netherlands is a more recent example of this kind of catastrophe. A storm in 1282 broke the natural dykes that protected this area of sub-sea-level land, and let in the North Sea, which submerged it in a single day.

In this century alone there have been a number of earthquakes that have taken in excess of 100,000 lives, and there are records of even more disastrous quakes in the past. The Chinese earthquake of 1556 is said to have killed 830,000 people. It would be surprising if similar quakes in ancient times did *not* give rise to catastrophe legends. To those living in the affected areas it must certainly have seemed as if the whole world were coming to an end.

Tidal Waves and Tsunamis

An earthquake beneath the sea may cause a tidal wave. In mid-ocean the gentle slopes of a tidal wave may go undetected, but as the wave approaches and meets the shore it surges up into a massive, sometimes skyscraper-high, wall of water. In 1737, a 210-foot tidal wave was recorded in Kamchatka (now part of the eastern Soviet Union), and many others have been reported between 50 and 100 feet tall. Volcanic eruptions, in addition to wreaking their own havoc, may also set up tidal waves. The Krakatoa eruption of 1883 caused a huge wave that drowned 36,380 people living on the shores of the nearby Indonesian islands.

So, our history is rich in natural disasters that have taken a tremendous toll of human life—as they still do—and that may well have given rise to the legends. But could any of these pestilences account for the sinking of a great continent such as Atlantis? Most scientists think it extremely unlikely. An earthquake might have destroyed part of the island continent, or caused landslides around its shores, but the total area devastated

Above: a tidal wave engulfing a British steamship off the West Indies in 1867. The widespread incidence of such disasters may account for their presence in the myths of so many different races.

by even a violent earthquake is relatively limited, and a quake that would have destroyed a huge landmass is unheard-of. Had Atlantis been an island with a very low profile it might have been at least partly submerged by flooding, but Plato describes Atlantis as a mountainous country. A tidal wave might have washed over Atlantis, but it would not have washed it away. And a volcanic eruption could have blown part of the continent into the ocean, but if Atlantis had been anywhere near the size claimed by Plato much would still be towering above the sea. In the scientists' view even a whole series of massive earthquakes, volcanic eruptions, and flooding would take many thousands of

Wegener and the Continental Drift Theories

Above: Alfred Wegener, German geophysicist who proposed the theory of continental drift. According to this theory, the continents we know today were once joined in a single landmass. When this broke up, the many pieces "drifted" to their present positions on the earth's surface.

years to sink an island of anything approaching continental size—and a low, flat island at that.

The only other possibility would seem to be that the earth's crust is capable of opening up and swallowing areas of land. Small islands have been submerged in living memory, and others have suddenly appeared. Could the same forces have been responsible for wiping Atlantis from the face of our planet? To answer this question we need to look at present opinion on the way the world has developed, and at the processes by which continents take shape.

According to current geological theory, the earth is encased in a crust of rock that becomes hotter and hotter as we go down toward the center of the planet. Some 50 to 100 miles beneath the surface the rock has become white-hot. From that point down the earth consists of a hot, glasslike substance called *magma*, which surrounds the nickel-iron core of the earth, a sphere about 4000 miles in diameter. The cool exterior rocks consist in general of two types: dense, heavy, magnesium-bearing rocks, called *sima*, which form most of the ocean floors, and light, aluminum-bearing rocks, called *sial*, which form most of the land areas. Geologists see the continents as beds of sial "floating" on a crust of sima. The continental blocks descend deeply into the sima, showing a comparatively small amount above the surface, just as icebergs do in water.

Over a century ago, it became apparent to some geologists that the face of our globe has not always been as it now appears. The evidence for this assumption was the same that led many biologists of the time to consider the possibility of a lost continent: namely, the existence of fossils of similar fauna and flora on continents thousands of miles apart.

Geologists who accepted fossil evidence of ancient land connections between the continents put forward the idea of a former gigantic landmass, which they called Gondwanaland, comprising present-day South America, Africa, India, Australia, and Antarctica. A second landmass, consisting of North America and Europe, was also suggested and given the name Laurasia. However, the proponents of this theory were unable to offer any convincing evidence as to how these two supercontinents might have broken up, and their idea attracted little support among fellow scientists.

Nevertheless, in the early years of the 20th century, a number of scientists began thinking along similar lines, and in 1915 the German astronomer, geophysicist, and meteorologist Alfred Wegener published the modern theory of continental drift. Wegener argued that if the continents float like icebergs on the sima crust, why should they not also drift like icebergs across the face of the earth? He suggested that all the modern continents were once joined in a single giant landmass. They have since drifted apart, and the drift is continuing; millions of years from now, the face of our planet will look very different from the way it does today.

Wegener's theory has rocked the geological establishment, and its revolutionary effect on the geological sciences has been compared to the effect of Darwin's theory of evolution on the biological sciences a century ago. But for several decades after its publication the majority of scientists continued to reject the idea of continental drift, mainly because they found it hard to envisage forces strong enough to move the continents around. (After all, even the smallest continent, Australia, weighs around 500 million million million kilograms.) In due course, however, a plausible explanation—involving convection currents driven by radioactive heat from within the earth—was put forward to account for the continental movements, and a mass of impressive evidence began piling up in support of Wegener's theory, so that most scientists now accept the reality of continental drift.

In the late 1960s computers were used to show how the continental jigsaw pieces might fit together to form the original gigantic landmass. This was not an easy task, because the shape of the continents has altered over the ages. Some minor parts of the jigsaw are missing, some have been added, and the true edges

Below: world map overprinted with lines representing the edges of the largest of the 19 "plates" that make up the earth's crust. Geological activity takes place mainly on the joins between the plates, and Atlantists believe that during such movement Atlantis could have sunk into the earth.

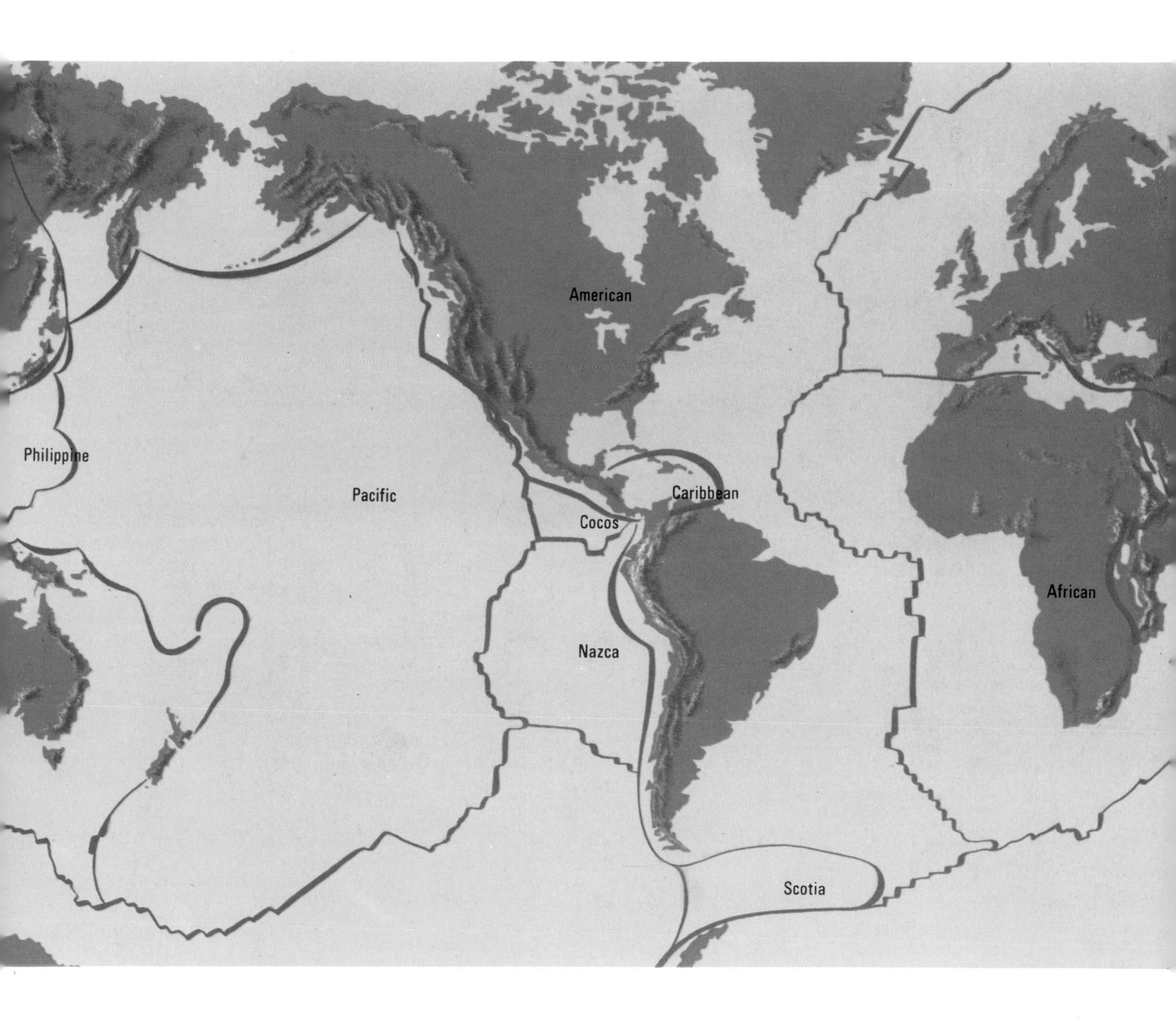

of the continents generally lie far below sea level and have not yet been plotted in detail. Nevertheless, the computer pictures showed an extremely good fit between South America and the western coast of Africa, and between Antarctica, Australia, and India. The fit of these last three continents against south and eastern Africa was less satisfactory, and some adjustment was needed to improve the fit across the North Atlantic, linking Britain and the rest of Europe with North America.

In their book *Continental Drift*, leading British geophysicist D. P. Tarling and his technical journalist wife M. P. Tarling write: "By studying the size and composition of particles in old sedimentary rocks it is possible to work out the direction and type of land from which they were derived. In Britain, we find that the source of many Caledonian Mountain sediments was a very extensive landmass which must have lain to the north and west where there is now the deep Atlantic Ocean. In North America, the sources of many Appalachian rocks lay to the south and east. To explain this before the acceptance of continental drift, geologists supposed that a continent, 'Atlantis,' must have occupied the present position of the Atlantic. This continent was thought to have sunk beneath the Atlantic waves. [But] there can be no question of the existence of a sunken continent in the Atlantic. By reconstructing the jigsaw we not only fit together the Caledonian Mountain chain, but also explain the sources of the sediments which formed it."

Most scientists agree that as we push the continents back to their original places, we effectively squeeze Atlantis off the map. So, could Atlantis have been North America, which, having drifted away, was thought to have been submerged in the Atlantic? No. The continents are moving apart at the rate of between one and six inches a year—hardly enough to give rise to Plato's account of the submergence of Atlantis in a day and a night. What is more, the original landmass is thought to have broken up before the Mesozoic era, some 200 million years ago, and the continents probably reached approximately their present positions by the beginning of the Cenozoic era, around 70 million years ago—long before man appeared on the face of the earth.

Could Atlantis have been in the Pacific, where Mu was said

Below: how the continental drift theory positions the continents on the earth's crust at various epochs. The landmasses were originally joined together in one vast supercontinent, Pangaea. Some 180 million years ago, this began to split into two smaller but still huge landmasses, Laurasia in the north and Gondwanaland in the south. These also broke up, and by 65 million years ago the shapes and positions of the continents began to resemble those we know today. The evidence of continental drift and of the geological composition of the earth's crust seems to rule out the possibility that continents other than ours ever existed. But does it? Might fresh geological evidence start the search again?

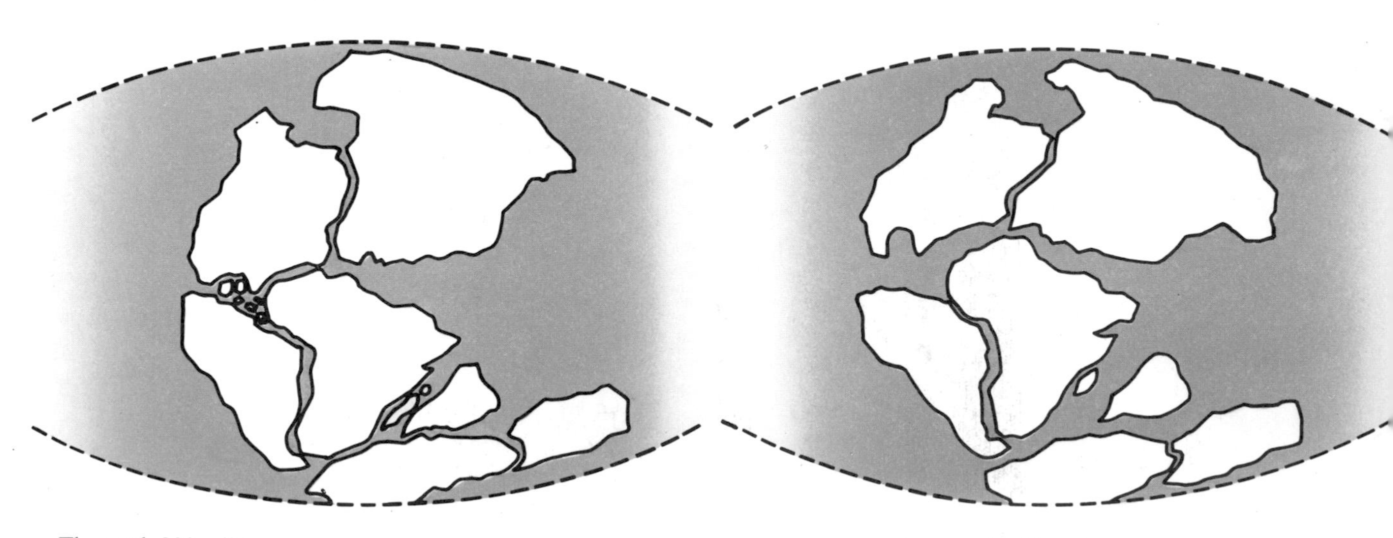

The earth 200 million years ago.

The earth 135 million years ago.

to have sunk, or in the Indian Ocean, where the early Lemuria enthusiasts placed yet another lost continent? Our present knowledge of the earth seems to rule out these possibilities, too. Bearing in mind the geologists' belief that the ocean floors are mostly formed of sima and the landmasses of sial, a sunken continent should be easy to detect because its rocks would be different from surrounding rocks in the deep ocean. However, geological investigation has so far revealed that the greatest areas of deep sima are in the Central Pacific, the southern Indian Ocean, and the Arctic Ocean, making these the least likely sites on earth for a vanished continent.

Not surprisingly, believers in Atlantis hotly contest the findings of modern science that seek to dismiss the existence of the lost continent. In considering the theory of continental drift they point to gaps and seeming misfits in the linking of continents across the Atlantic that might still leave room for Atlantis. Nor are they impressed by the failure of oceanographers to find evidence of a sunken civilization beneath the Atlantic. In his book *The Mystery of Atlantis*, Charles Berlitz points out that even the underwater cities of the Mediterranean have been discovered only comparatively recently and in relatively shallow water. How much more difficult, then, to discover the ruins of Atlantis beneath the far larger Atlantic, where they would be smothered by sedimentation and mud accumulated over thousands of years.

If a once-derided theory such as continental drift can eventually earn the backing of the respectable scientific community, the Atlantists argue, might not other theories, now regarded as nonsensical, one day gain the same acceptance? Perhaps man existed long before the scientists' estimates. Perhaps there was some extraordinary global catastrophe of a nature quite outside the bounds of cautious scientific conjecture. Perhaps Atlantis did exist after all.

Recent scientific findings and theories may have helped modern man put the search for Atlantis into perspective, but they have not proved the lost continent to be a myth. In fact, some investigators among scientists themselves believe they have now discovered the true site of Atlantis, far away from the huge ocean so long regarded as its resting place.

What Happened to Laurasia and to Gondwana?

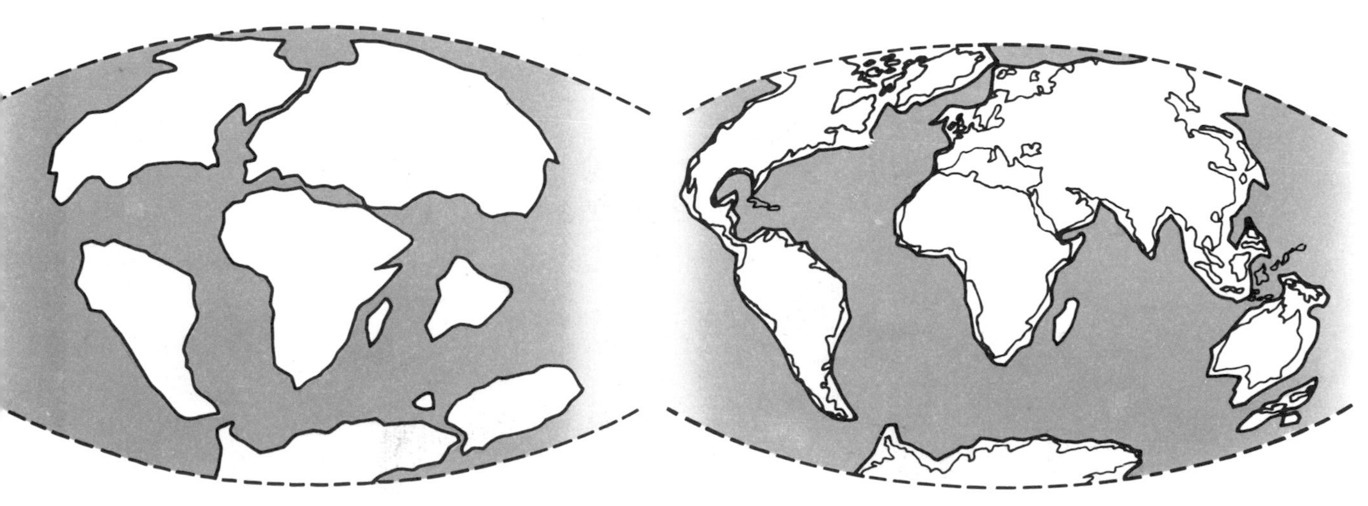

The earth 65 million years ago.

The earth's continents today.

Chapter 13
Has Atlantis Been Found?

"This is the best contender for the title of the real Atlantis. We know that there is something down there under the waves." This is how French underwater explorer Jacques Cousteau has summed up the theory that the volcanic island of Thera, just 75 miles north of Crete, is in fact the original Atlantis described by Plato. Many experts are now convinced that the Greek philosopher based his fabulous lost land upon ancient memories of Thera and Crete. What exactly is the evidence for such a theory? This chapter examines and assesses it all.

Until the beginning of this century most historians regarded the island of Crete as an unimportant place. True, the ancient Greeks had numerous stories and legends about this mountainous island at the southern end of the Aegean Sea. They looked upon Crete as the one-time home of a mighty seafaring people ruled by King Minos, the son of Zeus and the mortal maiden Europa. Legend had it that a bronze robot, with a man's body and a bull's head, patrolled Crete's rocky coastline, keeping invaders at bay by hurling boulders at them. There, too, was the labyrinth in which King Minos imprisoned the Minotaur, the monstrous bull-man who annually devoured seven Greek youths and seven Greek maidens, and who was finally slain by the Greek hero Theseus.

To most historians these stories were nothing more than colorful myths. It took the excavations of British archaeologist Sir Arthur Evans to prove that the legends were founded on fact. In 1900, Evans began uncovering astonishingly beautiful and sophisticated buildings on the island of Crete. His discoveries, together with subsequent finds, revealed that a highly advanced civilization had existed on Crete 4500 years ago. Evans gave this civilization the name Minoan for the legendary King Minos.

Minoans ruled the Aegean while the Greeks were still barbarians. Not only traders, but also colonizers, they were able to extract tribute from less advanced peoples such as the Greeks, and were known as far away as northern and western Europe,

Opposite: sunset over the Kameni Islands, photographed from Thera. In the Bronze Age, Thera was the home of a prosperous civilization closely linked with that of Minoan Crete. Then, in about 1500 B.C., its smoldering volcano erupted, smothering the island with pumice and ash and causing its central portion to sink into the sea. Today, Thera is the largest of three islands that mark the perimeter of the submerged crater or *caldera* of the volcano. In the center of the caldera rise the Kameni Islands, still-smoldering volcanic cones. Archaeologists excavating on Crete and Thera have found similarities between their civilizations and that of Atlantis as described by Plato. Some are convinced that the Greek philosopher based his fabulous continent on old memories of Thera and Crete.

The Real Atlantis?

as well as in Egypt and the eastern Mediterranean, for their seagoing power, their wealth, and their gracious style of living.

Knossos, near modern Heraklion, about three miles from the coast of northern Crete, was the Minoan capital, and in 2500 B.C. it probably housed about 100,000 people. The palace of Knossos, home of the king and queen and a center of Minoan government, was a magnificent complex of buildings covering six acres. The elaborate plan of its rooms, halls, and courts, with their stately porticoes, shrines, tapered columns, and terraces, built on many different levels and linked by stairways and twisting passages, could well have given rise to Greek tales of a labyrinth on the island of Crete. The palace's huge storerooms contained supplies of grain, wine, and oil. Some jars kept there were able to hold up to 79,000 gallons of olive oil. The palace was also a religious and

Below: part of the main staircase of the Palace of Knossos in Crete. In 1900, British archaeologist Arthur Evans began excavations at Knossos that revealed Crete as the home of one of the most striking civilizations of the ancient world. Evans called the civilization Minoan, after the legendary King Minos of Crete.

artistic center, with homes for priests and priestesses and workshops for artists and craftsmen, who held a highly respected place in Minoan society. The palace walls were resplendent with brilliantly colored paintings of birds, beasts, flowers, and young men and women in fashionable dress.

Frescoes and pottery found in Knossos and elsewhere express the Minoans' love of bright colors and swirling shapes, their keen observation of nature, and their zest for living. Their paintings show dancing and feasting, celebrations and sport, plants and animals, rather than battles or sieges—and everywhere their regard for the bull is apparent. Murals and vases show young, unarmed Minoans fearlessly leaping over the back of a bull, and a particularly striking ritual vessel is made in the form of a bull's head with golden horns. Other magnificent treasures, including beautifully wrought gold jewelry, and tools and ornaments inlaid with gold and ivory, testify to the reality of the Minoans' legendary wealth.

Not only did the Minoans live in beautiful surroundings but they enjoyed comforts unmatched until modern times. The palace in Knossos had flushing toilets, running water, and a well-planned drainage system for rainwater and sewage. Its rooms were ingeniously lit by windows opening onto light wells—possibly the earliest example of indirect lighting. The palace was surrounded by a town of 22 acres, containing the houses of sea captains, merchants, and shipowners, and a paved road with drains on either side ran all the way from Knossos to the south coast. Near the southern shore of Crete stood another magnificent city called Phaistos, and about 100 smaller cities or towns were scattered across the island. Archaeological studies have established that the civilization of Crete flourished for about 2000 years, but that it suffered an abrupt collapse around 1500 to 1400 B.C.

Here, for the first time, was evidence that a people very similar to the Atlanteans described by Plato had once existed. It was not long before some scholars were asking if a memory of this great culture had given rise to the Atlantis legend. Both Atlantis and Crete were island kingdoms and great sea powers, and both had suffered a sudden downfall. There seemed to be links, too, between the bull ceremonies depicted in Minoan art and the ritual hunting of the bull said to have taken place on Atlantis.

The first man to point out the similarities between Plato's Atlantis and the Minoan civilization was K. T. Frost, professor of classical history at Queen's University, Belfast. In 1909 Frost wrote in *The Times* of London about the need to reconsider the whole scheme of Mediterranean history as a result of the excavations on Crete, adding: "The whole description of Atlantis which is given in the *Timaeus* and the *Critias* has features so thoroughly Minoan that even Plato could not have invented so many unsuspected facts."

Recalling Plato's story, Frost went on to observe: "The great harbor, for example, with its shipping and its merchants coming from all parts, the elaborate bathrooms, the stadium, and the solemn sacrifice of a bull are all thoroughly, though not exclusively, Minoan; but when we read how the bull is hunted 'in the temple of Poseidon without weapons but with staves and

Above: the head of a Minoan woman, a fragment of a fresco found at Knossos. The Minoan civilization seems to have laid great emphasis on beauty and on pleasure—unlike contemporary civilizations, but like that of the Atlantis Plato described.

Below: the "Harvester Vase." Agriculture flourished in Crete, as in Plato's Atlantis.

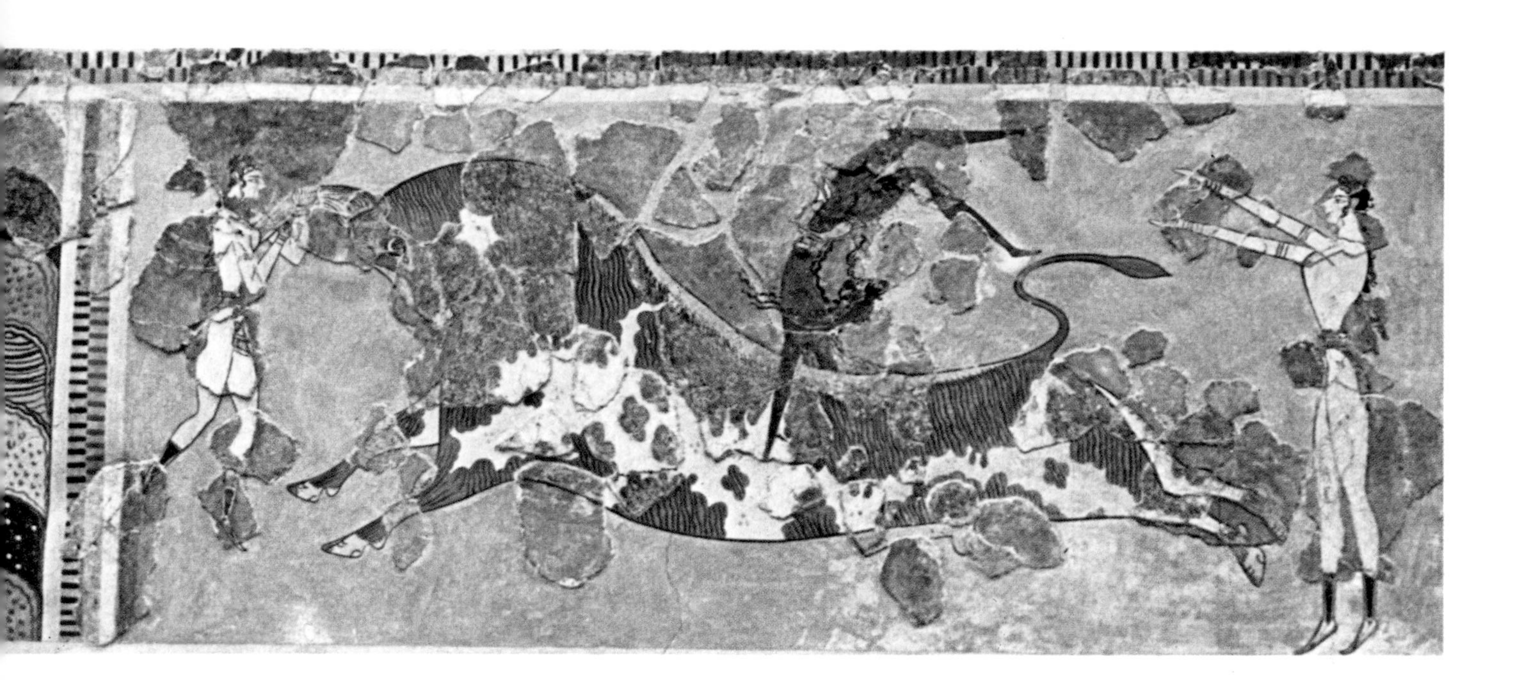

Above: the bull leap, a fresco from the Palace of Knossos depicting the dangerous but exhilarating bull games that the Minoans loved. As the excavations at Knossos progressed, it became clear that the bull was of immense importance to the life and mythology of Minoan Crete—and that it could provide some evidence to identify Crete with Atlantis. The bull, and bull ceremonies, also featured largely in the life of Plato's Atlantis.

nooses' we have an unmistakable description of the bull-ring at Knossos, the very thing which struck foreigners most and which gave rise to the legend of the Minotaur. Plato's words exactly describe the scenes on the famous Vapheio cups which certainly represent catching wild bulls for the Minoan bull-fight which, as we know from the palace itself, differed from all others which the world has seen in exactly the point which Plato emphasizes—namely that no weapons were used."

But Crete is not in the Atlantic. It is nowhere near the size of the great island continent described by Plato. And it has not disappeared beneath the waves. Frost argued that the sudden eclipse of Minoan power was probably caused by invasions from the Greek mainland—a point of view shared by most of his fellow scholars—but few were prepared to accept his suggestion that the loss of contact with their Minoan trading partners had led the Egyptians to believe that Crete had sunk beneath the sea. Frost's theory was therefore dismissed by the academic world, and after his death in World War I his ideas were forgotten.

Thirty years after the publication of Frost's theory, however, Professor Spyridon Marinatos, later Director-General of the Greek Archaeological Service, put forward new evidence that appeared to strengthen Frost's case. In an article entitled "The Volcanic Destruction of Minoan Crete," published in the British journal *Antiquity* in 1939, Marinatos told how, during his excavations in Amnisos, the site of an ancient harbor close to Knossos, he had discovered a pit full of pumice stone. He also found evidence that a vast mass of water had washed over the site, dragging large objects out of place. Marinatos became convinced that Crete's downfall was due not to foreign invaders, as most scholars still assumed, but to a tremendously violent natural catastrophe. He was also able to point an accusing finger at the probable source of this devastation: a small volcanic island named Thera, just 75 miles north of Crete, and the most southerly island in the archipelago of the Cyclades.

The Bull Link

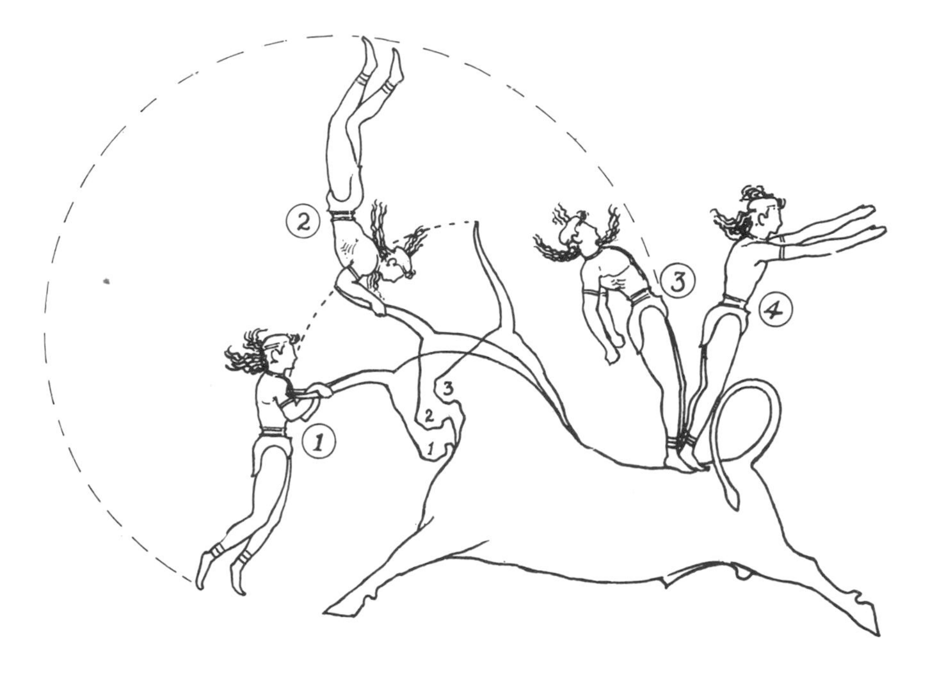

Left: the stages in the bull leap, reconstructed from the fresco opposite for Arthur Evans' book, *The Palace of Minos at Knossos.* First, the acrobat seized the bull by the tips of its horns (1), then somersaulted into the air over the animal's head (2). He would have gained impetus for his leap when the bull raised its head to toss him. Loosing the horns, he landed on his feet on the bull's back (3), then jumped or somersaulted to the comparative safety of the ground (4). It appears from paintings and sculptures discovered at Knossos that such games really took place in Crete—yet, as Evans wrote, they "transcend the power and skill of mortal man."

Thera has been given a number of names. Some people today know it as Santorini, a name derived from Saint Irene, the patron saint of the island. In the past, it has been called Kallistē ("the very beautiful island") and Strongulē ("the circular island"). Although these two names preserve a memory of how the island used to look, neither description is appropriate today. Once a circular island, about 11 miles across, covered by cone-shaped peaks, with woods and good vegetation, Thera now consists of three fragments of its former glory. The largest is a crescent-shaped island, Thera proper, which has a population of around 5000. A much smaller island, Therasia, situated to the northwest, has only two villages. The third portion, Aspronisi, is an uninhabited white fragment. Viewed from the air these three pieces

Below: reconstruction of the Palace of Knossos. It covered a vast area and—built as it was on different levels linked by twisting passages and stairs—could have given rise to the myth of the Cretan labyrinth where the bull monster, the Minotaur, dwelt. Plato tells of a bull hunt in the Temple of Poseidon in Atlantis, yet another example of remarkable coincidence between myth and fact.

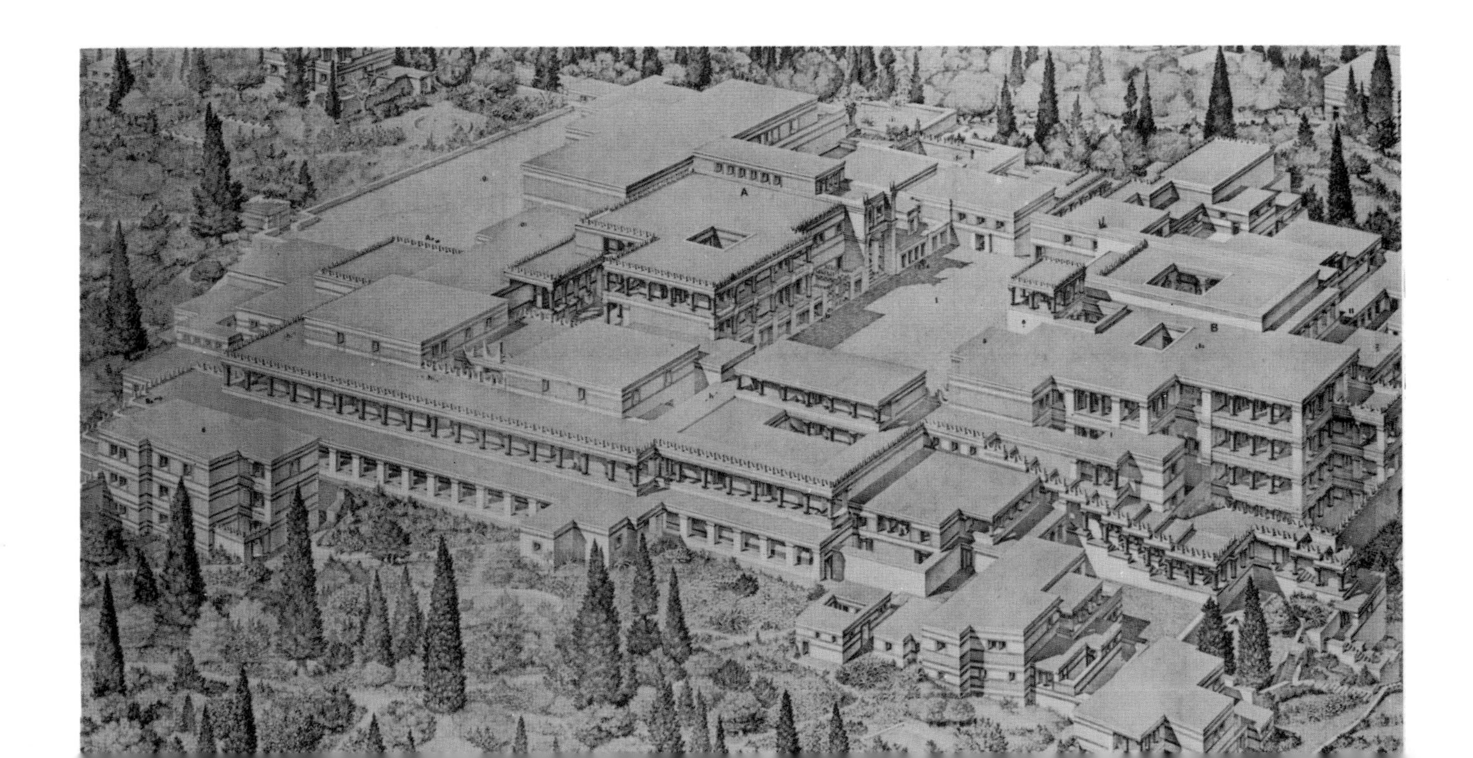

of land still show the circular outline of the former island, but the central area is now a deep bay. Towering cliffs form an inner rim around this expanse of sea, dropping steeply into the water as if sliced through by some gigantic knife. In the center of the bay a dark dome broods and smolders, a constant reminder that Thera is the only active volcano in the Aegean Sea.

The island has probably had a very long history of volcanic disturbance, but geological evidence suggests that the eruption, or series of eruptions, that tore out the center of the island and created the bay may well have been the greatest the world has ever known. It began with a burst of pumice, which built up to a height of 12 feet in some parts of the island. Then there was probably a period of quiescence, followed by another enormous outburst, which covered the island and a vast surrounding area in a mass of fine white ash known as *tephra*. On parts of Thera this tephra is over 200 feet thick. Once the vast magna chamber beneath the earth's crust had ejected this material, its roof—the island of Thera—collapsed, and part of it fell into the sea, forming the central, sea-filled bay known to scientists as a *caldera*.

We can gain some idea of the appalling, widespread devastation caused by such an eruption from eye-witness accounts of a similar event in 1883. In May of that year the island of Krakatoa —a volcano of the same type as Thera—began erupting. Krakatoa is situated in the Sunda Strait, between Java and Sumatra, close to a main sea route between the China Sea and the Indian Ocean. There were therefore a number of ships in the vicinity at the time

Is This How the Real Atlantis Fell?

"But afterward there occurred violent earthquakes and floods; and in a single day and night of destruction . . . the island of Atlantis . . . disappeard into the depths of the sea." So wrote Plato. But how did Atlantis really fall?

About 3500 years ago, violent earthquakes shook the Aegean. The volcano of Thera erupted, belching out great clouds of ash that buried the land on which it fell. Huge masses of pumice were thrown forth, rendering the sea "impassable and impenetrable," and white-hot lava fragments were hurled into the air.

The violence of the explosions caused catastrophic aerial vibrations that reverberated through the Aegean, shaking and destroying buildings. The entire central portion of Thera collapsed. setting up tsunamis that drowned all in their path.

Only 75 miles from Thera lay Crete. Between the two islands there was nothing to break the force of the explosion; no land to stem the first destructive fury of the tsunamis; no protection from the falling snow of lava and ash. It seems indisputable that it was the Thera eruption that ended Minoan power in the Mediterranean. Might the land it destroyed have been Atlantis? As yet, we cannot be sure.

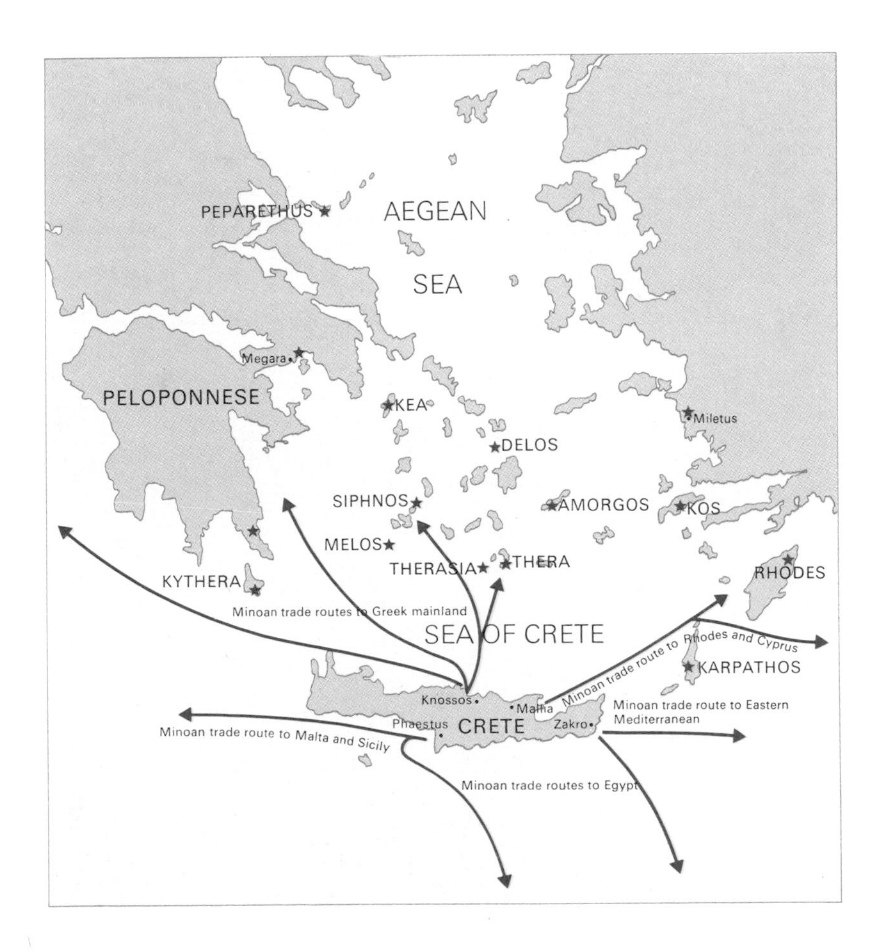

Opposite: the strangely colored cliffs that delineate the submerged caldera of the Thera volcano. Some of the rocks are black, some red, and some white—the three colors Plato specifically names in his description of the stone used in the building of Atlantis.

Left: Minoan ships spread the influence of their civilization far beyond Crete and the islands. On this map of Crete, Greece, and the Aegean, stars represent Minoan settlements, arrows trade routes.

Krakatoa and Thera Compared

Right: dust and vapor rising from Krakatoa at an early stage of the catastrophic eruption that took place in 1883. This drawing shows the scene on May 27, seven days after the eruption began. It did not reach its climax until August 27 when, early in the morning, four terrific detonations took place. They were so severe that they were heard as far as 3000 miles away, and their repercussions were felt on the other side of the world. The island of Krakatoa subsequently collapsed, leaving a submerged caldera similar to that of the Aegean island of Thera.

of the eruption, and their crews were able to give first-hand accounts of it. Krakatoa was uninhabited, and had been dormant for about 200 years, but the 1883 outbreak was preceded by six or seven years of severe earthquakes. Then, on May 20, 1883, the volcano began erupting with booming explosions that rattled doors and windows 100 miles away. Two days later a column of dust and vapor was seen rising from the island to an estimated height of seven miles, and falls of dust were recorded 300 miles away. Observers who landed on the island a week later found it covered by a thin layer of white ash, and the trees stripped of branches by the falling pumice. Activity continued throughout

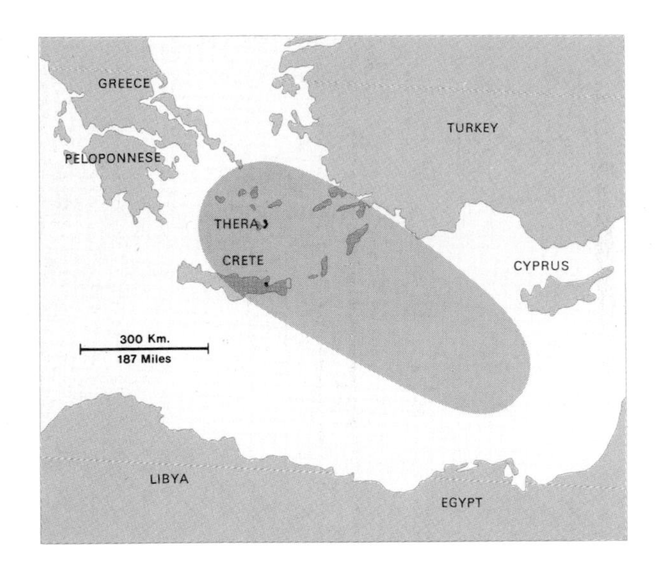

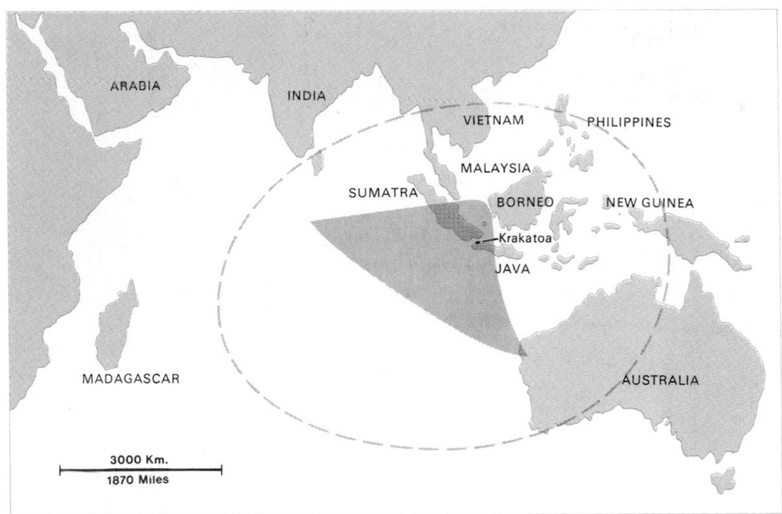

Above left: the eastern Mediterranean, showing the extent of the layer of *tephra* or ash produced by the Thera eruption. The map is based on the geological evidence of sediment cores from the seabed.
Above: this map shows the effects of the Krakatoa eruption of 1883: ash falls were reported within the triangular area, and the enormous explosion was heard as far away as the dashed line.

June and July, and at the beginning of August another visitor to Krakatoa reported that all vegetation had been completely destroyed. The climax came on August 26 and 27, beginning with a black, billowing cloud that rose to a height of 17 miles. Violent explosions were heard throughout Java, and warm pumice fell onto ships in the area. During the night of the 26th the crew of the ship *Charles Bal*, sailing about 15 miles east of Krakatoa, saw "balls of white fire" rolling down the rim of the island. The air became hot and choking with a sulfurous smell, and the sky was "one second intense blackness, the next a blaze of fire." Throughout the night the noise was so great that the inhabitants of western Java could not sleep. Krakatoa quietened a little toward dawn but early on the morning of the 27th there were four stupendous eruptions, the third of which was heard on the island of Rodriguez, 3000 miles away, and was the loudest noise ever recorded on earth. A cloud of dust rose 50 miles, dispersing its contents over a huge area. An estimated five cubic miles of material was blown out of the volcano, and two thirds of it fell within a 10-mile radius, piling white tephra to a height of 185 feet on the parts of Krakatoa that had survived the devastation. The rest of the ejected material caused a pall of darkness that rapidly spread, reaching Bandong, 150 miles away, late on the same day. Wind-borne dust was still falling 12 days later at a distance of 3300 miles.

Blast waves from the great explosion shattered windows and broke walls up to 100 miles away and were detected all over the globe. But it was the ensuing tidal wave that caused the greatest destruction. In areas bordering the Sunda Strait, 300 towns and villages were destroyed and 36,380 people died as a giant wave ripped through their lands. Tides rose steeply on shores as much as 7000 miles away, and a slight rise was recorded as far away as the English Channel. Sea-borne pumice floated over scores of thousands of square miles, and large amounts were reported all over the Indian Ocean for many months after the eruptions. For many months, too, people all around the world saw the strange phenomena created by dust retained in the upper atmosphere—the sun rose green and then turned blue, the moon was green or

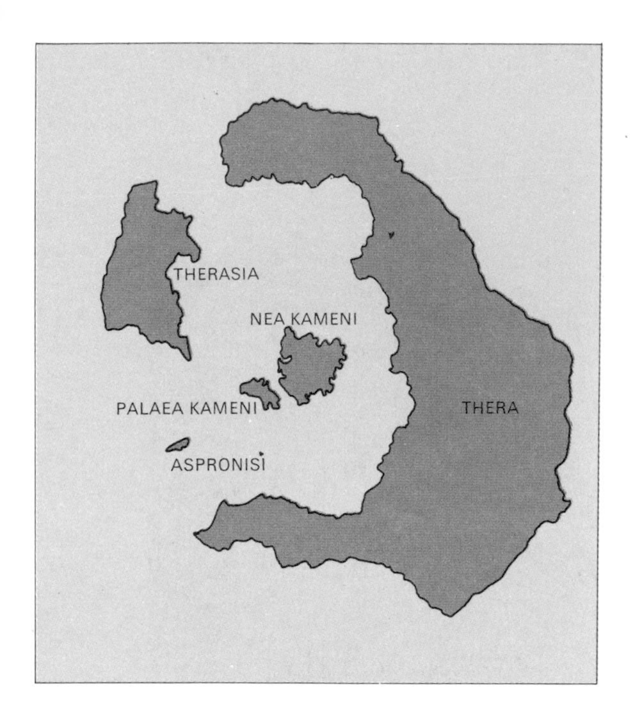

Above: the volcanic caldera of Thera, with the volcanic cones of Nea Kameni and Palaea Kameni in its center. The caldera is deeper than Krakatoa, and four times as large. Comparison with Krakatoa indicates that the destruction caused by the Thera eruption and its effects must have been immense.
Below: an eruption of Nea Kameni in 1866. Scientific investigations on Thera following this eruption proved for the first time when the caldera must have been formed.

blue, and glorious sunsets and afterglows set the sky ablaze.

When visitors ventured to the island after this great cataclysm they found that the northern part of Krakatoa had collapsed into the sea, creating a caldera, and the remainder of the island had been split in half.

How does the Thera eruption compare with the paroxysm of Krakatoa? The Thera caldera is deeper than that formed in Krakatoa, and its surface area is four times as large. Although this does not mean that the Thera eruption was four times as powerful, the structure of the caldera and the extent of the pumice deposits at Thera indicate that the eruption there was at least as violent as, and probably even more destructive than, that of Krakatoa.

Pumice dust from Thera, mixed with lime, produces a very durable cement, and during the 1860s Therasia provided vast quantities of pumice for the construction of the Suez Canal and the new harbor in Port Said. In the course of the quarrying operations, engineers found themselves hindered by numerous stone blocks that marked the lower limit of the pumice. These were the tops of ancient walls buried by fallout from the great eruption, and they might well have been destroyed in the interests of commerce had it not been for another eruption, which began in 1866 and brought a group of scientific observers to the island. As a result of their interest in the ancient walls, excavations were begun, notably by the French vulcanologist Ferdinand Fouqué, who went on to uncover part of a Bronze Age settlement in Akrotiri in northeast Therasia. Fouqué was the first to provide evidence that Thera had suffered its dramatic volcanic collapse sometime in the Bronze Age, 3000 to 1000 B.C.

Fouqué's finds were made before Sir Arthur Evans uncovered the glories of the Minoan civilization on Crete, and their full significance was not realized for a long time afterward. Indeed 100 years were to pass before Professor Marinatos began important new excavations in Akrotiri. In the meantime, however, Thera was not entirely neglected. In 1956 a severe earthquake disturbed the lower strata of a quarry on the main island of Thera, exposing the ruins of an ancient building. Human bones, teeth, and charred wood were found nearby and a Greek seismologist, Dr. Angelos Galanopoulos, arranged for these to be submitted to the carbon-14 dating test, which gives the approximate age of an object by detecting when it "died" and stopped absorbing carbon from the atmosphere. This showed the relics to be about 3500 years old. Further tests of this kind carried out in 1967 on a variety of objects found on Thera have enabled scholars to put the date of the Thera eruption at between 1500 and 1450 B.C. And that coincides with the period when the great Minoan civilization suddenly declined.

In his book *The End of Atlantis*, a scholarly study of the Atlantis legend, Professor J. V. Luce discusses the effects of the Thera eruption on Crete: "We do not know what happened on Crete and on the islands and coasts of the Aegean, but I consider it a safe guess that the loss of life and damage to property were no less [than from Krakatoa]. They may well have been many times as great. We can say with reasonable assurance that Crete had ceased to be a great maritime power after the middle of the

15th century B.C. Is it not reasonable to suppose that the Thera eruption was a major factor in her downfall?"

Supporting evidence for this point of view has come from cores of sediment taken from the floor of the Eastern Mediterranean. It was published in 1965 by two American scientists, D. Ninkovich and B. C. Heezen of the Lamont Geological Observatory, Columbia University, who concluded from the distribution of the volcanic ash found in these deposits that the Thera explosion was a major catastrophe for Minoan Crete. In their opinion, this catastrophe led directly to a transference of power in the area from the Minoans to the mainland Greeks—the Mycenaeans.

The remarkable buildings, frescoes, and pottery found on Thera indicate that it was part of the Minoan island empire. Discussing the 1967 excavations made by Professor Marinatos in Akrotiri, J. V. Luce comments: "Enough evidence has been accumulated for us to say with some assurance that the settlement has distinctly Minoan features, and was clearly in close contact with Crete. It is likely to have been a Minoan colony or dependency, possibly the seat of the Minoan ruler of the island."

Luce, like a number of other scholars who have studied the exciting finds on Thera and Crete, believes that Plato's Atlantis story is a composite picture of the Minoan downfall. The "disappearance" of Atlantis is really the sudden fall from power of the Minoans, coupled with the cataclysmic events on part of their island empire. Luce remarks that he does not look for the lost Atlantis under the surface of Thera bay. "For me 'lost Atlantis' is a historical rather than a geographical concept."

Greek seismologist Dr. Angelos Galanopoulos takes a more literal view of the legend, and has gone a long way toward satisfying many critics of the Atlantis-in-the-Aegean theory with an ingenious hypothesis. Galanopoulos interprets Plato's story as a description of two islands. The larger is the "royal state"—Crete. The smaller is the metropolis, or capital city and religious

Was it a Volcano?

Above: Greek archaeologist Professor Spyridon Marinatos. It was Marinatos who advanced the theory that the fall of the Minoan civilization was caused by an eruption of Thera. In 1967, he carried out excavations in Akrotiri on Thera which proved beyond doubt that a civilization had existed on the island contemporary with, and closely linked to, that of Minoan Crete.

Below: the Thera volcano during its eruption in 1938–41. This photograph shows clearly the ring-shaped submerged caldera with its central active volcanic islands.

Investigations at Thera Begin

Below: a fresco discovered in 1972–3 on Thera. The beauty and originality of the paintings discovered on Thera have astonished the world, and help support the argument advanced by Dr. Angelos Galanopoulos that Thera-Crete composed Atlantis, and that Thera was the chief town.

center—Thera. Plato says that the metropolis of Atlantis was about 11 miles in diameter. This is the same as the former size of Thera. But Galanopoulos noted that other measurements in Plato's account seemed to be far too great in comparison. However, he found that if all measurements over 1000 were divided by 10, they would neatly reduce Atlantis to a size consistent with that of the Minoan empire. Therefore Galanopoulos argued that at some time a tenfold error had crept into the Atlantis story—either when the Egyptians recorded it, or after they gave the story to Solon, who handed it down through a number of generations. Galanopoulos believes that in the translation of Egyptian scripts by Solon, or possibly of Minoan scripts from which the Egyptians obtained the story, the symbol for 100 was rendered as 1000. A modern example of this sort of confusion is the difference between the American billion, which is one thousand millions, and the English billion, which is one million millions.

This mistake, if it occurred, would affect not only the size of Atlantis and its population but also the date of its destruction. Take off the final zero in Plato's figures over 1000, says Galanopoulos, and we find that the date of the submergence of Atlantis coincides with that of the Thera eruption. Instead of sinking 9000 years before Solon's visit to Egypt—a date that caused most people to dismiss the account as a myth because there is no evidence of an advanced civilization existing at such an early period—Atlantis disappeared only 900 years before Solon's trip. Because Solon's journey took place around 600 B.C., this would mean that Atlantis was destroyed around 1500 B.C.—just when the experts believe Thera erupted and Crete suffered its downfall.

Galanopoulos first put forward his hypothesis in 1960, and it is interesting to recall that the 1500 B.C. date for the destruction of Atlantis had already been suggested 10 years earlier by Immanuel Velikovsky in his book *Worlds in Collision.* Writing before the present Atlantis-Thera-Crete theory had evolved, Velikovsky also believed that there was one zero too many in Plato's date.

If Atlantis was in the Aegean, why did Plato apparently situate it in the distant Atlantic Ocean? And why, if Atlantis sank so close to the Greek mainland, were the Greeks so vague about its

Right: the United States oceanographic research vessel *Chain.* In 1966, James W. Mavor used the *Chain* to make sonar soundings of the seabed in the sunken caldera of Thera in an attempt to prove Galanopoulos' theory. He hoped to find evidence of the existence of the harbors and canals described by Plato in his account of Atlantis, but although his voyage added considerably to knowledge of the caldera, and of the volcanic deposits on the seabed, no new evidence to prove the Thera-Atlantis theory emerged.

existence, having to rely on the Egyptians for information about the "lost continent"?

It has been suggested that Plato placed Atlantis in the Atlantic simply because, according to his figures, it was too big to fit anywhere else. Alternatively, there is the possibility of yet another misinterpretation originating with Solon. Plato's account states that Atlantis lay "beyond the Pillars of Hercules"—the name given to the Strait of Gibraltar in Plato's time. Thus his readers automatically assumed that Atlantis was in the Atlantic. But Dr. Galanopoulos has pointed out that the name "Pillars of Hercules" was also once applied to two promontories on the south coast of Greece (ancient Mycenae), facing Crete. If Plato's account refers to these, says Galanopoulos, then the Minoans are almost certainly the Atlanteans.

Archaeological evidence shows that the Minoan culture began to acquire strong Mycenaean characteristics around the time of its downfall, and that the Minoans were starting to lose their dominance of the Aegean. The Minoans and the Mycenaeans may well have been rivals, just as Plato described the Athenians and the Atlanteans to be. Whether the Mycenaeans had conquered parts of Crete, or whether the two cultures underwent a more peaceful integration, discoveries in Knossos show that, after the fall of Crete, the Mycenaeans took the Minoans' place as the major force in the Aegean. The Mycenaeans would even appear to have taken control of the palace in Knossos, which, though damaged, had survived because it was inland.

The Greeks, however, were still too young a people to recall the history of these events with any clarity, though with hindsight we can find some of the story in their legends. J. V. Luce comments that, "The Greeks remembered very little at all about the 15th century B.C. Their national consciousness was then only in an early formative stage. Their main saga cycles date from the 13th century when, under the leadership of Mycenae, they had become a major power in the eastern Mediterranean." Luce adds that "even the Mycenaean world as a whole was only dimly remembered by the later Greeks." The Egyptians, a much older race, had long been trading with the Minoans and recorded the visits of Minoans to Egypt. So it is perhaps not surprising if the Egyptians knew more than the Greek themselves about their talented forebears.

According to Plato, the Egyptian priests told Solon: "You remember only one deluge though there have been many, and you do not know that the finest and best race of men that ever existed lived in your country; you and your fellow citizens are descended from the few survivors who remained, but you know nothing about it, because of the many intervening generations silent for lack of written speech."

In the opinion of some scholars, that quotation supplies further evidence for the Atlantis-in-the-Aegean theory, and for the Egyptian origin of the Atlantis story. The Egyptians are apparently referring to a literacy gap that has since been confirmed. Scripts known as Linear A and B were used in Crete, Greece, and the Aegean islands during the second millennium B.C., but they disappeared from use after 1200 B.C. They do not appear to have been replaced by any other form of writing until around 850 B.C.,

Below: fresco found on Thera of a young woman, the "priestess." Such sophisticated art is common to Thera, Crete—and Plato's Atlantis.

An Atlantean Fresco Revealed?

Below: fresco of a coastal city, with ships offshore, from the West House on Thera. The city is surrounded by seas full of fish; on land deer run among the burgeoning trees. What other picture could so closely represent Plato's ocean-ringed land of milk and honey as this painting by an unknown Theran of long ago?

when the Greek archaic script appeared. So it seems that, even had there been any local records of the Thera explosion and the fall of Crete, they would have been written in a language that the Greeks of Plato's time would not have understood.

As a result of the discoveries in the Aegean, a number of scholars are now prepared to believe not only that Plato's account is based on historical reality, but that it is an astonishingly accurate record of events that occurred over 1000 years before he wrote his story. Until further information about the Minoan culture emerges, however, even the Atlantis-in-the-Aegean theory is open to different interpretations. Professor Galanopoulos, for example, believes that Thera was as important to the Minoans as Crete was. He regards Thera as the center of Minoan life and Crete as its larger adjunct. Galanopoulos pictures the slopes of the small volcanic island teeming with life and adorned with the white temples and palaces of a majestic city. When the eruption came, these great feats of architecture—equal to those discovered on Crete—would have been buried in fallout, then submerged beneath the waters that now fill the Thera basin.

Attempts to detect submerged harbors and canals at Thera similar to those described by Plato have been made, using the latest sonar equipment. In 1966 Dr. James W. Mavor of the Woods Hole Oceanographic Institution was given permission to carry out runs across the bay with the research vessel *Chain*.

The findings of the *Chain* are related in Mavor's book *Voyage to Atlantis*. Although they have added to our understanding of the shape and depth of the caldera and the volcanic deposits beneath the sea, they could not provide the evidence needed to support Galanopoulos's theory.

Clearly there is a need for deep-sea diving equipment to be used in the Thera basin, and in 1975 it was announced that the French underwater explorer Jacques Cousteau had received permission to dive and carry out research in the area. Cousteau was reported to be planning a year-long study off Thera and Delos (another island in the Cyclades), which would be recorded on film for television, and his research vessel was said to have been fitted with special "treasure-hunting" gear, including two lateral sonars that can scan the seabed for over 400 yards on either side of the ship. Speaking of Thera, Cousteau is quoted as saying: "This is the best contender for the title of the real Atlantis. We know there is something down there under the waves. We are determined to find out what."

Pending the discovery of new evidence, no one can say for sure that the Atlantis mystery has been solved. But excavations now in progress may soon be able to show whether the Minoans—possibly the most accomplished and inventive race the world has ever known—were not only the forefathers of Greek civilization, and ultimately of Europe, but also the lost and fabled Atlanteans.

Chapter 14
The Atlantis Mystery Deepens

In 1940 the American psychic healer and prophet Edgar Cayce predicted that Atlantis would "rise again" in 1968 or 1969. So in 1968, when it seemed that the site of the world's most famous lost land had finally been located in the eastern Mediterranean, news that underwater vast buildings off the Bahamas shook Atlantists everywhere. The whole question of Atlantis was reopened. Could this be Poseidia, described by Cayce as the "western section of Atlantis"? Were Plato and the other Atlantists right after all when they placed their lost civilization way out in the Atlantic Ocean? This final chapter examines the latest evidence in this greatest puzzle of the lost lands.

In 1968 two commercial airline pilots flying over the Bahamas spotted what appeared to be several underwater buildings coming to the surface. The pilots made their sighting just off the coast of Bimini and photographed the underwater formations from the air. Their discovery was immediately hailed by some as the fulfillment of a 28-year-old prophecy concerning the reappearance of Atlantis. Indeed one of the pilots had been keeping a lookout for underwater structures while flying his regular assignments because he believed Atlantis was about to reemerge from the Atlantic in this very area.

The man concerned is a member of the Association for Research and Enlightenment, an organization based in Virginia Beach, Virginia, which is dedicated to the study of the teachings and "psychic readings" of the late Edgar Cayce, the "sleeping prophet" and psychic healer. Between 1923 and 1944 Cayce made numerous references to Atlantis in the course of trance interviews concerning the alleged former lives of the people who consulted him. These interviews were recorded verbatim, and much of the material about Atlantis has been published in a book called *Edgar Cayce on Atlantis*, by Cayce's son Edgar Cayce. It includes this prediction, made in June 1940: "Poseidia will be among the first portions of Atlantis to rise again. Expect it in '68 and '69; not so far away!"

According to the Cayce readings, Poseidia was the "western section of Atlantis," and the area off Bimini is the highest point

Opposite: as the Surtsey volcano erupts, a new island gradually rises from beneath the waters of the Atlantic. The Atlantic seabed is notoriously unstable—Surtsey appeared for the first time little more than 10 years ago, and there are other recorded instances of islands appearing and disappearing. Surely, the Atlantists argue, this is how Atlantis might have been submerged by the waves.

Above: Dr. Charles Berlitz, like many other Atlantists, denies that the Thera discoveries have completely solved the mystery of Plato's lost continent. He has used his skill as a skin-diver to carry out archaeological investigations, and still hopes to prove that Atlantis was in the Atlantic.

of this sunken land. So the ARE is naturally delighted about the underwater find in the Bahamas, just where and when the famous prophet said something would appear. Until this and similar discoveries have been thoroughly explored, we have to admit that Thera may yet have an equally plausible rival for the title of Atlantis, right where most people always considered the long-lost continent to be—in the Atlantic.

In his book *The Mystery of Atlantis* Charles Berlitz comments that: "Other underwater ruins have subsequently been found near other Caribbean islands, including what appears to be an entire city submerged off the coast of Haiti, and still another at the bottom of a lake. What appears to be an underwater road (or perhaps a series of plazas or foundations) was discovered in 1968 off north Bimini beneath several fathoms of water. From these numerous findings, it would appear that part of the continental shelf of the Atlantic and Caribbean was once dry land, sunk or flooded during a period when man was already civilized."

Not everyone accepts these underwater features as being of man-made origin. The so-called "Bimini road" is dismissed by skeptics as nothing more than beach rock that just happens to have produced an unusual effect. Berlitz and Dr. Manson Valentine, the American archaeologist and oceanographer who discovered the "road," do not agree. "It should be pointed out," writes Berlitz, "that beach rock does not form great blocks which fit together in a pattern, that haphazardly splitting rock does not make 90-degree turns, nor does it normally have regularly laid-out passageways running between sections of it. Nor, above all, are 'natural' beach rocks, lying on the ocean floor, likely to be found supported by stone pillars precisely placed beneath them!"

Other sightings made off Bimini, at distances up to 100 miles from the shore, include what appear to be vertical walls, a great arch, and pyramids or bases for pyramids under the sea. Some 10 miles north of Andros, another island in the Bahamas, pilots have photographed formations on the seabed that look like great circles of standing stones, reminiscent of Stonehenge. Off the coasts of eastern Yucatán and British Honduras seemingly man-made roads stretch far out to sea, and off Venezuela a 100-mile "wall" runs along the ocean bottom. However, geologists have declared many of these to be natural features, and deem the Venezuelan wall "too big to be considered man-made." According to Berlitz, the Russians have explored an underwater building complex covering over 10 acres of the sea floor north of Cuba, and the French bathyscaphe *Archimède* has reported sighting flights of steps carved in the steep continental shelf off northern Puerto Rico.

Do these intriguing finds indicate that Atlantis was, after all, in the Atlantic? It seems we must keep an open mind until they have been investigated more thoroughly. Meanwhile, let us take a fresh look at the Atlantic Ocean to see if the theory of continental drift might still leave room for a missing continent there. When a computer was used to reassemble the continental jigsaw, the fit across the Atlantic was found, with some adjustment, to be fairly satisfactory. But that picture does not take account of a fascinating underwater feature known as the mid-Atlantic

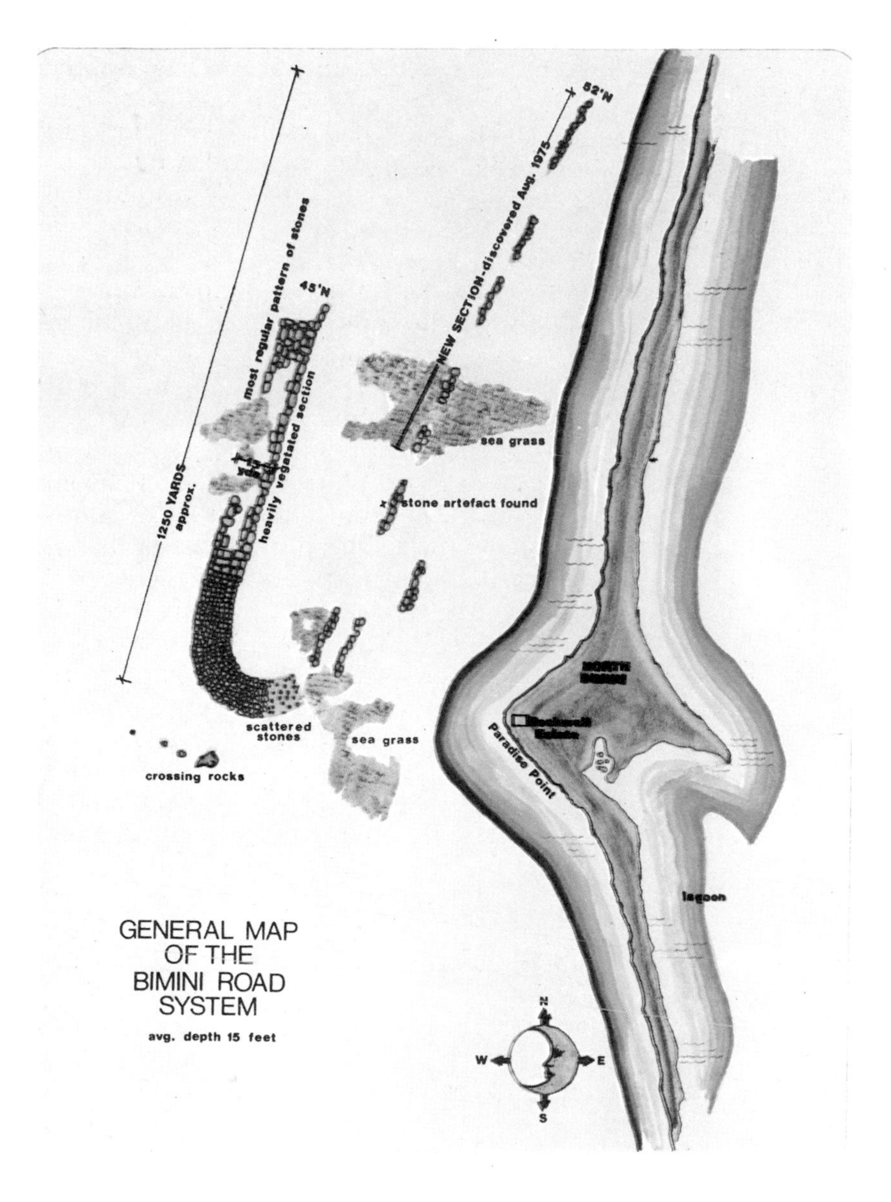

The Riddle of the "Bimini Road"

Left: map of the Bimini Road drawn after aerial and underwater surveys carried out by the Poseidia 75 expedition, sponsored by the Association for Research and Enlightenment. The road is magnified to approximately twice its actual size in relation to the island of Bimini. Shaped roughly like a letter J, it is some three quarters of a mile long and composed of huge stone blocks, often 15 feet square. On this map, the X marking the discovery of a stone artifact relates to a fragment of what appeared to be tongue-and-groove masonry discovered on the Poseidia 75 expedition by one of its members, Dr. David Zink.

Below: a diver taking part in ARE's Poseidia 75 expedition to Bimini in the Bahamas examines an encrusted marble column found about a mile south of the Bimini Road. Medical clairvoyant Edgar Cayce, who made predictions about Atlantis, foretold that the western part of the continent would rise from the sea in 1968 or 1969. In 1968, what appeared to be a vast underwater road was discovered off Bimini, and the next year the columns, of which this is one, were found.

Ridge. This mountainous ridge, nearly two miles high and hundreds of miles wide, runs in an S-curve down the Atlantic midway between the Americas and Africa and Europe, following the contours of those continents and marking its course above water with a number of islands, such as the Azores, Ascension Island, and Tristan da Cunha.

As early as 1883 Ignatius Donnelly suggested that the mid-Atlantic Ridge was a remnant of Atlantis. But most modern geologists and oceanographers consider that, far from being the relic of a continent that sank beneath the sea, the ridge was forced upward from the ocean floor, probably by volcanic activity. One theory is that as the continents drifted apart they produced a huge fault line that is a center of earthquake and volcanic action. Some of the earth's molten center has erupted through this crack and built up into a ridge, even rising above the waves in several places. However, there is evidence that this explanation may have to be reviewed before too long.

Seabed cores taken from the mid-Atlantic Ridge in 1957 brought up freshwater plants from a depth of two miles. And in

PHYSIOGRAPHIC DIAGRAM OF THE
SOUTH ATLANTIC OCEAN
The Caribbean Sea, The Scotia Sea, and the eastern margin of the South Pacific Ocean
BY BRUCE C. HEEZEN AND MARIE THARP
LAMONT GEOLOGICAL OBSERVATORY
Columbia University
0
4000

one of the deep valleys, known as Romanche, sands have been found that appear to have been formed by weathering when that part of the ridge was above water level. In 1969 a Duke University research expedition dredged 50 sites along an underwater ridge running from Venezuela to the Virgin Islands, and brought up granitic rocks, which are normally found only on continents. Commenting on this discovery, Dr. Bruce Heezen of the Lamont Geological Observatory said: "Up to now, geologists generally believed that light granitic or acid igneous rocks are confined to the continents and that the crust of the earth beneath the sea is composed of heavier, dark-colored basaltic rock. . . . Thus, the occurrence of light-colored granitic rocks may support an old theory that a continent formerly existed in the region of the eastern Caribbean and that these rocks may represent the core of a subsided, lost continent."

A recent report on the nature of the Atlantic seabed appears to confirm that there is at least part of a former continent lying beneath the ocean. Under the headline "Concrete Evidence for Atlantis?" the British journal *New Scientist* of June 5, 1975 reported: "Although they make no such fanciful claim from their results as to have discovered the mythical mid-Atlantic landmass, an international group of oceanographers has now convincingly confirmed preliminary findings that a sunken block of continent lies in the middle of the Atlantic Ocean. The discovery comes from analyzing dredge samples taken along the line of the Vema offset fault, a long east-west fracture zone lying between Africa and South America close to latitude 11°N."

The report goes on to state that in 1971 two researchers from the University of Miami recovered some shallow-water limestone fragments from deep water in the area. Minerals in the limestone indicated that they came from a nearby source of granite that was unlikely to occur on the ocean floor. More exhaustive analysis of the dredge samples revealed that the limestones included traces of shallow-water fossils, implying formation in very shallow water indeed, a view confirmed by the ratios of oxygen and carbon isotopes found in the fragments. One piece of limestone was pitted and showed evidence of tidal action.

The researchers believe that the limestone dates from the Mesozoic era (between 70 and 220 million years ago) and forms a cap "on a residual continental block left behind as the Atlantic spread out into an ocean." The *New Scientist* observes that "the granitic minerals could thus have come from the bordering continents while the ocean was still in its infancy. Vertical movements made by the block appear to have raised it above sea level at some period during its history."

It would therefore seem that there *is* a lost continent in the Atlantic, but unfortunately for Atlantists, it evidently disappeared long before man appeared on earth. Most scientists remain convinced that there is no likelihood of finding the Atlantis described by Plato in the area of the mid-Atlantic Ridge. As L. Sprague de Camp comments in his *Lost Continents*, nearly all of the ridge, except for the small and mountainous Azores region, is under two or three miles of water, "and there is no known way to get a large island down to that depth in anything like the 10,000 years required to fit in with Plato's date for the

Remnants of a Sunken Land

Opposite: diagram of the physical features underlying the Atlantic Ocean. The mid-Atlantic Ridge curves from north to south down the middle of the ocean. Atlantist Ignatius Donnelly suggested that the ridge might be a remnant of the sunken continent of Atlantis, but scientific opinion today holds that, rather than being formed above the surface of the waters and sinking, it was in fact pushed up from beneath the ocean floor. Recent research does seem to indicate that there is a sunken continent in the Atlantic, lying between Africa and South America, but this continent sank long before man's appearance on earth.

Below: the French bathyscaphe *Archimède*. The crew of *Archimède* produced what could be fresh evidence to support the existence of a sunken continent in the Caribbean area when they reported seeing flights of steps carved in the continental shelf off the island of Puerto Rico.

Evidence for a Lost Atlantic Continent

Below: volcanic eruption on Surtsey, just south of Iceland. Atlantists believe that recorded changes in the physical features of the Atlantic Ocean caused by volcanic eruptions provide ample evidence for siting the lost Atlantis in the Atlantic. Volcanic activity not only explains how the continent might have disappeared, but also explains it in exactly the way Plato described.

sinking of Atlantis." He also points to a report published in 1967 by Dr. Maurice Ewing of Columbia University, who announced that "after 13 years of exploring the mid-Atlantic Ridge," he had "found no trace of sunken cities."

Atlantists reply that Dr. Ewing could have been looking in the wrong places, or perhaps too close to the center of the destructive forces that plunged Atlantis into the ocean. Some Atlantists have suggested that the original Atlantic landmass broke up into at least two parts, one of which sank long after the other. Perhaps Plato's Atlantis was a remnant of the continent that oceanographers now appear to have detected in the Atlantic, and perhaps it was not submerged until very much more recent times. The bed of the Atlantic is, after all, an unstable area and one that has given birth to numerous islands, then swallowed them up again. In 1811, for example, volcanic activity in the Azores resulted in the emergence of a new island called Sambrina, which shortly sank back again into the sea. In our own time, the island of Surtsey, 20 miles southwest of Iceland, has slowly risen from the ocean. Surtsey was formed during a continuous underwater eruption between 1963 and 1966.

If Atlantis did exist in the Atlantic above the great fault line

that runs between the present continents, it would certainly have been plagued by earthquakes and volcanic eruptions. Is it mere coincidence that Plato should have situated his lost continent in an ocean that does apparently contain such a continent, and in an area subject to the very kind of catastrophe he describes? Atlantists think not.

On the other hand, there are some Atlantists who believe that the destruction of Atlantis was brought about not by geological events but by a man-made disaster, such as a nuclear explosion. According to the Cayce readings the Atlanteans achieved an astonishingly high level of technology before the continent sank, around 10,000 B.C. They invented the laser, aircraft, television, death rays, atomic energy, and cybernetic control of human beings, and it was the misuse of the tremendously powerful natural forces they had developed that caused their destruction.

Cayce is best-known for his apparent ability to diagnose illness even in people whom he had never met. This ability was tested by a group of physicians from Hopkinsville and Bowling Green, Kentucky. They discovered that when Cayce was in a state of trance, it was sufficient to give him the name and address of a patient for him to supply a wealth of information about that person, often drawing attention to medical conditions of which the physicians were then unaware, but that subsequent tests on the patient proved to be correct. This work alone would appear to justify the description of Cayce as America's most talented psychic. And if one aspect of his clairvoyant powers could prove so successful, it seems reasonable to give a fair hearing to other psychic statements he made, however fantastic.

Cayce's sons, who help run the organization set up to study his work, admit that their life would be far simpler if Edgar Cayce had never mentioned Atlantis. Hugh Lynn Cayce comments: "It would be very easy to present a very tight evidential picture of Edgar Cayce's psychic ability and the helpfulness of his readings if we selected only those which are confirmed and completely validated. This would not be fair in a total, overall evaluation of his life's work. My brother and I know that Edgar Cayce did not read Plato's material on Atlantis, or books on Atlantis, and that he, so far as we know, had absolutely no knowledge of this subject. If his unconscious fabricated this material or wove it together from existing legends and writings, we believe that it is the most amazing example of a telepathic-clairvoyant scanning of existing legends and stories in print or of the minds of persons dealing with the Atlantis theory." Edgar Evans Cayce makes the comment that "unless proof of the existence of Atlantis is one day discovered, Edgar Cayce is in a very unenviable position. On the other hand, if he proves accurate on this score he may become as famous an archaeologist or historian as he was a medical clairvoyant."

If, as his sons and thousands of followers believe, Edgar Cayce's readings were supernormal, and not the product of reading the works of others, it is certainly an intriguing case. There are, for example, some fascinating similarities between Cayce's descriptions of Atlantis and those of occultists such as Madame Blavatsky, Rudolf Steiner, and W. Scott-Elliot, including references to the Atlanteans' telepathic and other supernormal

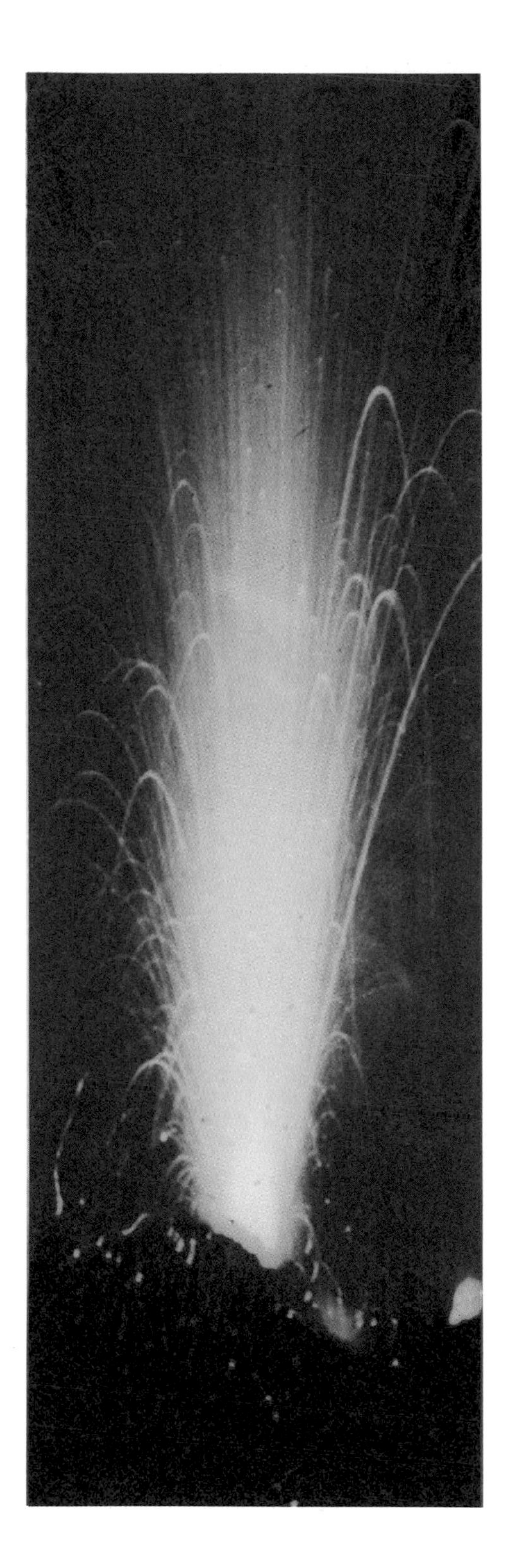

Above: volcanic eruption in the Lipari Islands, off southwestern Italy. The volcanic activity explanation for Atlantis' disappearance could support a Mediterranean Atlantis as effectively as an Atlantic one. Volcanic eruptions also occur in the Mediterranean, and in the Thera caldera they have created totally new islands.

The Persistent Legend of the Lost Atlantis

powers, their advanced technology, their moral disintegration, and the civil strife and misuse of their powers that finally caused their demise. Cayce's readings also mention Lemuria, or Mu. Either Cayce was psychically reading the works of these earlier writers, or he—and they—really were "tuning in" to the past.

Whatever the result of future investigations around the splendid temples and palaces of Crete, or in the depths of the Thera basin, there will still be people who continue to look for Atlantis in the Atlantic Ocean. Scholars may have made out a convincing case for the identification of Plato's Atlantis with the Minoan civilization of the Aegean, but their opponents argue that the existence of such a civilization—however striking its similarities with Atlantis—does not preclude the existence of an even greater civilization in the Atlantic. The finds in the Bahamas remain to be verified, and the discovery of what appears to be a submerged continent in the Atlantic adds a new dimension to the Atlantis mystery.

Whatever prompted Plato to write about Atlantis, he could never have dreamed that he would start a worldwide quest for the lost continent. Perhaps, as his pupil Aristotle hinted, "he who invented it also destroyed it." Yet through a fortuitous accident—or a canny understanding of the human spirit—Plato hit upon a story that has struck a responsive chord in people's minds and hearts down the centuries. Whether his story was fact or fiction, a distorted version of real events or a fable that just happened to tie in with reality, it has managed to enchant, baffle, and challenge mankind for over 2000 years.

The persistence of the Atlantis legend is almost as intriguing as the lost continent itself. What is it that keeps the Atlantis debate alive? Is it a longing for reassurance that men and women once knew the secret of happiness, and really did inhabit a Garden of Eden? Is it the thrill of the search—the hope of finding a master key to unlock the secrets of the past? Or is it simply man's thirst for mystery itself—for something grand and inexplicable, larger than himself? Certainly popular interest in the mystical side of Atlantis is always most intense when the life of the spirit is in greatest disarray—during the latter half of the 19th century, in the aftermath of Darwin's bombshell, for example, and during our own time.

The day may yet come when the key is found and the mystery of Atlantis is solved once and for all. The solution may be simple or complex. It could be sensational or disappointingly dull. We may already suspect the answer, or it may surprise us. Either way, it would rob the world of one of its most fascinating enigmas. Atlantis has intrigued and inspired people for a very long time. Perhaps, for the time being, we should be glad that the answer has not yet been found, and that Plato's lost continent remains just beyond our grasp.

Opposite: the fisher, a fresco from the West House on Thera. The evidence seems to point to Thera as the origin of Plato's Atlantis, but the mystery still lingers, for the evidence is not yet conclusive. Until new discoveries are made, or fresh proof uncovered, we can pursue our quest for the lost utopia. We can wonder whether this figure is really an Atlantean.

Index

References to illustrations are shown in italics.

Picture Credits

Key to picture position: (T) top (C) center (B) bottom; and in combinations, e.g. (TR) top right (BL) bottom left.

Aldus Archives 10, 13(L), 23(T), 24, 49(L), 69, 78(T), 106–109, 134, 139, 140(L), 142(L), 143(B), 145(B), 146(R), 152(T), 170(R), 180, 181(B), 182, 184(L), 202, 203; © Aldus Books 149, 152(B), 154, 158, (Bruno Elletori) 129, (Christopher Foss) 206, (Hawke Studio/Michael Turner) 224–225, (Alan Hollingbery) 150(T), 184(R), 186(R), 196, 216, 233, 235, 236(T), (David Nockels) 223, (Peter Tomlin) 200, (Eileen Tweedy) 48; Aerofilms Ltd. 14; Ashmolean Museum, Oxford 132(L); Associated Press 237(T); *Athens Annals of Archaeology* 238(L), 239–241, 251; Barnaby's Picture Library 132(R); Bodleian Library, Oxford 160(R), 219; British and Foreign Bible Society (Photo Eileen Tweedy © Aldus Books) 22; Reproduced by permission of the Trustees of the British Museum 21, 153, 156, 162, (Ray Gardner © Aldus Books) 73, (Michael Holford Library photo) 42(L)(TR), (Mansell) 40(L), 44(B), (Mansell/Alinari) 40(C), (Mansell/Anderson) 40(R); Trustees of the British Museum (Natural History) 192; Else Wegener, *Alfred Wegener*, 1960, with permission of F. A. Brockhaus, Wiesbaden 222; Brown Brothers 138; Zdenek Burian 148(R); Camera and Pen 145(T); Camera Press 189(T), (Alexander Lawrence) 91(R), (David South) 174, (Wim Swaan) 2–3, 78(B), 90, 93, 96(L), 97; J. Allan Cash Ltd. 60(B), 61, 112(B); Raymond Cauchetier, Paris 83, 86, 87(B), 89, 94, 96(R); Photos J.-L. Charmet 121, 141, 181(T); Photo Peter Clayton 125; Culver Pictures 150(B); Ecole Française d'Extrême-Orient, Paris 80–81, 85(B), 92, 95; Photo Jacques Arthaud, from B. P. Groslian, *Angkor*, Editions Arthaud, Paris 84–87(T); The Executors of Sir Arthur Evans, deceased 133, 231(T); Mary Evans Picture Library 197(R); FPG 135; From photos in the possession of Brian Fawcett 164, 165, 166(R); Werner Forman Archive 15, 33, 159, 170(L), 210, 213; Peter Fraenkel 111, 113, 117; Heinrich Schmidt, *Ernst Haeckel*, Frommannsche Buchhandlung, Jena, 1934 197(L); Bruce C. Heezen and Marie Tharp, *Physiographic Diagram of the South Atlantic Ocean*, The Geological Society of America, 1962 246; Musée du Louvre, Paris/Giraudon 131(B); *Glasgow Herald* 148(L); © G. Goakimedes 237(B); Groninger Museum 101; Museo Nacional de Historia, Madrid/Photo Pulido Gudino 173; Hale Observatories 214(R); Sonia Halliday Photos 11(B), 18, 23(B), 27, 28(R), 29; The Hamlyn Group/Photos Constantino Reyes-Valerio 168(T), (National Museum of Anthropology, Mexico City) 160(L); Robert Harding Associates 30, 32(L), 56, 65, 67, 68(L), 74(L), 136, 157, 168(B), 171, 188(R), 194–195, 228, (Robert Cundy) 13(R), (F. Jackson) 17, (F. L. Kennet) 26, (John Stathatos) 75; Photos Dimitrios Harissiadis 226, 232; Photo Roger Haydock 245(R); Photos Thor Heyerdahl 190–191; Hirmer Fotoarchiv, München 11(T), 25, 31, 32(R), 124; Historisches Museum, Basel 58; Michael Holford Library photo 144, 146(L), 161(L), 172; Pierre Honoré, *In Quest of the White God*, Hutchinson & Co. Ltd., London, 1963 178; Icelandic Photo and Press Service 242, 248; International Publishing Company, Israel 20; A. F. Kersting 60(T), 63, 64, 66, 68(R), 70(B), 71; Keystone 163(T), 247; Laing Art Gallery, Newcastle upon Tyne (Tyne and Wear Museums Service) 208, 212; Frank W. Lane (S. Jonasson) 211, (Tomas Micek) 249; Documents Henri Lhote's expedition, Tassili-n-Ajjer 16; The MacQuitty International Collection 28(L); The Mansell Collection 72, 131(T), 198, 221, 236(B), (Alinari) 46(L), 52; Photo Mas 179; Chr. Mathioulakis and N. Gouvoussis, Athens 231(B); Minnesota Historical Society 142(R), 143(T), 147; John H. Moore 166(L); Musée de l'Homme, Paris 177; Museo Historico Regional del Cuzco, Calle Heladeros, Peru 161(R); Museo Nacional di Antropologia, Mexico 169; NASA 215; Nasjongalleriet, Oslo 120; The National Archives of Rhodesia 100, 105, 116; National Gallery, London 8; William Hodges 1744–1797. Woman of Easter Island. Drawn from nature by W. Hodges. Engraved by J. Caldwell. Line engraving 25.2 x 19.5cm (in James Cook, *A Voyage towards the South Pole and round the world . . .*, London, 1777). From the Rex Nan Kivell Collection in the National Library of Australia 188(L); National Portrait Gallery, London 50(L), 140(R); Photo Fima Noveck 214(L); The Ny Carlsberg Glyptotek, Copenhagen 70(T), 122(B); The Parker Gallery, London 176; Picturepoint, London 229, 230; Popperfoto 163(B); *Psychic News* 167; Mauro Pucciarelli 36, 38, 39(B), 41, 42(B), 43, 45, 47, 50(R), 53, 54; *Radio Times* Hulton Picture Library 204; James Wellard, *The Search for the Etruscans*, The Rainbird Publishing Group Limited, London 55; Library, Royal Commonwealth Society 103, 104; By courtesy of the Royal Geographical Society 59, 62, 79; Courtesy The Royal Norwegian Embassy, London 189(B); *Royal Society Report on Krakatoa, 1889* 234; Scala (Galleria Borghese, Rome) 46(R), (Museo Archeologico, Florence) 44(T), (Museo di Villa Giulia) 34, (Museo Etrusco, Chiusi) 37, (Museo Nazionale, Naples) 118, (Museo Pio Clementino, Vatican) 122(T), (National Museum, Athens) 126, (Stanze di Raffaello, Vatican) 123, (Tomba dei Leo-Tarquinia) 51, (Vatican Museum) 39(T); Christopher Scarlett, London 76, 87(T), 88, 91(L); Flip Schulke/Seaphot 12(B); James Churchward, *The Lost Continents of Mu*, Neville Spearman Ltd., 1942 183, 185, 186(L), 187; Photo John Steele 245(L); The Tate Gallery, London/Photos John Webb 130, 218; Barbara Pfeffer *People* © Time Inc. 1976 244; Transafrica-Pix, Brescia 102, 112(T), 114, 115; Universitätsbibliothek, Heidelberg. Cod. Pal. Germ. 60, fol. 179v 151; Victoria & Albert Museum, London/Photo Eileen Tweedy © Aldus Books 220; Wiener Library 217; Woods Hole Oceanographic Institution 238(R); Courtesy Cecil Woolf 49; ZEFA (J. Rushmer) 98, (K. Scholz) 12(T).